Great Chefs®
~of the South~

Great Chefs®
~of the South~

From the television series
GREAT CHEFS OF THE SOUTH

Edited by

MARLENE OSTEEN

A Cumberland House Hearthside Book

CUMBERLAND HOUSE
Nashville, Tennessee

Great Chefs® is a registered trademark of Great Chefs® Television/Publishing,
a division of G.S.I. Inc. Great Chefs® Trademark
Reg. U.S. Pat. Off. and in other countries.

A free catalog of other Great Chefs products is available.
Call 1-800-321-1499, or contact www.greatchefs.com

Published by Cumberland House Publishing, Inc.,
431 Harding Industrial Drive
Nashville, Tennessee 37211

Design by Bruce Gore, Gore Studio, Inc., Nashville, Tennessee.

Library of Congress Cataloging-in-Publication Data

Osteen, Marlene
    Great chefs of the south : from the television series Great Chefs
of the south / compiled by Marlene Osteen.
    p.   cm.
    Includes index.
    ISBN 1-888952-45-8 (hc : alk. paper)
    1. Cookery, American.   2. Cooks—South (U.S.)   I. Title.
TX715.O77   1997
641.5973—dc21   97–39902
                                                                    CIP

Printed in the United States of America
1 2 3 4 5 6 7 — 01 00 99 98 97

CONTENTS

Credits   vi

Acknowledgements   vii

Mail Order Sources   ix

Introduction   xi

APPETIZERS   1

SALADS   45

FISH & SEAFOOD   55

MEATS & POULTRY   91

DESSERTS   115

The Chefs   173

Basic Recipes   215

Glossary   223

Index   235

CREDITS

Television Series

Presenter	Mary Lou Conroy
Announcer	Andres Calandria
Camera Assistants	Mark Farley
	Milton Perque, Jr.
	Mark Schenck
Editor/Animation	George Matulik
Assistant Editor	Maria D. Estevez
Post-Production Audio	Andres Calandria
	C. Caldwell Sainz
Original Music	The Charlie Byrd
	Quartet
	Charlie Byrd, guitar
	Hendrik Meurkins,
	harmonica
	Johnny Frigo, fiddle
	Bill Huntington, bass
Theme performed by Carol Sloane	
Recording Studio	Ultrasonic Studios

Recording Engineer	Steve Reynolds
Additional Footage	Paul Cornbel
Transportation General	Bryan Dupepe
Assistant to the Executive Producer	
	Cybil W. Curtis
Associate Producer	C. Caldwell Sainz
Producer/Director/Writer	
	John Beyer
Executive Producer	John Shoup

Book

For Great Chefs

Photography	Eric Futran
Project Coordination	Linda Anne Nix

For Cumberland House Hearthside Publishing

Editor-in-Chief	Julia M. Pitkin

ACKNOWLEDGMENTS

Many, many thanks to John Shoup who has been more than generous in giving me this opportunity, and even more saintly to put up with my delays in completing it. I owe considerable gratitude to Linda Nix, who was ever ready with assistance, solutions, and terrific good cheer.

Ron and Julie Pitkin deserve no fewer acolades for their patience. Deenie Cooper was my great savior in the pastry kitchen, testing and tasting, and of course, my husband Louis and my children Lara and Heather are due equal thanks for their assistance and understanding.

MAIL ORDER SOURCES

BALDUCCI'S
P.O. BOX 10373
NEWARK, NJ 07193-0373
1-800-225-3822

The mail order division of the famed New York gourmet market, with everything from fresh pastas and excellent sauces to prime meats, desserts, and such foods as pâté de foie gras, capon, pheasant, squab, venison, and imported and domestic caviars.

CHICKORY FARMS
723 HILARY STREET
NEW ORLEANS, LA 70118
1-800-605-4550

All manner of mushrooms, both cultivated and wild.

D'ARTAGNON
399-419 ST. PAUL AVENUE
JERSEY CITY, NJ 07306
1-800-327-8246

Fresh foie gras, plus sausages, ducks and duck fat, and other specialty items.

THE FARMS AT MT. WALDEN
P.O. BOX 515
THE PLAINS, VA 22171
1-800-64-TROUT

This small smokehouse in the foothills of the shenandoahs offers fine smoked trout, as well as hot-smoked salmon.

GWALTNEY'S
P.O. BOX 1
SMITHFIELD, VA 23431
1-800-292-2773

While many people substitute prosciutto in recipes calling for Smithfield ham, there really is no comparable product. The hams available at Gwaltney's are cooked and presliced.

HOPPIN JOHNS
30 PINCKNEY STREET
CHARLESTON, SC 29401
1-800-828-4412

For southern ingredients—from stone ground grits and cornmeal to country hams and pickles and relishes, Charleston's John Taylor at Hoppin' Johns has it all, including books about food, with a heavy emphasis on southern food and cooking classes for hands on instructions in how to do it all.

LEONARD SOLOMON'S WINES AND SPIRITS
L&L DISTRIBUTING
1456 NORTH DAYTON
CHICAGO, IL 60622
312-915-5911
312-915-0466 FAX

Grains, including spelt; rattlesnake and other beans, vinegars, crème fraîche, smoked fish, pâtés, caviars, special sausages, smoked duck breast, pastrami, imported cheeses, Amazon spices, frozen purées, and vanilla beans.

L'ESPRIT DE CAMPAGNE
P.O. BOX 3130
WINCHESTER, VA 22604
703-955-1014

Dried vine-ripened tomatoes in various forms, including halves marinated in extra-virgin olive iol with herbs, purées, and sprinkles. The company also offers dried apples, cherries, blueberries, and cranberries, all unsulphured and with no preservatives.

MONTDOMAINE CELLARS
R.R. 6, P.O. BOX 188A
CHARLOTTESVILLE, VA 22902
1-800-829-4633

Wines from the land of Thomas Jefferson, including Chardonnay, Cabernet Sauvigon, Merlot, blush, Viogies, Marsanne, and Cabernet Franc.

MORE THAN GOURMET
115 W. BARTGES STREET
AKRON, OH 44311
1-800-860-9392

Demi-Glace Gold® and Glace de Poulet Gold®, two classic French sauces of four-star quality that are made in the classic manner of Escoffier. An ultimate shortcut for the home cook.

PENZEYS, LTD.
P.O. BOX 1448
WAUKESHA, WI 53187
414-574-0277
414-574-0278 FAX

A wonderful source of spices and herbs by mail. A mail order catalog is available.

S. WALLACE EDWARDS & SONS, INC.
P.O. BOX 25
SURRY, VA 23883
1-800-290-9213

Hickory-smoked aged Virginia hams, bacon, and Surry sausages, as well as dry-cured duck breast and Virginia seafood including crab cakes, smoked tuna, and Chesapeake Bay oysters.

SWEET CELEBRATIONS
P.O. BOX 39426
EDINA, MN 55439
1-800-328-6722
612-943-1688

A complete catalogue of confectioners' supplies, including chocolate and other ingredients, and equipment.

ALBERT ULSTER IMPORTS, INC.
9211 GAITHER ROAD
GAITHERSBURG, MD 20877
1-800-231-8154

A professional source for confectionery and bakery supplies and tools, including edible gold dust.

WILTON ENTERPRISES, INC.
2240 WEST 75TH STREET
WOODRIDGE, IL 60515
708-963-7100, EXT. 320

Pastry and cake decorating supples, paste food colors, and icing ingredients.

INTRODUCTION

A Southerner Eats

I could never have written this book had I not met John Egerton. Over the years John has taught me about southern food and made me understand that, unlike any other region in the country, it is only through an appreciation of the southern table that one can comprehend its society. After too long a time unopened on my bookshelf, I opened John's 1987 classic *Southern Food* before writing this introduction. As I did so, three pieces of paper drifted out. The first was a typed note from the producer (although I suspect that John really wrote it) about the ham that John was sending as a gift to my husband, Louis Osteen. The second, in John's hand was his scrawl about the same ham, the third was Louis' thank you note. The story of that ham tells, in a small way, the story about the significance of southern food in a Southerner's life, about the people who produce it, those that cook it, and the folks who simply love to eat it.

The typed note read, "The time-honored country hams produced by southern craftsmen like Kentucky farmer Douglas Freeman are unsurpassed works of comestible art. Like the great winemakers of provincial France, the master pork smiths of the south have for generations combined traditional curing techniques with well-guarded family secrets to turn out signature hams of great distinction and universal appeal. This Freeman ham was dry-cured with salt (and certain undisclosed ingredients) in the winter of 1992–93, hung for a specified period in a dense fog of green hickory and sassafras smoke, and then left to age in the smokehouse for an additional twelve months. Thus baptized in the alternate extremes of frost and heat, it comes to the table as a product representative of almost four centuries of Southern culinary history." Dated April 4, 1994, John's scrawl read, "The ham weights 17 lbs. I'll try to call you before I ship this UPS today. Hope it's as good as they usually (but not always) are. Let me know how it goes. "

The day the ham arrived, my husband began the preparation—first soaking and then cooking. It sat on a our kitchen table for a while (less time than it might have), and every day Louis would slice off a piece of that ham and pop it in his mouth. As he chewed a huge and generous smile would illuminate his face. John needn't have worried. The ham was at least as good as "they usually are." In his thank you note, Louis wrote, "I certainly appreciated and savored the ham that you sent. I had been anxious to try a ham of Mr. Freeman's since I was introduced to them by way of your book. . . . It was truly a fine ham, I cannot remember any that have been better. Since most of my family eats only nuts, twigs, and things of that sort, I was able to enjoy as much ham as two people should have."

A couple of years later I was talking to John, reminiscing about that ham, and asked him about Doug Freeman. Doug had gone through a bad winter. He was ill and had been "whip sawed" by the weather, which had not been cold enough long enough to cure the hams "to the bone." He said that there had no been no sausage that winter either because his wife just couldn't handle the whole process alone. "More's the pity. Maybe next winter," he added. John was clearly worried, and although a man of modest means, I suspect that John was helping Doug out. It was important that Doug and his hams survive, because " a genuine country ham. . .is a cause in itself for joyful celebration."

In much the same way as John Egerton is perpetuating the mystique of southern food and Doug Freeman is preserving its traditions in his smokehouse, southern chefs are regaining the south's identity in their kitchens, stockpots, and skillets. The spirit of the South that many fear was lost in its assimilation into commercial centers is daily being reestablished in its restaurants.

In 1968, the authors of *The Horizon Cookbook* lamented that American cookery had been abased by technological developments, succumbed to bland efficiency. "It is easy—perhaps all too easy—to wish the revival of traditional individualized cuisine such as that found today only in the finest European restaurants." Happily since the eclipse of the generation of which they spoke, southern chefs have taken up the banner, searching for perfection in every vegetable bin and fishmonger's stall, refining their cuisine and in general inspiring a remarkable display of gastronomic enthusiasm for southern cookery.

The chefs represented in this book are truly the most passionate, energetic and enthusiastic of the many that are bringing the art of southern food into the American consciousness today. They have been evangelists for southern food, and it is to their credit that the region's diet is no longer thought of as greasy, "country" food unfit for the refined restaurant table. The creations of these chefs have spawned an international awareness, a hunger and appreciation of American southern food. That these chefs have succeeded so well in arousing an enthusiasm for their cuisine is not surprising. What the reader will discover here is food as spicy, bright, flavorful, and energetic as the chefs who have created it. I have been fortunate enough to have dined at the tables of many of these men and women, and I can assure you that those of you who enjoy a good table must not escape the delights of this southern one.

—Marlene Osteen

Appetizers

Esteemed culinary littérateur Joseph Weschberg believed that a great meal could only be had after serious contemplation. It might also be said that it could only be had after a notable prelude or preamble. And so, you are presented here with some intriguing and creative southern specialties to titillate your appetite, stimulate your palate, and forewarn you of some of the great delicacies that will follow this very auspicious beginning. In combination, these appetizers would make for an inspired cocktail party or holiday celebration or, in smaller assortment, a delectable culinary grazing of the South.

Asparagus Charlotte

Guenter Seeger

THE DINING ROOM, THE RITZ CARLTON BUCKHEAD
ATLANTA, GEORGIA

SERVES 4

This is a quick and dramatic way to serve asparagus. Green asparagus can be substituted for white with equal success.

2	pounds white asparagus, peeled, tough ends removed	1	tablespoon chopped chervil
			Salt and pepper to taste
1	egg, boiled 12 minutes, peeled, yolk and white separated, and grated		Juice of 1 lemon
		3	tablespoons olive oil
2	tablespoons peeled, seeded, and diced tomato	1	teaspoon sugar
			Fresh chervil for garnish

🍃 Tie the asparagus in bundles, 6 to 7 asparagus per bundle. In a large stockpot bring a large quantity of lightly salted water to boil, add the asparagus, and cook 6 to 7 minutes or until tender. Remove the asparagus with a long-handled strainer and plunge into a bowl of ice water. Drain and dry the asparagus on paper towels. Cut the tips of the asparagus into 2-inch lengths and the stems into small pieces. In a small mixing bowl combine the asparagus stem pieces with the egg white, tomato, and chervil. Season with salt and pepper, dress with the lemon juice and olive oil, and sprinkle with sugar.

🍃 Place a round 2-inch cookie cutter in the center of the serving plates and stand the asparagus tips in the cutter. Fill the center with the salad. Remove the cookie cutter, leaving the asparagus standing on the plate. Sprinkle with the grated egg yolk and garnish with fresh chervil.

GRILLED VEGETABLE TERRINE WITH LOBSTER AND RED PEPPER COULIS

Jean Banchet
THE RIVERIA
ATLANTA, GEORGIA

SERVES 4

Terrine

3	carrots, peeled and sliced ¼-inch lengthwise
2	Japanese eggplants, sliced ½-inch thick
2	medium zucchini, sliced ½-inch thick
2	yellow squash, sliced ½-inch thick
5	portabello mushrooms, dark gills removed and sliced ½-inch thick
3	carrots, peeled and sliced ½-inch thick
1	pound thin asparagus, ends trimmed
2	leeks, cleaned
4	large tomatoes
2	red bell peppers, roasted and peeled (see page 217)
2	green peppers, roasted and peeled (see page 217)
32	leaves fresh basil
1	cup olive oil
½	cup sherry vinegar
	Salt and pepper

Red Pepper Coulis

2	red bell peppers, roasted, seeded, and peeled (see page 217)
2	cloves garlic, peeled and minced
1	tablespoon olive oil
1	tablespoon sherry vinegar
	Salt and pepper to taste

Lobster

1	2-pound live lobster
	Salt

🍃 ***To make the terrine:*** In a small steamer set over simmering water (the water should not reach the vegetables), arrange the ¼-inch sliced carrots. Steam 4 to 5 minutes or until tender and pliable. Remove and reserve for later use.

🍃 Preheat the broiler or preheat the oven to 400°. Lightly brush a large roasting pan with a little of the olive oil. With the remaining oil brush the sliced eggplant, zucchini, squash, mushrooms, remaining uncooked carrots, asparagus, and leeks on both sides. Place the vegetables in a single layer in the prepared roasting pan. Cook the vegetables 3 to 4 minutes under the broiler, or about 10 minutes in the oven, until the vegetables have softened and are lightly colored. Remove from the oven and set aside.

🍃 Reduce the oven temperature to 350°. Core the tomatoes, cut in half, and place cut side down on a small roasting pan. Place them in the oven and cook about 20 minutes until the skins are blistered. Remove from the oven, remove the seeds, and cut into strips the size of the grilled vegetables.

🍃 Lightly brush a 3 x 8-inch loaf or terrine pan with olive oil. Line with parchment paper and brush again with the olive oil. Line the mold with lengthwise slices of the steamed carrot, allowing the ends to hang over the edges of the pan. Add a layer of each of the remaining grilled vegetables: eggplant, zucchini, squash, mushrooms, asparagus, leeks, tomatoes, and red and green peppers. Sprinkle some of the basil leaves on each layer before proceeding to the next. End with a layer of the grilled carrots. Fold in the overhanging ends of the steamed carrots. Press the top of the terrine gently with your fingers to make sure that the corners are completely filled and the top is flat. Lightly brush the shiny side of a sheet of aluminum foil with olive oil and wrap the terrine tightly with it. Place the terrine on a baking sheet and place another baking sheet on top. Add a 5-pound weight to the top pan and chill the terrine in the refrigerator for 4 hours or overnight.

🍃 ***To make the coulis:*** In a blender or food processor combine the red bell peppers, garlic, olive oil, sherry vinegar, and salt and pepper to taste, and purée until smooth.

🍃 ***To make the lobster:*** Set a rack or colander inside a large stockpot (12 or more inches deep), fill with 1½ inches of water and 1 tablespoon of salt, and bring to a boil. Add the lobster, cover, and if necessary weight down the cover to keep the steam inside. Lower the heat and continue to cook the lobster about 8 minutes or until the shell has turned bright red and the meat is just tender. Test for doneness by pulling off one of the little legs and tasting the meat. Drain the lobster. When cool enough to handle, twist off the claws and large knuckles and legs where they join the body. Lightly crush the tail shell with your hands and carefully remove the meat. Slice the tail into ½-inch-thick medallions. Remove the meat from the claws by cracking the shell with a lobster cracker or the back of a knife. Slice the claw meat into ½-inch-thick slices, and lightly brush all the lobster pieces with olive oil. Cover and reserve until ready to serve.

To serve: Unmold the terrine and slice into eight ½-inch-thick slices. Place 2 slices of the terrine on each serving plate; surround them with some of the coulis, and garnish with the lobster medallions.

SCALLOP ESCABECHE

Johnny Earles
CRIOLLA'S RESTAURANT
GRAYTON BEACH, FLORIDA

SERVES 4

Slaw
1   cup sliced fresh or canned hearts of palm
1½ cups peeled, seeded, and julienned green papaya
2   Scotch bonnet (habañero) chilies, seeded and minced
4   scallions, thinly sliced on the diagonal
¼   cup cilantro leaves
½   cup fresh tangerine juice
3   tablespoons lime juice
3   tablespoons rice vinegar
½   cup cold pressed peanut oil
    Salt and pepper to taste

Marinade
¾   cup fresh tangerine juice
¼   cup fresh lime juice
¼   cup rice vinegar
2   teaspoons kosher salt
1   Scotch bonnet (habañero) chile, seeded and minced
    Black pepper

Scallops
16 diver-harvested scallops
2   tablespoons grapeseed oil
    Salt and pepper to taste

Hibiscus Oil
¼   cup dried Jamaica flower petals (hibiscus)
    Reserved scallop marinade
½   cup grapeseed oil

Fried Plantain Strips
1   very ripe plantain
1   cup canola or other vegetable oil

Garnish
2   tangerines, peeled, sectioned into segments, white pith removed
4   fresh cilantro sprigs
    Crushed pink peppercorns

🌿 **To make the slaw:** In a nonreactive bowl combine the hearts of palm, papaya, Scotch bonnet, green onions, and cilantro leaves. Season with salt and pepper. In a separate bowl combine the juices and vinegar, then slowly whisk in the peanut oil. Season with salt and pepper. Pour this vinaigrette over the slaw, toss well to combine, and refrigerate 1 hour.

🌿 **To prepare the marinade:** In a medium shallow bowl combine the juices, vinegar, salt, chile, and fresh ground pepper.

🌿 **To make the scallops:** Place a dry large heavy steel or iron skillet over high heat for 3 minutes. Add the grapeseed oil and heat to nearly smoking. Pat the scallops dry with paper towels, season with salt and pepper, and place in the pan. Do not overcrowd the pan; cook the scallops in 2 batches if necessary. Sear the scallops on one side for about 2 minutes, then turn them with tongs and cook for 2 minutes on the other side. Remove the scallops from the pan and allow to cool.

🌿 Slice each scallop horizontally into 5 slices. Add the scallop slices to the marinade and chill 20 minutes in the refrigerator. With a slotted spoon remove the scallops from the marinade and reserve all of the marinade for later use.

🌿 **To make the hibiscus oil:** In a medium nonreactive saucepan combine the hibiscus and reserved marinade and reduce over medium-high heat until reduced to ¼ cup. Remove from the heat and let cool 5 minutes. Pour into a small mixing bowl and slowly, in a steady stream, whisk in the grapeseed oil. Set aside at room temperature.

🌿 **To fry the plantain:** Cut the plantain crosswise into 2½-inch pieces. Make a lengthwise cut in each and peel off the skin by sliding your thumbnail under the slit to pry off the skin. (Alternately you may run the plantain under running water to wash away the milky liquid that sometimes seeps from the skin. If you do, pat the plantain sections dry with paper towels before proceeding.) In a large heavy frying pan over high heat bring ½ inch of oil to 350°. Add more oil if necessary. Add the plantain slices and fry about 1 minute per side until they have formed a skin and turned golden brown. With a long-handled strainer remove the plantains to paper toweling to drain.

🌿 **To assemble:** Place a 3-inch round ring mold in the center of one of the four serving plates. With a slotted spoon, place one-fourth of the slaw into the mold and pack loosely. For the next layer, arrange 8 to 10 tangerine segments on top of the slaw. Follow with 5 slices of scallop arranged in a pinwheel pattern. Remove the ring mold and spoon the hibiscus oil around the plate and garnish with fried plantain strips, a sprig of cilantro, and crushed pink peppercorns.

STUFFED COLLARD GREENS WITH ROASTED CHICKEN, CAROLINA GOAT CHEESE, AND BLACK-EYED PEA SALAD

Casey Taylor
THE RHETT HOUSE INN
BEAUFORT, SOUTH CAROLINA

SERVES 4

Horseradish Yogurt Sauce
⅔	cup plain yogurt
1	tablespoon grated fresh or drained bottled horseradish
	Salt and freshly ground pepper to taste

Barbecue Sauce
1	tablespoon olive oil
½	cup peeled, seeded, and chopped plum tomatoes
½	cup minced garlic
¾	cup seeded and chopped poblano pepper
¼	cup seeded and chopped red bell pepper
2	tablespoons chopped cilantro
1	tablespoon paprika
2¼	teaspoons chile powder
½	tablespoon chopped coriander
¾	teaspoon ground cumin
2	cups Veal or Chicken Stock (see page 218)
3	tablespoons Lea and Perrins Worcestershire sauce
2	tablespoons plus 1 teaspoon Dijon mustard
¼	cup plus 2 tablespoons tomato catsup
¼	cup firmly packed dark brown sugar
	Salt and pepper to taste

Red Pepper Purée
2	roasted red bell peppers
1	small chopped onion
3	garlic cloves, chopped
3	tablespoons olive oil
2	tablespoons chopped fresh basil leaves
	Salt and pepper to taste

Collards
2	bunches collards
1	cup apple cider vinegar
1	smoked ham hock
1	large red onion, coarsely chopped
2	tablespoons Tabasco sauce
	Enough chicken stock to cover collards (approximately 12 cups)

Black-eyed Peas
½	pound dried black-eyed peas
4	cups water
2	teaspoons salt
½	teaspoon pepper
2	tablespoons fresh oregano, chopped
¼	cup balsamic vinegar
1	large red bell pepper, diced (¾ cup)
1	large red onion, diced
½	cup olive oil

Chicken
1	pound bonelesss, skinless chicken thighs
2	tablespoons olive oil
	Salt and pepper

8	ounces goat cheese

🐟 **To make the horseradish sauce:** In a small bowl combine the yogurt, horseradish, salt, and pepper. Set aside.

🐟 **To make the barbecue sauce:** In a nonreactive, heavy-bottomed saucepan heat the olive oil over medium-high heat and sauté the tomatoes, garlic, poblano and red peppers, and cilantro for 5 minutes or until softened. Add the spices and continue to cook for 4 minutes. Add the veal or chicken stock, Worcestershire sauce, mustard, catsup, and dark brown sugar, and bring to a boil. Reduce the heat and simmer for 20 minutes, stirring occasionally. Adjust the seasoning for salt and pepper. Pour through a fine mesh strainer into a clean container and reserve until ready to use.

🐟 **To make the red pepper purée:** Begin roasting the peppers by broiling on a rack about 2 inches from the heat, turning every 5 minutes until the peppers are charred and blistered (about 15 minutes total). Transfer the peppers to a brown paper bag, close, and let steam in the bag until cool enough to touch. When cooled, remove the peppers from the bag and peel. Remove the tops and discard the seeds and ribs. In a skillet cook the onion and garlic in 1 tablespoon of oil over moderate heat until softened. Transfer the mixture to a food processor and add the roasted peppers, basil, 2 tablespoons of olive oil, salt, and pepper to taste. Blend the sauce until smooth and transfer to a small bowl.

🐟 **To make the collards:** Wash and drain the collard greens. Remove leafy parts from the thicker stems. The darker, heavier outer leaves will be used for this dish. Rinse the leaves, removing any dirt and grit. Place the collards in a large stockpot with the apple cider vinegar, smoked ham hock, red onion, and Tabasco. Add the chicken stock and bring to a boil over medium-high heat. Reduce the heat, cover, and simmer until the collards are tender, approximately 1 hour. Drain well in a colander, pressing with the back of a spoon to release excess water.

🐟 **To make the peas:** Wash and pick over the peas. Soak overnight in cold water to cover. (Or quick-soak the peas. Bring the water and peas to a boil. Boil 2 minutes. Cover, remove from the heat, and set aside for 1 hour.)

🐟 Drain thoroughly. Return the peas to a large saucepan, add water to cover, and bring to a boil. Reduce the heat, cover, and simmer over low heat for 45 minutes to 1 hour until tender.

🐟 Remove the peas from the heat, drain, and transfer to a mixing bowl. To the mixing bowl add seasonings, oregano, vinegar, diced red pepper, red onion, and olive oil. Toss all together. Marinate at least 1 hour.

🐟 **To make the chicken:** Trim the thighs of all sinew and fat. Place in a tray, toss with olive oil, and season with salt and pepper. Roast in a 350° oven for approximately 18 to 20 minutes. Let cool, then julienne the meat.

✍ *To assemble:* Preheat the oven to 350°. Arrange the collard leaves on a work surface, being careful not to tear the leaves. Discard any leaves that have holes. Spread the leaves with 2 tablespoons of chicken, add 1 tablespoon of goat cheese, and cover with 2 tablespoons of the pea salad. Starting at the long end, carefully roll up each collard leaf to enclose the filling. Fold the ends over and square it off. The finished product will resemble a burrito. Place seam side down in a pan and place in the oven until heated through. Slice the rolls on the bias, arrange attractively on individual plates, and garnish with the three sauces.

ROASTED PORTABELLO CAPS

Richard Grenamyer
THE GOVERNOR'S CLUB
TALLAHASSEE, FLORIDA

SERVES 4

Sun-dried Tomato Tapenade

2	cups sun-dried tomatoes, soaked in boiling water 15 minutes
3	tablespoons capers
1	tablespoon garlic, peeled
2	tablespoons fresh basil
1	teaspoon salt
1/3	cup olive oil

Portabello Mushrooms

4	portabello mushroom caps, stems removed
4	ounces goat cheese, crumbled
1/4	cup Basil Oil (see page 215)
8	teaspoons balsamic vinegar
	Fresh basil leaves for garnish

✍ *To make the sundried tomato tapenade:* In a blender or food processor combine the reconstituted tomatoes, capers, garlic, basil, and salt and briefly process until mixture forms a coarse purée. With the machine running, add the oil in a slow and steady stream. Transfer the tapenade to a clean container and refrigerate. The tapenade can be made up to 2 weeks in advance.

✍ *To roast the portabello caps:* Preheat the oven to 400°. Place the mushroom caps on a clean work surface and, using a sharp thin-bladed knife, slice the caps horizontally into 3 pieces. Spread 1 tablespoon of the tapenade on the bottom slice, crumble on 1 tablespoon of the goat cheese, and top with the middle mushroom slice. Layer with the tapenade and goat cheese as before, and cap with the mushroom top. Transfer the mushrooms to an oiled baking sheet and bake for 8 to 10 minutes or until the caps are heated through.

🐟 **To serve:** Drizzle 3 teaspoons of basil oil on the bottom of each serving plate, and swirl 2 teaspoons of balsamic vinegar in the oil. Center a mushroom on each plate and garnish with fresh basil leaves.

RISOTTO WITH BACON, SILVER QUEEN CORN, AND CATFISH

Scott Howell

NANA'S
DURHAM, NORTH CAROLINA

SERVES 8

Bacon and Broth

3	tablespoons butter
1/4	pound bacon, cut into 1/2-inch cubes
1/4	cup chopped celery, cut into 1/4-inch cubes
1/3	cup chopped onion, cut into 1/4-inch cubes
2	bay leaves
6	cups chicken broth
1/3	cup thinly sliced and peeled shallots
2	tablespoons Roasted Garlic Purée (see page 218)
6	catfish fillets, about 6 ounces each

Silver Queen Corn

2	cups Silver Queen corn
3	tablespoons butter
	Salt and pepper

Risotto

7	tablespoons butter, divided
2	cups Arborio rice
1/2	cup dry white wine
	Reserved broth
1/2	cup freshly grated Parmesan cheese

🐟 **To make the bacon and broth:** In a medium skillet heat the butter over medium-high heat. Add the bacon and cook until the fat is rendered and the bacon is crisp. With a slotted spoon remove the bacon onto absorbent toweling.

🐟 To the skillet in which the bacon cooked add the chopped celery, chopped onion, and bay leaves and sauté for 5 minutes, being careful not to brown. Add the chicken stock, shallots, and roasted garlic, and bring to a boil. Reduce to a simmer. Taste and add salt and pepper as necessary. The broth should be a little salty. After 15 minutes add the catfish and gently simmer for 4 minutes or until the catfish is cooked through, but not overcooked. Carefully remove the fish to a plate, cut into chunks, and keep warm. Remove and discard the bay leaves and strain the broth, reserving the solids. In a food processor purée the solids, and add back to the broth.

🐟 **To prepare the corn:** In a small saucepan melt the butter and add the corn. Season with salt and pepper. Gently simmer for 5 minutes. Remove the pan from the heat and reserve.

🍂 *To make the risotto:* In a saucepan heat 3 tablespoons of the butter and add the rice. Cook, stirring until the rice is opaque and thoroughly coated with the butter. Add the white wine and stir constantly until the liquid has all absorbed into the rice.

🍂 In a separate medium saucepan heat the broth to a simmer. To the rice add the hot broth ½ cup at a time, constantly stirring after each addition until the liquid is completely absorbed. The risotto will become more creamy with each addition of hot broth. Toward the end, add the reserved bacon, half of the catfish fillet pieces, and the cooked corn. At the very end add the remaining 4 tablespoons of butter and the Parmesan. Taste and add salt and pepper as necessary.

🍂 *To serve:* Divide the risotto among 4 serving plates and place reserved catfish pieces on top of each portion. Serve very hot.

POTATO CRISP PIZZA

Cory Mattson

THE FEARRINGTON HOUSE
PITTSBORO, NORTH CAROLINA

SERVES 4

Mushrooms

1½   cups assorted dried mushrooms (such as
        shiitakes, morels, or cèpes)
¼   cup olive oil
1   cup dry white wine
      Salt and pepper to taste

Potato Cake

6   tablespoons olive oil
6   cups shredded unpeeled Yukon Gold
        potatoes
      Salt and pepper to taste

Tomatoes and Basil

1½   cups very ripe cherry tomato halves
1   cup basil leaves cut into chiffonade (very
        thin strips)

⅓   cup grated Parmesan cheese
1   tablespoon balsamic vinegar

🍂 *To prepare the mushrooms:* Soak the mushrooms for 40 minutes in very hot water to cover. Carefully lift the softened mushrooms out of the water, leaving the sand and grit behind. Squeeze dry. Heat the olive oil in the skillet and sauté the mushrooms on high heat until lightly browned. Add the white wine and simmer until the mushrooms are cooked dry. Season to taste with salt and pepper. Reserve.

🌱 **To make the potato cake:** In a heavy skillet heat the olive oil. Toss the potatoes with the salt and pepper and add to the hot skillet. Press lightly to about ⅓-inch thickness. Cook for 4 minutes, then flip the potatoes to brown the other side. When brown on both sides, transfer the potato cake to an absorbent paper towel and drain for 1 minute. Transfer the potato cake to an ovenproof plate.

🌱 **To make the pizza:** Scatter the mushrooms evenly over the potato crust (formerly called a potato cake, but it is now transforming into a classy pizza crust), then top with the tomatoes and basil. Sprinkle the Parmesan evenly over the pizza. Finish in a 350° oven for 5 minutes.

🌱 Sprinkle with 1 tablespoon of balsamic vinegar if desired before serving.

GNOCCHI STUFFED WITH FONDUTA IN PARMESAN CHEESE–CREAM SAUCE

Jamie Adams
VENI VIDI VICI
ATLANTA, GEORGIA

SERVES 4

Fonduta

1	pound Italian fontina cheese, rind removed, diced, soaked in 1 cup milk
3	egg yolks
2	tablespoons all-purpose flour

Gnocchi

4	pounds Idaho potatoes
3	eggs
½	teaspoon salt
1	tablespoon olive oil
¾	cup all-purpose flour (approximately)

Sauce

1	tablespoon butter
1	cup heavy cream
½	cup grated Parmigiano-Regiano cheese
	Pinch of salt and pepper
	Pepper to taste
1	truffle, peeled and thinly sliced

🌱 **To make the fonduta:** In a double boiler or a metal bowl set over a pan of simmering water melt the Fontina with its soaking milk until smooth. Whisk in the egg yolks and flour and cook, stirring constantly with a whisk, about 7 minutes until smooth and thickened slightly. Be careful not to overcook, as the eggs will curdle and the mixture will separate. Remove the pan from the heat and remove the bowl from the pan. Stir the sauce for 1 minute while the water in the pan cools slightly. Transfer the mixture to a clean bowl and allow to cool for 30 minutes.

🌒 When the cheese is cooled enough to handle, but still slightly warm, transfer to a lightly floured work surface and roll into pencil width strips.

🌒 *To make the gnocchi:* Bring a large pot of lightly salted water to boil over high heat. Add the potatoes and cook about 35 minutes until very tender. Remove the potatoes from the water and peel. While potatoes are still warm, pass them through a food mill. Allow the potatoes to cool completely.

🌒 Spread the milled potatoes on a board and make a well in the center. Put the eggs, salt, and olive oil in the well. Little by little mix in the flour, incorporating it into the potatoes and liquids. Add the minimum amount of flour possible. When a solid dough is formed, start kneading. Gently knead for about 5 minutes, being careful not to overknead, as this will develop the gluten in the flour, making the gnocchi tough.

🌒 Remove a small piece of the gnocchi and roll out into a strip the same width but slightly thicker than the fonduta strips. Press a fonduta strip into the gnocchi dough and roll out into a strip. Repeat with the remaining gnocchi and fonduta. Cut the strips crosswise into 1/2-inch pieces. (Be careful not to place the strips too close together when cutting into pieces, as they will stick to each other.)

🌒 Bring a large pot containing a large quantity of salted water to a boil over high heat. While the water is coming to a boil, make the sauce.

🌒 *To make the sauce:* In a medium saucepan melt the butter over medium heat until golden. Add the cream and bring the mixture to a simmer. Cook until reduced slightly. Add the cheese, salt, and pepper to taste and cook until the cheese has melted and the sauce is smooth. Keep the sauce warm on the back of the stove while completing the dish. If necessary, reheat over very low heat.

🌒 When the water is boiling, quickly drop all the gnocchi into the pot. Lightly stir the water with a wooden spoon to keep the gnocchi from sticking. After a few seconds, they will come to the surface of the water; let them cook for 1 minute longer. With a strainer, remove the gnocchi to the pan containing the sauce. Toss them briefly in the sauce to coat, and transfer to a serving dish. Garnish with the truffle.

SHRIMP AND PLANTAIN TORTE

Guillermo Veloso
YUCA RESTAURANT
MIAMI BEACH, FLORIDA

SERVES 6

The torte is made with the basic cooking sauce, "sofrito," that is the essential ingredient in many Spanish recipes and was brought to North America centuries ago by the Spanish settlers. The important sauce base is the oil made from the seed of the annatto (known in Spanish-speaking countries as achiote), a red flowering tree. Because the seed makes an excellent dye, the American Indians mixed it with oil and used it to paint their bodies. Its purpose was only ornamental, causing some historians to speculate that it was the Indians' use of this dye that earned them the name "redskins." As a culinary resource, the annatto seed, like saffron, lends a strong color and delicate flavor to food.

Annatto Oil

1/2	cup vegetable oil
1/4	cup annatto (achiote seeds)

Sofrito

2	ounces salt pork, finely diced
1	teaspoon Annatto Oil
1 1/2	cups finely chopped onions
1	tablespoon minced garlic
2	medium green bell peppers, seeded, deribbed, and coarsely chopped
4	ounces lean boneless ham, cut into 1/2-inch dice (about 1 cup)
2	large tomatoes, peeled, seeded, and coarsely chopped (or substitute 1 1/2 cups drained, chopped, canned tomatoes)
1 1/2	teaspoons finely chopped cilantro
1/2	teaspoon crumbled dried oregano
1	teaspoon salt
	Freshly ground black pepper

Shrimp

9	tablespoons butter
1	onion, peeled and diced
1	garlic clove, peeled and minced
2	tomatoes, diced
2	pounds shrimp, peeled, deveined, and roughly chopped
2	cups Shrimp Stock (see page 219)
1 1/2	cups white wine
1/2	cup Sofrito
1	bunch fresh basil, cut into chiffonade

Plantains

2	sweet plantains
3	tablespoons butter
1	egg, beaten until frothy
1/4	cup grated Manchego cheese (see Note)

Sauce

1	cup (2 sticks) butter
4	shallots, peeled and minced
2	cups Spanish sherry
1/4	cup sherry vinegar
1	vanilla bean, split and scraped
	Pinch of saffron
1/4	cup heavy cream

🍂 ***To make the annatto oil:*** In a small saucepan heat the oil over medium-high heat until a light haze forms on the surface. Stir in the annatto seeds and when they are evenly coated with oil, reduce the heat to medium, cover, and simmer for 1 minute. Remove from the heat, uncover, and let the oil cool to room temperature. Strain the annatto oil into a jar and discard the seeds. Cover tightly and refrigerate until ready to use. Although the annatto oil will keep for several months, its flavor and color will diminish as it ages.

🍂 ***To make the sofrito:*** In a large heavy skillet fry the salt pork over medium heat, stirring with a spoon until crisp and brown. With a slotted spoon remove and discard the salt pork. Add the annatto oil to the fat remaining in the skillet. Add the onions, garlic, and peppers and cook, stirring frequently, about 5 to 10 minutes until the vegetables are tender but not yet brown. Add the diced ham and stir until all the pieces are coated with the oil. Then stir in the chopped tomatoes, coriander, oregano, salt, and a few grindings of black pepper. Reduce the heat to low, cover, and simmer 30 minutes, stirring occasionally to prevent the vegetables from sticking. Ladle the sofrito into a large clean jar or bowl, cover, and refrigerate until ready to use. It may be kept for 1 to 2 weeks.

🍂 ***To cook the shrimp:*** In a large sauté pan melt 1 tablespoon of the butter over medium-high heat. Add the onion and garlic and cook briefly until the onions are just tender. Add the tomato and stir thoroughly. Add the shrimp and cook about 1 minute, stirring, until the shrimp are almost cooked. Transfer the shrimp mixture to a platter, raise the heat to high, and pour in the shrimp stock, white wine, and sofrito. Bring the mixture to a boil, and continue to boil vigorously until the mixture is reduced by half. Reduce the heat until the mixture is just at a simmer. Using a wire whisk, beat in the butter quickly, one piece at a time. Be careful not to continue to reduce the mixture as the butter is beaten in. Return the shrimp to the sauté pan and finish cooking the shrimp, about 1 minute or just until the shrimp turn bright pink. Add the basil and check the seasonings.

🍂 ***To cook the plantains and assemble the torte:*** Peel the plantains and cut each lengthwise into ¼-inch thick strips. In a heavy-bottomed skillet melt the butter over medium-high heat. When the foam begins to subside, add the plantains. Cook them about 1 minute per side or until golden brown, turning the strips with a slotted spatula. Transfer to paper towels to drain.

🍂 Preheat the oven to 350°. Place six 4-inch metal ring molds on a baking sheet, and fit 2 plantain strips inside each mold. Fill with the shrimp mixture, brush with 1 tablespoon of the egg wash, and sprinkle with the Manchego cheese. Bake the tortes in the preheated oven 20 minutes or until warmed through and the cheese has browned.

🍂 ***To make the sauce:*** In a small saucepan melt 1 tablespoon of the butter over medium-high heat. Add the shallots and sauté until translucent. Raise the heat to high, pour in the sherry, sherry vinegar, vanilla bean, and saffron and reduce by half. Add the heavy cream and reduce by half again. Reduce the heat to very low and beat in the butter, 1 tablespoon at a time, until well incorporated. Do not let the sauce begin to bubble; remove from the heat if necessary. Serve immediately.

🐚 Remove the tortes from the oven. Spoon 2 tablespoons of the sauce on each of the serving plates and place the ring mold in the center. Carefully remove the ring and serve immediately.

🐚 *Note:* Manchego, Spain's most famous cheese, was named because it was originally made from the milk of Manchego sheep from the plains of La Mancha. This unctuous, semi-firm cheese has a mellow flavor. The two most popularly exported are curado and viejo. The latter is aged longer.

CRAWFISH SPRING ROLLS WITH ROOT VEGETABLES AND CRAWFISH BEURRE BLANC

Hallman Woods **III**

LE ROSIER
NEW IBERIA, LOUISIANA

SERVES 4 TO 6

Crawfish Beurre Blanc

2	cups dry white wine
2	tablespoons champagne or rice vinegar
1	tablespoon lemon juice
1	cup crawfish fat, removed from the processed tails and rinsed with water
½	medium yellow onion, peeled and sliced
4	cloves garlic, peeled and sliced in half
2	bay leaves
8	parsley stems
3	tablespoons heavy whipping cream
½	cup Tabasco brand Bloody Mary mix or tomato juice
1	cup (2 sticks) unsalted butter, cut into 1-inch pieces

Tabasco sauce to taste

½	teaspoon ground coriander
	Salt and white pepper to taste
½	jalapeño pepper, minced and seeded
2	tablespoons peeled and minced fresh garlic

Crawfish Spring Rolls

¼	cup olive oil
1	carrot, peeled and julienned
¼	cup cleaned and julienned leek
¼	cup peeled and julienned celery root
½	red bell pepper, julienned
½	yellow bell pepper, julienned
1	cup finely shredded green cabbage
2	tablespoons thinly sliced scallions

½	teaspoon peeled and minced fresh ginger	1	pound crawfish tails with fat
½	teaspoon minced lime zest		Egg roll or spring roll wrappers
1	teaspoon minced garlic	1	egg yolk, beaten with 3 tablespoons water
¼	teaspoon finely chopped cilantro		and 3 tablespoons all-purpose flour
5	dashes Tabasco sauce	2	quarts vegetable oil for deep fat frying
⅛	teaspoon ground coriander		Baby greens for garnish
	Salt and white pepper to taste		Chive sprigs for garnish

To make the beurre blanc: In a small saucepan boil the white wine, vinegar, lemon juice, crawfish fat, onion, garlic, bay leaves, and parsley stems until the wine mixture is completely reduced and only 2 tablespoons remain.

Add the heavy whipping cream and Bloody Mary mix and cook over high heat until reduced by half. Reduce the heat to low and whisk in the butter, one piece at a time, making sure each piece is incorporated before adding the next one. Add the garlic, salt, Tabasco, coriander, jalapeño, and white pepper. Taste and adjust the seasonings if necessary. Remove the pan from the heat and strain the sauce through a fine mesh strainer or chinois into a stainless steel mixing bowl. Set the bowl over barely simmering water set over low heat, and keep warm until ready to use.

To make the spring rolls: In a medium saucepan heat the olive oil over medium heat and sauté the julienned vegetables briefly, about 3 to 5 minutes or until just tender. Remove the pan from the heat. Add all remaining ingredients, including the crawfish. Taste and adjust the seasoning by adding salt, pepper, and Tabasco. Remove the mixture to a tray and let cool for 15 minutes before proceeding.

Separate the egg or spring roll wrappers and place them on a counter. Place a heaping tablespoon of the crawfish-vegetable mixture on one wrapper toward the edge of the wrapper closest to you. Spread the filling out evenly over the wrapper to within 2 inches of each end. Spread some of the egg mixture on the opposite end. (The egg mixture will act as a sealer.) Fold in the sides and roll up the wrapper to enclose the filling. Press to secure. Repeat for the remaining wrappers and filling.

Preheat the oven to 400°. In a large saucepan heat the oil to 375°. Add half the egg rolls and deep-fry, turning constantly over high heat for about 5 minutes or until golden brown. Remove with a long-handled strainer and drain on paper towels. Reheat the oil and deep-fry the remaining spring rolls in the same way. Place the spring rolls on a sheet pan and rewarm in the preheated oven for approximately 3 minutes.

To serve: Ladle ¼ cup of crawfish beurre blanc onto warmed dinner plates. For a decorative touch, position 2 to 3 pieces of exotic baby greens, such as frisee, on the sauce. Remove the spring rolls from the oven and cut each in half on the diagonal. Position the spring rolls on top of one another and garnish with chive sprigs.

SUGAR CANE–SPEARED GULF SHRIMP WITH TAMARIND–ORANGE HONEY GLAZE

Wilhelm Gahabka

THE REGISTRY RESORT
NAPLES, FLORIDA

SERVES 4

Shrimp

8	Gulf shrimp (under 15-per-pound size)
1	8-inch strip sugar cane
1	ounce (2 tablespoons) spiced rum
2	ounces (¼ cup) coconut milk
3	ounces (6 tablespoons) pineapple juice

Slaw

1	small jicama, peeled and julienned
1	chayote squash, julienned
½	yellow bell pepper, julienned
½	red bell pepper, julienned
½	green bell pepper, julienned
¼	teaspoon chipotle pepper oil (or smoked, dried jalapeño pepper)
1	tablespoon pineapple juice
	Juice of ½ lime
1	teaspoon chopped fresh cilantro
	Salt and pepper to taste

Sauce

1	teaspoon sesame oil
1	teaspoon olive oil
1	shallot, peeled and diced
1	garlic clove, peeled and diced
8	shrimp shells
1	teaspoon chopped unpeeled fresh ginger
2	teaspoons Madras curry powder
1	cup white port wine
1	14-ounce can unsweetened coconut milk
2	cups heavy cream
	Salt and pepper to taste
¼	teaspoon Thai curry paste

Glaze

1	teaspoon tamarind paste
2	teaspoons orange honey
3	teaspoons orange marmalade
1	pinch chopped Scotch bonnet (habañero) chile

Garnishes

1	plantain
2	tablespoons butter
¼	cup roasted coconut flakes
4	tablespoons cilantro leaves

✍ **To prepare the shrimp:** Peel the shrimp, reserving the shells for the sauce. Devein and wash the shrimp in cold water. Set aside.

✍ Cut the sugar cane into 8-inch strips. In a medium mixing bowl combine the rum, coconut milk, and pineapple juice. Add the sugar cane to the mixing bowl. Let the sugar cane marinate while preparing the slaw, sauce, and glaze.

🍃 **To prepare the slaw:** In a medium mixing bowl toss together the jícama, chayote squash, and peppers. Add the chipotle pepper oil, pineapple juice, fresh lime juice, and cilantro. Season to taste with salt and pepper. Combine well and set aside to marinate at room temperature.

🍃 **To prepare the sauce:** In a medium saucepan heat the sesame and olive oils over medium heat. Add the chopped shallot and garlic and sauté 3 to 4 minutes or until softened. Add the shrimp shells, ginger, and curry powder to the saucepan, and stir well. Raise the heat to medium-high, add the port wine, and bring to a simmer. Simmer this mixture for about 2 to 3 minutes. Add the unsweetened coconut milk. Stir in the heavy cream and add the Thai curry paste. Reduce the heat to low and cook at a slow simmer for about 10 minutes or until the sauce is reduced by half. Season with salt and pepper. Strain the sauce through a fine mesh strainer and keep warm over very low heat until ready to use.

🍃 **To make the glaze:** In the top of a double boiler over simmering water combine the tamarind paste, orange honey, orange marmalade, and Scotch bonnet pepper. Warm just until the ingredients are combined. Set aside at room temperature until ready to use.

🍃 **To cook the shrimp:** Preheat the oven to 350°. Remove the sugar cane from the marinade and, using the sugarcane as a skewer, spear one shrimp on each piece of sugarcane. Season the shrimp with salt and pepper. In a large sauté pan or skillet heat the chipotle and olive oils over medium-high heat. Sear the shrimp in the hot skillet about 30 seconds per side or until they just begin to stiffen. Be careful not to overcook (the shrimp will cook some more in the oven). Remove the shrimp from the skillet, brush with the glaze, and place in a medium roasting pan. Roast the shrimp in the preheated oven for 5 minutes. Remove from the oven.

🍃 **To assemble the dish:** Peel and slice the plantain. In a medium skillet melt the butter over medium-high heat and add the slices of plantain. Sauté the plantain until lightly browned. Remove from the pan and set aside.

🍃 Divide the slaw between 4 plates, placing in the center of each plate. Top the slaw with 2 pieces of sugar caned shrimp per dish. Drizzle the curry sauce around the plate. Garnish with roasted coconut flakes, cilantro leaves, and crisp slices of plantain.

Yuca-stuffed Shrimp with a Sour Orange Mojo and Scotch Bonnet Tartar Salsa

Norman Van Aken
NORMAN'S
CORAL GABLES, FLORIDA

SERVES 4

Stuffing

2 pounds yuca
1 Scotch bonnet (habañero) chile, stem and seeds removed, minced
3 garlic cloves, peeled and minced
Salt and pepper to taste

Shrimp

12 fresh very large shrimp, peeled, deveined, and butterflied
1 tablespoon olive oil
Salt and pepper to taste
½ cup all-purpose flour
1 egg yolk, beaten with 3 tablespoons water
½ cup finely ground dried breadcrumbs

Mojo

6 garlic cloves, peeled and minced
1 to 2 Scotch bonnet (habañero) chilies, stems and seeds discarded, minced
½ teaspoon salt

2 teaspoons whole cumin seeds, freshly toasted
1 cup pure olive oil
⅓ cup sour orange juice (or lime juice)
2 teaspoons Spanish sherry vinegar
Salt and pepper to taste

Scotch Bonnet Tartar Salsa

3 egg yolks
1 tablespoon champagne vinegar
1 teaspoon pickling juice from the Scotch bonnets
½ cup virgin olive oil
½ cup canola oil
1 bottled Scotch bonnet (habañero) chile, stem and seeds discarded, minced
3 tablespoons diced sweet butter pickles
2 tablespoons peeled and diced red onion
1 hard-boiled egg
Salt and pepper to taste

¼ cup peanut oil

☙ **To make the stuffing:** Cut the yuca crosswise into 3-inch pieces and peel with a paring knife. Cut a shallow x in the end of each section to help the yuca expand while cooking. Place the yuca in a medium-size saucepan with 1 teaspoon salt and cold water to cover. Boil the yuca until soft, about 15 minutes.

☙ Drain in a colander and return to the saucepan. Place the pan over very low heat and coarsely mash the yuca pieces with a potato masher or 2 large meat forks or force through a ricer. Combine the mashed yuca with the Scotch bonnet, garlic, salt, and pepper to taste and set aside.

❧ *To prepare the shrimp:* In a medium mixing bowl toss the shrimp with the olive oil, salt, and pepper. Remove them to a plate. Stuff the cavity of each shrimp with 1 tablespoon of the yuca stuffing. Pack the stuffing firmly into place. In separate shallow bowls place the flour, egg yolk mixture, and breadcrumbs. Dredge the shrimp in the flour, then dip in the egg yolk mixture, and then into the breadcrumbs. Remove the shrimp to a rack until ready to cook.

❧ *To make the mojo:* Mash the garlic, chilies, salt, and cumin together in a mortar with the pestle until a smooth paste is formed. Scrape the paste into a small heat resistant mixing bowl and set aside.

❧ In a small saucepan heat the olive oil over medium-high heat until fairly hot and pour it over the garlic-chilies mixture. Allow this mixture to stand 10 minutes.

❧ Whisk in the sour orange juice and the vinegar. Season with salt and pepper to taste and set aside until ready to use. (Mojo tastes best when served within a couple of hours of making, but it will keep for several days in the refrigerator.)

❧ *To make the Scotch bonnet tartar salsa:* Place the 3 egg yolks in the mixing bowl of an electric blender and beat until pale. Whisk in the vinegar and the pickling juice. In a steady stream, slowly add the olive and canola oils, mixing slowly until the oils are incorporated and an emulsion has been formed. Remove the mixture to a medium mixing bowl. Add the Scotch bonnet, sweet butter pickles, and red onion. Separate the white from the yolk of the hard-boiled egg. Pass the egg white through a fine sieve and add to the mixing bowl. Season to taste. Cover and refrigerate until ready to serve.

❧ *To serve:* In a small saucepan heat the mojo over medium heat until quite hot. While the mojo is warming, in a large frying pan heat the peanut oil over medium heat. Add the shrimp and cook until golden and cooked through, about 1 minute per side. Remove the shrimp to a plate lined with paper towels, and then arrange on the 4 serving plates.

❧ Pour the mojo into a dipping bowl or pour it directly onto the plated shrimp. Spoon the Scotch bonnet tartar in small dots between the shrimp or into individual bowls on the side.

❧ *Note:* Leftover mojo and tartar sauces can be stored in covered containers in the refrigerator for up to 3 days.

SPICY SCALLOPS WITH CHILE SAUCE

Nick Apostle

NICK'S
JACKSON, MISSISSIPPI

SERVES 8

Cabbage in Vinaigrette

6	tablespoons olive oil
2	tablespoons rice vinegar
	Kosher or sea salt to taste
	Ground black pepper to taste
½	head red cabbage, thinly sliced
½	bunch scallions, cut on the bias
½	bunch cilantro, leaves only

Chili Sauce

¾	cup mayonnaise, homemade or good quality store-bought
3	tablespoons chile paste
	Juice of 1 lemon
2	tablespoons (approximately) cold water

Scallops and Breading

1¼	pounds large sea scallops
½	cup all-purpose flour
½	cup cornmeal
1½	teaspoons paprika
¼	teaspoon cayenne pepper
1½	teaspoons ground cumin
1½	teaspoons kosher or sea salt
1½	teaspoons ground white pepper
1½	teaspoons pure chili powder
	Oil for deep-frying
	Salt and pepper to taste
2	lemons, cut into wedges

🐟 **To make the vinaigrette:** In a large mixing bowl combine the oil, vinegar, salt, and pepper. Add the cabbage, scallions, and cilantro to the vinaigrette and toss together to combine and dress the vegetables.

🐟 **To make the chili sauce:** In a small mixing bowl combine the mayonnaise, chili paste, and lemon juice and mix well. Add the water a little at a time, using only as much as necessary to make a slightly thick sauce.

🐟 **To cook the scallops:** Remove the connecting muscles from the sides of the scallops and check for fragments. In a medium bowl combine the flour, cornmeal, paprika, cayenne, cumin, salt, pepper, and chili powder. Mix well and pass through a sieve into a shallow bowl. In a heavy 4-quart saucepan or heavy kettle heat 1½ inches of oil to 365°F. on a deep-fat thermometer. Working in batches of 6, roll the scallops in the breading, shaking off any excess. Fry the scallops in the hot oil, stirring gently, for 2 minutes or until browned and cooked through. Transfer the scallops with a slotted spoon to paper towels to drain. Season to taste with salt and pepper. To serve, arrange the dressed cabbage on small plates and top with the scallops. Drizzle the chile sauce over the scallops and garnish with lemon wedges.

SHRIMP WITH SUGAR CANE AND PAPAYA KETCHUP

Jose Gutierrez

CHEZ PHILLIPE, THE PEABODY HOTEL
MEMPHIS, TENNESSEE

SERVES 4

Papaya Ketchup

1/3	cup sugar
1/3	cup water
2	cups white wine
1/2	papaya
1/4	cup chopped lemon grass
1/4	cup chopped ginger
1	tablespoon minced hot red pepper
1	cup water
1	tablespoon tomato paste
1/2	teaspoon salt

Fried Leeks

4	cups peanut oil
	White part of 1 leek

Shrimp

4	8-inch pieces fresh sugar cane
1	medium zucchini
1	large turnip
1	large carrot
	Olive oil
10	medium asparagus
	Salt to taste
	Green part of 1 leek, steamed 1 minute
12	large shrimp, peeled and deveined
3	tablespoons firmly packed light brown sugar

❧ **To make the papaya ketchup:** In a small heavy-bottom saucepan heat the sugar until it turns a nice mahogony brown. Quickly and carefully add the water and wine. Add the papaya, lemon grass, ginger, red pepper, water, tomato paste, and salt. Simmer for 10 minutes. Pour into an electric blender and purée. Strain through a fine mesh strainer and keep warm in the top of a double boiler over simmering water until needed.

❧ **To fry the leeks:** In a medium saucepan heat the peanut oil over high heat to 350°. Cut the white part of the leek into 1/8-inch wide julienne and deep fry in the oil for 2 to 3 minutes or until golden brown. With a long-handled strainer, remove to absorbent toweling until ready to use.

❧ **To cook the shrimp:** Prepare a charcoal fire. Cut the sugar cane in half lengthwise, and then in half widthwise. Cut the zucchini, turnip, and carrot into 1/8 x 2-inch shapes and toss in a large mixing bowl with olive oil. Cut the blanched asparagus into 2-inch lengths and add to other vegetables in the bowl. Add a little salt to taste. Over hot coals, grill the vegetables for 2 minutes, turning once.

🍃 Preheat the oven to 350°. Cut the blanched leek green into ⅛-inch strips. Lay 1 section of sugar cane across a green leek strip, then place one of each vegetable across the sugar cane. Top with a second piece of sugar cane and tie securely with the leek green. Do the same for the shrimp: place a section of sugar cane across a leek strip and place 3 shrimp on top of the sugarcane and top with another section of sugar cane and tie securely with the leek.

🍃 Sprinkle the vegetable and shrimp packages with salt and brown sugar. In a heavy sauté pan heat the olive oil until almost smoking and add the packets in batches so they won't be overcrowded. Cook for 3 minutes on each side. When each is finished, remove to an absorbent towel while finishing the others. Place all packages on a baking tray and finish in the preheated oven just until heated through.

🍃 Place one vegetable package on a plate, crossing it with a shrimp package on top. Pour over 4 tablespoons of the papaya ketchup and top the whole with one-fourth of the fried leeks.

STONE CRAB CAKES WITH RED PEPPER REMOULADE

Dawn Sieber
CHEECA LODGE
ISLAMORADA, FLORIDA

SERVES 4

Red Pepper Remoulade

2   red bell peppers, roasted, peeled (see page 217), and finely chopped
2   tablespoons sour cream
½   bunch fresh basil, julienned
     Pinch of cayenne pepper
     Salt and pepper to taste

Crab Cakes

1   egg
1   teaspoon key lime juice
1   tablespoon Dijon Pomery mustard
     Salt and pepper to taste

1   tablespoon Old Bay Seasoning
½   bunch fresh basil, julienned
½   bunch fresh cilantro, cleaned, stemmed, and chopped
¼   bunch fresh parsley, cleaned, stemmed, and chopped
½   cup prepared mayonnaise
½   cup fresh breadcrumbs
½   red bell pepper, roasted, peeled (see page 217), and diced
1   pound stone crab meat

2   tablespoons butter

✍ **To make the remoulade:** In the work bowl of a food processor or in a blender combine the red peppers, sour cream, basil, cayenne, salt, and pepper, and purée until smooth. Transfer to a serving dish, cover, and refrigerate. This mixture will last up to one week.

✍ **To make the crab cakes:** In a large bowl beat together the egg, key lime juice, mustard, salt, pepper, and Old Bay seasoning. Beat in the basil, cilantro, parsley, mayonnaise, and half the fresh breadcrumbs until well combined. Add the red pepper and crabmeat. Toss very gently to mix, taking care not to break up the crab chunks. The mixture should just barely hold together; if it does not, add a little more breadcrumbs and mayonnaise.

✍ **To cook the crab cakes:** Form the crab mixture into 4 patties about 1 inch thick and about 2½ to 3 inches in diameter. In a large nonstick skillet heat 2 tablespoons of butter over medium-high heat. Add the crab cakes and cook about 4 to 5 minutes on each side or until golden brown on the outside and warmed through on the inside. Serve with a dollop of the red pepper remoulade.

STONE CRAB CAKES
WITH CURRIED POTATOES AND THAI BUTTER

Michael McSweeney
THE PEABODY
ORLANDO, FLORIDA

SERVES 4

Curried Potatoes

3/4   pound small red potatoes
1   tablespoon plus 1 teaspoon peanut oil
2   teaspoons Madras curry powder
2   tablespoons Thai red curry paste
2   teaspoons salt

Thai Butter

1/4   pound butter, at room temperature
4   tablespoons Thai sweet chili sauce
2   teaspoons Thai red curry paste

Stone Crab Cakes

1/2   cup (about 1 small) seeded and diced red
     bell pepper

3   tablespoons peanut oil
2   large eggs
1/2   cup heavy cream
2   tablespoons chopped fresh chives
2   tablespoons Thai sweet chili sauce
1   pound cleaned stone crab meat
1 1/2   cups panko (Japanese breadcrumbs), or
     any coarsely ground dried breadcrumbs
1   tablespoon butter

4   large leaves from 1 head butter lettuce
1   bunch fresh chives
4   cracked stone crab claws

❦ **To make the potatoes:** In a 4-quart saucepan bring 3 quarts of salted water to a boil. Add the potatoes and boil until just tender, about 8 minutes. Transfer the potatoes with a small strainer or slotted spoon to a bowl of ice and cold water to stop the cooking. Cut the potatoes into 1/4-inch thick slices.

❦ In a medium sauté pan heat the peanut oil over medium-high heat. Add the potatoes and sauté, stirring constantly, for 6 to 8 minutes until golden. Season with curry powder, curry paste, and salt, and keep warm until service.

❦ **To make the Thai butter:** In a small saucepan over medium heat melt the butter. Add the chili sauce and curry paste and stir to combine. Remove the pan from the heat and set aside until ready to use.

❦ **To make the crab cakes:** Preheat the oven to 375°. In a small nonstick skillet sauté the red pepper in 1 tablespoon of the peanut oil over moderately high heat, stirring constantly, for 2 minutes or until softened. In a medium bowl whisk together the eggs, heavy cream, chives, and sweet chili sauce. Gently stir in the stone crab meat, bell pepper, and the panko. Form ½-cup measures of the mixture into 8 ¾-inch thick cakes and transfer the crab cakes as they are made to a baking sheet. To help prevent crumbling during cooking, cover the crab cakes loosely and chill for at least 1 hour and up to 1 day.

✍ In a 12-inch skillet heat 1 tablespoon of oil and ½ tablespoon of butter over moderately high heat until hot but not smoking and sauté half of the crab cakes 3 to 5 minutes until golden brown. Turn the crab cakes carefully and brown the other side. Transfer the sautéed crab cakes to a baking sheet. Add the remaining 1 tablespoon of oil and ½ tablespoon of butter to the skillet and sauté the remaining crab cakes in the same manner. Bake the crab cakes for 6 minutes or until heated through.

✍ *To serve:* Shape the lettuce leaves into cups, place the warm potatoes inside, and set on individual serving plates. Lean a crab cake against each lettuce cup, drizzle with Thai butter, and garnish with fresh chives and the crab claws.

STONE CRAB COBBLER
WITH COCONUT MILK, CHILIES, KEY LIME, AND CORIANDER

Allen Susser

CHEF ALLEN'S
NORTH MIAMI, FLORIDA

SERVES 6

Stone Crab Mixture

8	large stone crab claws
2	tablespoons olive oil
2	large shallots, peeled and minced
4	medium tomatillos, minced
1	cup fresh corn
1	large Anaheim chile, minced, seeds removed
1	tablespoon ground coriander
½	teaspoon ginger, peeled and chopped
½	teaspoon curry powder
3	tablespoons rum
1	cup coconut milk
3	teaspoons salt

Cobbler Crust

1	cup all-purpose flour
¼	teaspoon salt
1	teaspoon sugar
1½	teaspoons baking powder
3	tablespoons butter, at room temperature
1	tablespoon fresh or dried key lime zest

🐚 **To prepare the stone crab mixture:** Using the back of a chef's knife, crack the knuckle, crack again, and remove all of the meat from the shell and cartilage. Reserve the claw meat and knuckle meat separately. In a medium saucepan warm the olive oil and sweat the shallots until translucent. Add the tomatillos, corn, and Anaheim chile. Flavor this mixture with the coriander, ginger, curry, rum, and ¾ cup of coconut milk. Add the knuckle meat and simmer for 3 to 4 minutes. Season with salt.

🐚 **To prepare the cobbler crust:** In a medium mixing bowl mix the flour, salt, sugar, and baking powder. Add the butter and mix, using your fingertips, until the consistency of sand. Add the key lime zest and enough of the remaining ¼ cup of coconut milk to bind the ingredients.

🐚 **To bake the cobbler:** Preheat the oven to 350°. Spoon the stone crab mixture into individual ovenproof dishes. Place 2 whole stone crab claws over the filling. Top with dollops of the cobbler crust. Bake in the preheated oven for 10 minutes or until the top is nicely browned. Serve immediately.

Fresh Cracked Conch with Vanilla Rum Sauce and Spicy Black Bean Salad

Mark Militello
MARK'S PLACE
NORTH MIAMI, FLORIDA

SERVES 4

Black Bean Salad

¼ cup dried black beans
1 garlic clove
1 tomato, peeled, seeded, and finely diced
1 mango, peeled, seeded, and finely diced
3 green onions, thinly sliced, including some greens
½ Scotch bonnet (habañero) chile, seeded and minced
3 tablespoons extra-virgin olive oil
2 tablespoons fresh lime juice
1 tablespoon chopped fresh cilantro
1 tablespoon chopped fresh mint
1 tablespoon peeled and chopped red onion

Salt and freshly ground black pepper to taste

Vanilla Rum Sauce

¼ cup white Bacardi rum
¼ cup dark Bacardi rum
1 tablespoon fresh lime juice
3 tablespoons sugar
1 small shallot, peeled and minced
½ vanilla bean
1 cup (2 sticks) unsalted butter, cut into ½-inch pieces
Salt and freshly ground black pepper

Cracked Conch

4	to 5 shelled conchs (1 to 1½ pounds)
	Salt and freshly ground black pepper
2	eggs, beaten
¼	cup milk
1	cup all-purpose flour
½	cup clarified butter (see page 215)
1	cup fresh breadcrumbs

Garnish

3	tablespoons finely diced red bell pepper
3	tablespoons finely diced green onion (white and tender green part)
6	key lime wedges

✌ **To make the black bean salad:** Two days before serving, rinse and carefully pick over the black beans, cover them with cold water, and let them soak overnight.

✌ Place the beans in a saucepan with the garlic and water to cover. Bring the beans to a boil over high heat, reduce the heat, and simmer for 1 to 1½ hours or until tender. Drain the beans and rinse with cold water. Drain again and place them in a medium bowl. Add the tomato, mango, green onions, chile, oil, lime juice, cilantro, mint, and onion. Season with salt and pepper, mix well, and adjust the seasoning as necessary. Cover and chill overnight.

✌ **To make the sauce:** In a heavy medium saucepan over medium heat combine the rums, lime juice, sugar, and shallot. Split the vanilla bean in half lengthwise and scrape the seeds into the rum mixture with the point of a knife. Add the vanilla pod and boil the mixture, stirring so that the sugar melts but does not caramelize. When the mixture has reduced to 3 tablespoons, whisk in the butter a few pieces at a time. Do not let the sauce boil; if the pan gets too hot, pull it off the heat as the final butter is added. Strain the sauce into a bowl, season with salt and pepper, and keep warm over a simmering water bath.

✌ **To prepare the conch:** Cut the conch on the diagonal into ¼-inch slices. Place a sheet of plastic wrap over each medallion and pound it as thinly as possible, using a meat tenderizer or scaloppine pounder. Conch is very tough; pounding helps tenderize it. Season with salt and pepper. In a shallow bowl combine the eggs and milk and whisk until blended. Place the flour in another shallow bowl. Place the breadcrumbs in a third shallow bowl.

✌ Just before serving, in a heavy sauté pan heat the clarified butter over medium heat. Dip each piece of conch first in the flour, shaking off the excess, then in the egg mixture, and finally in the breadcrumbs. The breading should be only a light, thin layer. Fry the conch until lightly golden brown on both sides, about 45 seconds on the first side, and another 30 seconds on the second side. Drain the conch on paper towels and lightly salt it.

✌ **To serve:** Place about 2 tablespoons of the bean salad in the center of each serving plate. Spoon 3 pools of vanilla sauce around the salad and place 3 slices of conch between the pools of sauce. Sprinkle some of the red pepper and green onion over the sauce and place a wedge of lime on each plate.

Spicy Crawfish and Black Bean Phyllo Burritos with Cilantro Cream and Fresh Salsa

Jeff Tuttle
PAWLEYS PLANTATION
PAWLEYS ISLAND, SOUTH CAROLINA

SERVES 8

Salsa

6	ripe plum tomatoes, chopped
½	red onion, peeled and minced
¼	red bell pepper, finely diced
¼	yellow bell pepper, finely diced
½	bunch cilantro, stemmed and chopped
1	jalapeño pepper, seeded and minced
	Juice of 1 lime
	Salt and pepper to taste

Black Beans

¾	cup black beans, picked through and washed
5	cups Fish Stock (see page 219) or bottled clam juice
2	teaspoons ground cumin
2	shallots, peeled and minced
2	garlic cloves, peeled and minced
2	tablespoon Texas Pete hot sauce

Phyllo Burritos

12	sheets phyllo dough
2	cups unsalted butter, melted
1	red bell pepper, roasted, skinned, seeded, and cut lengthwise in eighths
1	yellow bell pepper, roasted, skinned, seeded, and cut lengthwise in eighths
1	pound jalapeño pepper cheese, shredded
1	pound crawfish tails, cooked and peeled

Cilantro Cream

2	tablespoons clarified butter
2	shallots, peeled and minced
	Salt and white pepper
2	cups heavy cream
1	bunch fresh cilantro, stemmed and chopped

Garnish

8	sprigs of fresh cilantro

☙ **To make the salsa:** In a large bowl combine the tomatoes, onion, diced bell peppers, cilantro, and jalapeño. Add the lime juice and mix thoroughly. Season with salt and pepper to taste. Let sit for 30 minutes before serving. The salsa can be made up to 1 day in advance.

☙ **To cook the black beans:** In a large heavy pot soak the beans in cold water to cover by at least 3 inches for not less than 4 hours or overnight. Drain the beans in a colander, rinse, and return to the cooking pot with the fish stock, cumin, shallots, garlic, and hot sauce. Bring to a boil over high heat. Skim off any foam that rises to the surface. Reduce the heat and gently simmer the beans, uncovered, stirring occasionally until tender, 1 hour to 1 hour and 15 minutes. Add more stock or clam juice as necessary to keep the beans submerged in liquid. Season the beans with salt and pepper during the last 10 minutes of cooking. Drain the beans in a colander. Cover and store in the refrigerator for up to 3 days.

🡒 **To make the burritos:** Preheat the oven to 350°. Line a baking sheet with parchment paper or aluminum foil. Place 1 sheet of phyllo dough on a large cutting board. Keep the remaining dough covered with a towel to keep it moist. Lightly brush the phyllo sheet with melted butter, and top with another sheet. Brush again with the melted butter. Repeat again with a third sheet. Cut the phyllo in half. Place one piece of roasted red pepper on a stack of phyllo, top with 1 tablespoon of prepared black beans, sprinkle with ¾ ounce of jalapeño pepper cheese, top with 1 ounce of crawfish meat, 1 tablespoon of black bean mixture, and 1 piece of roasted yellow pepper. Fold the phyllo over the filling and roll up burrito style, tucking in the short ends as you roll. Seal the ends with a little more butter. Repeat with the remaining 9 sheets of phyllo dough. Place the 8 burritos on the prepared baking sheet and bake in the preheated oven for 10 to 12 minutes until the burritos are well browned. While the burritos are baking, prepare the cilantro cream.

🡒 **To make the cilantro cream:** In a medium sauté pan or skillet heat the butter over medium-high heat and sauté the shallots 2 to 3 minutes until they are soft but not browned. Season with salt and pepper to taste. Add the cream, stir, and bring to a boil. Reduce heat to a simmer and cook until reduced by half, 10 to 15 minutes. Stir in the chopped cilantro and remove the pan from the heat.

🡒 **To serve:** Pour 3 tablespoons of cilantro cream in the center of 8 plates. Cut each burrito in half on the diagonal and place one piece standing up, cut side down. Position the second half lying down. Garnish the base of the burritos with the salsa and a sprig of fresh cilantro.

BARBECUED SPICED OYSTERS ON CREAMY SUCCOTASH

Daniel O'Leary
BUCKHEAD DINER
ATLANTA, GEORGIA

SERVES 4

Creamy Succotash

1   tablespoon peeled and chopped shallots
½   cup dry white wine
½   cup heavy cream
½   cup (1 stick) butter, at room temperature, cut into 8 pieces
¼   cup cooked fresh lima beans (or substitute thawed frozen lima beans)
¼   cup fresh whole corn kernels (or substitute thawed frozen whole kernels)
¼   cup cooked fresh green beans, cut into ½-inch lengths (or substitute thawed frozen green beans)
¼   cup green bell pepper, deribbed, seeded, minced, and cooked until soft in 1 tablespoon butter
     Salt and pepper to taste

Seasoned Flour

1   cup all-purpose flour

1   tablespoon ground black pepper
1   tablespoon salt
2   tablespoons cornstarch

Oysters

16   plump oysters, removed from shells, shells reserved
     Peanut oil for frying

BBQ Spice Mix

2   tablespoons paprika
1   tablespoon chili powder
1   teaspoon ground cumin
1   teaspoon ground coriander
1   teaspoon sugar
1   teaspoon salt
½   teaspoon dry mustard
½   teaspoon black pepper
½   teaspoon curry powder
½   teaspoon cayenne pepper

🐚 **To make the creamy succotash:** In a small saucepan combine the shallots and white wine and cook over medium-high heat until most of the liquid has evaporated. Add the cream, bring to a boil, and continue to cook until reduced by half. Remove the pan from the heat and gradually whisk in the butter, 1 tablespoon at a time, until it is completely incorporated.

🐚 Add the lima beans, corn kernels, green beans, and bell pepper to the pan, and return the pan to medium-high heat. Bring to a simmer, season to taste with salt and pepper, and continue to simmer until the vegetables are warmed through. Keep warm over very low heat.

🐚 **To cook the oysters:** In a shallow bowl combine the flour, pepper, salt, and cornstarch. Dredge the oysters in the flour mixture, shaking off any excess. Pour enough oil in a heavy-bottomed saucepan set over high heat to rise ¼-inch up the pan. When the oil is hot but not smoking (350° on a fat thermometer), fry the oysters, turning, until lightly browned and crispy, about 1 minute per side. Transfer to paper towels to drain.

🖝 **To make the BBQ spice mix:** In a small mixing bowl combine the paprika, chili powder, cumin, coriander, sugar, salt, dry mustard, pepper, curry powder, and cayenne pepper and sprinkle the fried oysters with the spice mixture. Season to taste with additional salt and pepper.

🖝 **To serve:** Spoon a tablespoon of the succotash into each of the reserved oyster shells. Top with a cooked oyster and serve.

CRÊPINETTE OF TURBOT AND FOIE GRAS ON SALSIFY MOUSSELLINE WITH WHITE ASPARAGUS AND MOREL JUS

Robert Waggoner
WILD BOAR RESTAURANT
NASHVILLE, TENNESSEE

SERVES 4

More commonly used in Europe than in the United States, salsify is a root plant that resembles a parsnip and may be found here from June through February. It is also frequently referred to as an oyster plant, because its taste resembles a mildly flavored oyster.

Salsify

¼	cup (½ stick) unsalted butter
2	pounds salsify, peeled and diced
¼	cup white wine
1	cup chicken stock
	Salt and pepper to taste

Caramelized Onions

¼	cup (½ stick) unsalted butter
2	onions, halved lengthwise and thinly sliced crosswise
	Salt and pepper to taste

Asparagus

12	ounces white asparagus, peeled and tough ends removed
6	ounces green asparagus, peeled and tough ends removed
2	tablespoons butter
	Salt and pepper to taste

| 4 | 3-ounce slices fresh foie gras |
| | Salt and pepper to taste |

Turbot

1	pound caul fat
4	7-ounce fillets fresh, skinless turbot
1	bunch fresh chervil
1/4	cup pork fat
1 1/2	cups chicken stock

1/2	cup heavy cream
10	fresh morels (or 1 ounce dried morels that have been soaked in boiling water for 15 minutes)
1	bunch fresh chives, use the tips only

✍ **To prepare the salsify:** In a medium sauté pan melt the butter over medium-high heat. Add the salsify and brown for a total of 4 to 6 minutes. Add the white wine and chicken stock, bring to a boil, and continue cooking until reduced to 1/4 cup. Reduce the heat to medium low and cook for 15 minutes or until tender.

✍ Remove the pan from the heat and pour the salsify into a blender or the work bowl of a food processor fitted with a metal blade. Pulse the salsify just until smooth. Season with salt and pepper. Return the salsify to the pan, cover, and keep warm over very low heat. Taste and adjust the seasoning.

✍ **To prepare the onions:** In a large skillet melt the butter over medium-low heat. Add the onions and stir 1 minute. Cover and cook about 15 minutes until the onions are tender, stirring occasionally. Uncover and sauté until the onions are deep golden, about 5 minutes. Season with salt and pepper. Remove the pan from the heat and let the onions cool before using to finish the dish.

✍ **To prepare the asparagus:** Pour 1/2 inch of lightly salted water into a medium sauté pan or skillet and bring to a boil. Place a stainless steel steamer in the bottom of the pan and add the asparagus. Cover the pan and steam the asparagus for 5 to 8 minutes, depending on thickness.

✍ Meanwhile, in a medium sauté pan melt the butter over medium-high heat. When the asparagus is tender, remove it from the steamer, and place it in the sauté pan in which the butter has melted. Season with salt and pepper, and cook just until warmed through.

✍ **To prepare the foie gras:** Season the foie gras slices well on both sides with salt and pepper. Heat a dry cast-iron skillet or heavy-bottomed sauté pan to very hot over medium-high heat. Place the foie gras slices in the pan and sear on each side 10 seconds. Remove the foie gras from the heat and blot on paper towels.

✍ **To cook the turbot:** Preheat the oven to 400°. Cut the caul fat into four 5 x 5-inch squares. Place a turbot fillet in the center of each square. Top with foie gras, one-fourth of the caramelized onions, and a few sprigs fresh chervil. Fold the corners of the caul fat together in the middle of each package to seal.

🐚 In a cast-iron skillet heat the pork fat over medium-high heat. Add the crêpinettes, folded side down, and sear quickly, just until browned. Place the skillet in the preheated oven and bake 10 minutes or until the turbot is just cooked through. Remove the skillet from the oven and transfer the crepinettes to a side dish while you finish the sauce. Place the turbot cooking skillet over medium-high heat, and pour in the chicken stock. Bring to a boil, and boil about 5 minutes until the stock is reduced by half. Add the cream and morels, and boil until the sauce is thick enough to coat a spoon, about 5 minutes.

🐚 **To serve:** Place one-fourth of the salsify purée in the center of each serving plate. Top with a crepinette and arrange the asparagus on top of the crepinette. Cover lightly with morel sauce and garnish with the chive tips.

ROULADE OF SALMON WITH EGG AND CAPERS

Joe Castro
THE ENGLISH GRILL
LOUISVILLE, KENTUCKY

SERVES 4

To make the salmon roulade the chef uses nori—paper-thin sheets of dried seaweed. Nori can range in color from dark green to dark purple to black, and has a sweet ocean taste. It is commonly used for wrapping sushi and rice balls. If the nori is too brittle to handle, warm in a 350° oven for about 10 minutes or until it is softened.

Egg Rolls

2	tablespoons white wine
1	tablespoon cornstarch
3	eggs
1	tablespoon capers
2	tablespoons clarified butter (see page 215)
4	6-ounce salmon fillets
	Sea salt and pepper to taste
4	sheets nori
4	cups peanut oil

Tempura Batter

1	egg white
1	egg
1	cup ice water
1	cup all-purpose flour
1/2	cup cornstarch
2	tablespoons baking soda

Beurre Blanc

2	tablespoons unsalted butter
1/4	cup shallots, peeled and minced
2	cups dry white wine
1	bay leaf
1 1/2	cups unsalted butter, cut into tablespoon-size pieces
1	tablespoon cucumber, peeled, seeded, and diced
1	tablespoon tomato, peeled, seeded, and diced
3	sprigs fresh dill, chopped

✎ **To make the egg rolls:** In a small mixing bowl combine the white wine with the cornstarch to make a slurry (the word *slurry* refers to a thin paste of water and flour, which is stirred into hot liquids and used as a thickener. After the slurry is added, the mixture should be stirred and cooked for several minutes so that the flour loses its raw taste). In a separate mixing bowl whisk the eggs until frothy, add the capers, and blend in the slurry.

✎ Wipe a medium sauté pan or nonstick skillet with enough clarified butter to coat the surface and place over high heat. Ladle one-fourth of the batter into the pan and swirl the pan so that the bottom coats the pan evenly. Cook the crêpe for 30 to 45 seconds or until the surface of the crêpe looks dry. Flip with a thin metal spatula and cook another 20 to 30 seconds. Transfer the crêpe to a cutting board and roll into a cigar shape. Cover with a damp towel. Repeat with the remaining batter to make 4 egg rolls.

✎ **To prepare the salmon roulades:** Season the salmon with sea salt and black pepper to taste. Place the egg roll along the long side of the salmon and roll up jelly roll fashion. With a long side of the nori sheet facing you, place the salmon on the sheet, leaving a ½-inch border on the long sides. Beginning with the long side tightly roll up the nori jelly roll fashion.

✎ **To make the tempura batter and fry the roulades:** In a large bowl combine the egg white and the egg. Add the ice water. In a small bowl combine the flour, cornstarch, and baking soda. Add the dry ingredients to the egg mixture and stir without combining completely. The batter should be lumpy with a consistency just thick enough to coat your finger. You can thin the batter by adding more ice water, or thicken with additional flour. Dip the roulades into the tempura batter. At this point either proceed to cooking the roulades or keep in the refrigerator until ready to fry.

✎ In a deep, heavy pot or deep-fryer heat the peanut oil over high heat until the oil is hot but not smoking (350° on a fat thermometer). Deep-fry the roulades for about 2 minutes or until very lightly colored. Drain on paper towels while making the beurre blanc.

✎ **To make the beurre blanc:** In a small saucepan melt the butter over medium heat and sauté the shallots until translucent. Add the white wine and bay leaf, increase the heat to high, and cook at a fast boil until the liquid is reduced by half. Remove the pan from the heat and remove the bay leaf. Whisk in the butter one tablespoon at a time, making sure each piece has been incorporated before adding the next one. Keep the pan off the stove but have a burner set on low to reheat the sauce briefly if it becomes too cool to melt the butter. The sauce should be kept hot enough that steam rises from the surface, but should not be bubbling. Add the cucumber pieces, tomato concassée, and fresh chopped dill. Reheat briefly over low heat before serving and season to taste with salt and pepper.

✎ **To serve:** Cut the roulade with a sharp knife into ¾-inch-thick diagonal slices and serve with the beurre blanc.

TEMPURA–BATTERED FROG LEGS WITH ARUGULA CREAMY TARTAR SAUCE

Gene Bjorkand
AUBERGINE
MEMPHIS, TENNESSEE

SERVES 4

Mayonnaise

½   teaspoon mustard
2   egg yolks
     Salt and pepper to taste
2   cups peanut or vegetable oil
½   teaspoon red wine vinegar
2   tablespoons lemon juice

Sauce

1   hard-boiled egg
½   cup heavy cream, whipped
1½   cups Mayonnaise
1   ounce capers
2   shallots, peeled and minced
2   cornichons or gerkins
2   tablespoons chopped fresh herbs (one or
         more of the following: parsley, chervil,
         tarragon, or chives)

1   teaspoon fresh lemon juice
     Salt and pepper to taste

Garnish

2   cups peanut oil
1   bunch fresh parsley, stems removed, flow-
         ers separated

Frog Legs

1   pound frog legs (6 to 8 per pound)
1   8-ounce box purchased tempura batter
     Pinch of saffron
2   quarts peanut oil

🔊 **To make the mayonnaise:** In a medium bowl beat the mustard, egg yolks, salt, and pepper with a whisk or an electric beater until thick. Gradually whisk the oil into the egg mixture, starting with 1 drop at a time. When 2 or 3 tablespoons of the oil have been whisked into the eggs, pour in the rest of the oil in a fine stream while whisking constantly. Add the vinegar and lemon juice to the mixture 1 teaspoon at a time, whisking constantly until smooth. Cover and store up to 1 week in the refrigerator.

🔊 **To make the sauce:** Separate the yolk from the white of the hard-boiled egg, and finely chop the egg white. In a deep bowl whip the cream until soft peaks form. Place the prepared mayonnaise in a second mixing bowl and quickly fold in the whipped cream. Continue folding until the mixture is stiff and forms a liaison. Add the capers, shallots, cornichons or gerkins, and chopped egg white. Add the fresh herb mixture. Season with lemon juice, salt, and pepper.

🐌 ***To make the garnish:*** Wash and dry parsley flowers. In a medium saucepan heat the peanut oil to 350° over high heat. Quickly add the dried parsley, a few handfuls at a time. Be careful, as the parsley will kind of explode. With a long-handled strainer remove the parsley to paper towels and drain.

🐌 ***To prepare the frog legs:*** Wash the frog legs and blot dry. Season with salt and pepper. Separate each pair into single legs. Remove the shank with its meat attached, and reserve for another purpose. The shank is the smallest of the two joints with the least meat attached. Beginning at the cut end, scrape the meat down to form a sort of ball with most of the bone clean and exposed. The shape will be something of a drumstick. You will have a nice clump of meat with its own "handle."

🐌 Prepare the tempura batter according to the manufacturer's directions, adding a pinch of saffron. Just before serving, pour the oil into a large saucepan and heat to 350° over high heat. Dip the frog legs into the tempura batter, shaking off any excess batter. Fry the frog legs until golden brown, turning with a wire skimmer, 1 to 2 minutes total. Work in several batches so as not to crowd the pan. Drain the frog legs on paper towels.

🐌 ***To assemble:*** Place 2 tablespoons of the sauce in the center of each plate. Divide the frog legs among 4 dinner plates, placing on top of the sauce. Sprinkle the fried parsley around the plate and serve immediately.

DUCK AND SWEET POTATO HASH
WITH QUAIL EGGS, SUNNY SIDE UP

Dean Mitchell
MORELS RESTAURANT
BANNER ELK, NORTH CAROLINA

SERVES 4

This tasty, innovative dish is equally scrumptious at breakfast or as an appetizer or entrée at dinnertime.

2	cups Duck Stock (see page 220)	¼	cup chopped Italian parsley
4	4-ounce duck breasts, skin removed (the		Salt and pepper to taste
	chef suggests leaving some fat on for	2	tablespoons clarified butter (see page 215)
	added flavor)	4	fresh quail eggs (or chicken eggs)
2	medium sweet potatoes, peeled and diced	1	tomato, skinned, seeded, and chopped
1	small onion, peeled and diced	2	tablespoons mixed, chopped, fresh parsley
4	sprigs fresh thyme		and celery leaves

🍤 In a small saucepan bring the duck stock to a simmer over medium-high heat. Continue to simmer the stock about 15 minutes or until reduced by half.

🍤 Cut the duck breasts into 2-inch pieces, and transfer to the mixing bowl of a food processor fitted with a metal blade. Chop the meat coarsely, being careful not to over-process.

🍤 Place the sweet potatoes in a large pot. Add lightly salted water to cover by 1 inch. Bring the water to a boil over high heat. Reduce the heat to a simmer and cook the potatoes uncovered for 5 to 7 minutes or until barely cooked. They should still be firm. With a long-handled strainer remove the potatoes to a stainless steel bowl. Add the duck, onion, thyme, parsley, salt, and pepper and mix together. Form the mixture into 4 patties.

🍤 In a medium sauté pan or skillet heat the clarified butter over medium-high heat and place the patties in the skillet with a pancake turner. Sauté the duck patties 2 minutes on each side or until browned, but not overbrowned. They are done to medium rare when just barely resilient to the touch. Remove to hot plates.

🍤 While the duck patties are cooking, begin the eggs. In a second small skillet warm 2 tablespoons of clarified butter, and fry the eggs sunny side up until set, or to the desired firmness.

   Place a duck patty on each of 4 serving plates. Place one egg on top of each of the duck patties. Drizzle ¼ cup of the reduced duck stock around the patty. Garnish each plate with 1 tablespoon of chopped tomatoes and ½ tablespoon of the chopped greens.

GRILLED MISSISSIPPI QUAIL, MARINATED IN HOISIN, SZECHUAN CHILIES, AND SESAME WITH SWEET POTATO POLENTA

Wally Joe
KC's
CLEVELAND, MISSISSIPPI

SERVES 4

Marinade

1 tablespoon hoisin sauce
2 teaspoons Szechuan chili paste
   Drizzle of sesame oil
   Salt to taste

4 semi-boneless quail (breast bone and back-bone removed)

Polenta

1 large sweet potato, about 8 ounces
1 tablespoon cream
2 tablespoons butter
3¼ cups water
2 teaspoons salt
1 cup polenta
¼ cup firmly packed brown sugar
¼ teaspoon ground cloves
¼ teaspoon ground cinnamon

¼ teaspoon grated nutmeg
¼ teaspoon ground ginger
¼ teaspoon ground mace

   Cracker crumbs
½ cup olive oil

Five-Spice Oil

1 tablespoon five-spice powder
2 cups grapeseed oil

Balsamico Syrup

1½ cups balsamic vinegar
1 teaspoon brown sugar

   Fresh thyme
   Fresh rosemary
   Fresh chives

To make the marinade: In a shallow bowl combine the hoisin sauce, Szechuan chili paste, sesame oil, and salt and blend well. Add the quail to the marinade, coating well. Cover and marinate in the refrigerator for at least 2 hours.

To make the polenta: Prick the sweet potato with a fork and roast in a 400° oven for 1 hour or until tender. Cool the potato slightly until it can be handled, and scoop out the flesh. In a rice mill or food processor purée the sweet potato until smooth. Add the cream and butter, and purée until smooth. In a large saucepan bring the water and salt to a boil. Reduce the heat to low so the water simmers. Pour in the polenta, brown sugar, and all spices in a steady stream, stirring constantly with a whisk, keeping the water at a bare simmer. Crush any lumps that may occur against the side of the pan. Cook about 10 minutes or until the mixture is thickened and pulls away from the side of the pan. Add the sweet potato purée to the cooked polenta. Pour onto a sheet pan, and smooth the surface. Cool the polenta at least 1 hour in the refrigerator.

*Cut the polenta into wedges with a cookie cutter or a sharp knife. Dredge the polenta in cracker crumbs. In a sauté pan heat the olive oil and sauté the cut outs, turning on all sides, until crisp and golden. Drain the polenta on paper towels.

To make the five-spice oil: In a skillet combine the five-spice powder and oil and bring to a slow simmer. Simmer over low heat for 10 minutes. Pour into a clean jar and let sit overnight or longer in order to allow the spices to infuse the oil.

To make the balsamico syrup: In a small saucepan combine the vinegar and sugar and bring to a boil over medium-high heat. Reduce the heat to low and simmer until the volume is reduced by three-fourths, about 20 minutes.

To make the quail: Prepare a charcoal fire. When the coals are mostly white, lay the quail skin side down and grill 5 minutes. Flip and grill another 5 minutes until medium rare.

To assemble: Place the cooked polenta on the center of 4 plates. Decorate with sprigs of fresh thyme and rosemary. Split the quail in half lengthwise through the back bone and place around the polenta. Drizzle five-spice oil and balsamico syrup over and around the quail. Garnish with fresh chopped chives.

Blackberry-glazed Quail

John Fleer
THE INN AT BLACKBERRY FARM
WALLAND, TENNESSEE

SERVES 4

Vinaigrette

¼ cup apple cider vinegar
¼ cup malt vinegar
¾ cup olive oil
1 teaspoon chopped fresh tarragon
½ teaspoon chopped fresh lemon thyme
½ tablespoon hot sauce (chef uses Durkee's)
½ teaspoon salt

Black-eyed Pea Salad

¾ cup dried black-eyed peas
1 ham hock
2¼ cups chicken stock (or as needed)
⅓ cup diced red bell pepper
⅓ cup diced green bell pepper
⅓ cup diced yellow bell pepper
¼ cup diagonally sliced scallions
½ teaspoon peeled and chopped garlic

Marinade

¾ cup Madeira wine
½ cup vegetable oil
¼ cup peeled and minced shallots
1 teaspoon thyme
¼ teaspoon black pepper
8 semi-boneless quail

Glaze

1 tablespoon butter
2 tablespoons peeled and chopped Vidalia or
    other sweet onions or shallots
½ tablespoons peeled and chopped garlic
½ cup blackberry juice
2 tablespoons water
2 tablespoons sugar
1 tablespoon balsamic vinegar
½ tablespoon soy sauce

🖎 **To make the vinaigrette and black-eyed pea salad:** In a bowl or container with a cover combine the apple cider vinegar, malt vinegar, olive oil, tarragon, thyme, hot sauce, and salt. Mix well, and let stand overnight.

🖎 Pick over the peas, removing any dark ones. Place the peas in a large bowl and cover with water by at least 2 inches. Cover the bowl and let the peas soak overnight. Drain the peas and place them in a large saucepan with the ham hock and enough chicken stock to cover. Set the pan over medium-high heat and bring to a simmer. Reduce the heat to medium, cover, and simmer the beans slowly 45 minutes or until done, stirring occasionally. The peas are done when a pea is tender to the core when tasted. Add salt to taste. Strain the peas and let cool. When the peas have cooled, combine with the diced peppers, scallions, and garlic. Add vinaigrette to taste. The salad may be served cold or at room temperature.

✎ *To prepare the quail:* In a shallow bowl combine the wine, vegetable oil, shallots, thyme, and pepper, and blend well. Add the quail to the marinade, coating well. Cover and marinate for at least 2 hours or overnight.

✎ Remove the quail and drain off the excess marinade. Fold the quail legs under the breast, and place on a sheet pan.

✎ *To make the glaze:* In a small saucepan melt the butter over medium heat. Add the onions and garlic and cook until softened. Add the blackberry juice, water, sugar, vinegar, and soy sauce. Increase the heat to medium-high and bring to a simmer. Cook, stirring constantly, until the sugar is dissolved. Remove the pan from the heat. When the glaze has cooled, brush the quail with the mixture. Let the quail rest for 2 hours before proceeding.

✎ *To cook the quail:* Preheat the oven to 400°. Place the quail in a shallow roasting pan. Roast in the preheated oven for about 12 minutes or until browned. Baste with the glaze during the roasting. Remove the quail from the oven, and let sit 5 minutes before serving.

LAMB RIBS WITH SHALLOT–PEPPER BUTTER SAUCE

Louis Osteen

LOUIS'S CHARLESTON GRILL
CHARLESTON, SOUTH CAROLINA

SERVES 4

In 1994 these lamb ribs were awarded the prestigious "Golden Dish Award," presented by Alan Richman of GQ magazine to the 10 best dishes of the year from around the world. The chef has kept them on the menu since, and the lamb ribs continue unfailingly to offer a unique excitement to his guests, giving nod to the notion that eating with your hands gives pleasure.

4   *racks of lamb ribs*

Marinade

¼	*cup extra-virgin olive oil*
2	*tablespoons chopped garlic*
4	*sprigs fresh thyme*
1	*sprig fresh rosemary*
2	*sprigs fresh Italian parsley*
1	*tablespoon freshly ground black pepper*

Shallot-Pepper Butter

¼	*cup white wine*
½	*cup champagne vinegar*
⅓	*cup finely diced shallots*
¼	*cup freshly ground coarse black pepper*
½	*teaspoon salt*
12	*tablespoons (1½ sticks) unsalted butter, cut into 8 pieces*
	Salt to taste

🐾 *To marinate the lamb ribs:* Place the lamb ribs in a nonreactive shallow dish. Sprinkle with the olive oil, garlic, thyme, rosemary, parsley, and black pepper. Cover and refrigerate overnight.

🐾 *To cook the lamb ribs:* Heat the grill to medium. Slowly grill the ribs over the medium-hot fire. For a medium-rare rib, grill about 6 minutes on each side, for a total of 12 minutes per rack. Sprinkle the ribs with a little salt. Place them on a platter, cover, and keep warm until ready to serve.

🐾 *To slice the ribs:* Since lamb ribs are rather small, they do not have an abundance of meat. Therefore, they require a special, rather tricky slicing technique. Slice the first rib bone off the rack, cutting as close to the bone as possible—leaving as much meat as you can attached to the second rib. Slice the second rib off the rack by cutting as close as possible to the third rib bone. This gives the second rib lots of nice meat on both sides of the bone. Continue to cut the ribs in this manner, discarding every other bone, yielding succulently meaty ribs with the remaining.

🐾 *To prepare the shallot-pepper butter sauce:* In a small, heavy-bottomed saucepan combine the wine, vinegar, shallots, pepper, and the salt and bring to a boil over medium-high heat. Maintain a vigorous boil and let the mixture reduce until it thickens and the bubbles start to enlarge. Reduce the heat until the mixture is just at simmer. Using a wire whisk, beat in the butter quickly, one piece at a time. Be careful not to continue to reduce the mixture as the butter is beaten in. Check the seasonings and add salt to taste. Keep the sauce warm on the back of the stove until ready to use.

🐾 *To serve:* Stack 4 of the cut ribs "tent style" on each of 4 serving plates. Drizzle the sauce over the top and enjoy.

POACHED VIDALIA ONIONS WITH FOIE GRAS AND MARMALADE

Mathew Medure

THE DINING ROOM, THE RITZ CARLTON
AMELIA ISLAND, FLORIDA

SERVES 4

Marmalade

1   large Vidalia onion, peeled and diced
1   bunch chives, sliced
¼   cup sugar
¼   cup honey

Onion Confit

4   Vidalia onions, peeled and sliced in
     ½-inch thick slices
½   cup rice wine vinegar
¼   cup olive oil

Juice of 1 lemon
Salt and pepper to taste
Pinch of saffron

Foie Gras

4   4-ounce foie gras portions, 1-inch thick,
     vein removed
   Salt and pepper to taste
1   tablespoon sliced chives

¼   cup balsamic vinegar

To make the marmalade: In a medium saucepan combine the onion, chives, sugar, and honey and bring to a simmer over medium-high heat. Simmer, stirring occasionally, for 15 minutes or until the contents combine into a thick marmalade.

To make the onion confit: Preheat the oven to 350°. Place the sliced onions in a small roasting pan. Add the rice wine vinegar, olive oil, and lemon juice. Cook the mixture in the oven, stirring occasionally, for about 15 minutes or until the onion is very soft and almost all the liquid has evaporated. Stir in the salt, pepper, and saffron, and cook for 1 minute. Remove from the oven and set aside. The confit may be made one day in advance, covered and chilled, and reheated as needed.

To prepare the foie gras: Season the foie gras with salt, pepper, and chives. Preheat a medium dry skillet over high heat. Cook the foie gras for about 15 seconds on each side. Immediately remove from the heat and set aside.

To assemble: Place 2 tablespoons of the onion confit in the center of the plate. Top with 1 piece of foie gras and 1 tablespoon of marmalade. Drizzle 1 tablespoon of balsamic vinegar around the plate.

SALADS

❦

*F*or nearly a generation after the Civil War, green salads were not eaten in the South and, up until the beginning of the nineteenth century, were eaten only by the well-to-do. Perhaps it is for this reason that salads are not frequently associated with southern cooking. What is more frequently brought to mind in any consideration of southern salads is coleslaw or potato salad.

But here southern chefs have rendered their salads wonderful with traditional and nontraditional southern ingredients. And although in the South the salad is traditionally served as a first course, these salads could serve as an equally important second course in a four-course menu that includes dessert, or in many instances in larger portion as a light luncheon entrée. I can think of no occasion that would not be right for either Ben Barker's Wild and Exotic Mushroom Salad with Marinated Tomatoes or Paul Abrecht's Maine Lobster with Celery Root and Apple Salad.

WILD AND EXOTIC MUSHROOM SALAD ON MARINATED TOMATOES WITH WARM SHERRY BACON VINAIGRETTE

Ben Barker

MAGNOLIA GRILL
DURHAM, NORTH CAROLINA

SERVES 4 TO 6

Roasted Tomato Fondue

1	pound very ripe, flavorful tomatoes
3	tablespoons olive oil
2	tablespoons fino sherry
2	tablespoons sherry vinegar

Tomatoes

2	pounds yellow tomatoes or any low- to medium-acid tomatoes, yellow or red
2	shallots, peeled and minced
1	teaspoon tarragon, stems removed and minced
1/3	cup extra-virgin olive oil
	Freshly ground black pepper to taste

Mushroom Salad

1	pound mixed wild and exotic mushrooms (choose at least 3 different varieties from the following list: shiitakes, chanterelles, hedgehogs, black trumpets, oysters, cremini)
1/4	cup olive oil
	Salt and pepper to taste

4	to 5 cups watercress, frisee, endive, or arugula or any combination
1	3- to 4-ounce sweet onion, peeled and shaved paper-thin using a mandolin or Japanese benri-slicer
1/4	cup stemmed and chopped combined fresh tarragon and parsley

Vinaigrette

4	ounces country-sliced smoked bacon, cut crosswise into julienne
1/4	cup plus 2 tablespoons extra-virgin olive oil
1	teaspoon minced garlic
1	tablespoon minced shallot
1/4	cup sherry vinegar
2	tablespoons fino sherry
	Kosher salt
	Black pepper

Garnish

2	tablespoons extra-virgin olive oil
	Reserved bacon, chopped
1	tablespoon fresh tarragon leaves, cut into chiffonade (thin slices)

❧ **To roast the tomatoes:** Preheat the oven to 350°. Cut the tomatoes in half, toss with olive oil, and roast on a sheet pan lined with parchment paper or aluminum foil for 35 to 40 minutes. The tomatoes are ready when they have softened and lightly browned and the skins are begining to pull away. Purée the tomatoes through a food mill into a medium non-reactive saucepot. Add the sherry and vinegar to the tomatoes, and set the saucepot over medium-high heat. Bring to a boil, reduce the heat to medium, and cook until thickened to the consistency of crème anglaise. Season with salt to taste and reserve.

🐦 **To marinate the tomatoes:** Slice tomatoes as thinly as possible, and remove to a large platter or sheet pan. In a small container combine the shallots, tarragon, olive oil, and freshly ground black pepper and drizzle the mixture over the tomatoes. Cover and reserve at room temperature for up to 6 hours.

🐦 **To prepare the mushrooms:** Clean, trim, and slice the mushrooms, discarding the trimmings. Heat a heavy-bottomed sauté pan over medium-high heat. Add the olive oil and sauté the mushrooms seasoned with salt and pepper, until browned. (If your pan is not large enough to hold the mushrooms comfortably in one layer, sauté in batches.) With a slotted spoon remove the mushrooms to paper toweling and reserve.

🐦 **To prepare the greens:** Clean the greens thoroughly, and dry in a salad spinner or by hand with paper toweling. Tear into small pieces and refrigerate in plastic bags until ready to use. Remove from the refrigerator no more than 15 minutes before using.

🐦 **To make the vinaigrette:** In a heavy-bottomed steel or cast-iron pan cook the bacon over medium heat until crisp. Remove the cooked bacon to paper towels, leaving the rendered fat in the pan. Add the olive oil to the fat remaining in the pan and heat over medium-high heat until aromatic but not smoking. Add the minced garlic and shallot, and cook for 15 seconds without scorching. Pour the oil into a heavy bowl and immediately add vinegar, sherry, and salt and pepper to taste. Season to taste and adjust the acidity, adding more vinegar if necessary. The dressing should be tart.

🐦 **To serve:** Divide the marinated tomatoes among the serving plates. In a large stainless steel bowl combine the greens, shaved onion, chopped parsley, and tarragon. Heat a 10-inch sauté pan over medium-high heat, splash with olive oil, and sauté the mushrooms to warm through. Stir the vinaigrette well and add to the mushrooms. Pour over the greens. Toss to wilt lightly, and divide among plates. Drizzle tomato fondue and extra-virgin olive oil around. Sprinkle with reserved crisp bacon and tarragon chiffonade.

MAINE LOBSTER WITH CELERY ROOT AND APPLE SALAD

Paul Albrecht

PANO'S AND PAUL'S
ATLANTA, GEORGIA

SERVES 4

Lobsters

   Water
1   cup white vinegar
1   teaspoon cracked peppercorns
1   small onion, peeled
1   bay leaf
   Several fresh dill branches
2   2-pound Maine lobsters

Celery Root and Apple Salad

½   cup mayonnaise
1   teaspoon Dijon-style mustard
3   teaspoons lemon juice
2   tablespoons chopped fresh parsley

   Salt and pepper to taste
1   1-pound celery root, peeled and julienned
2   Granny Smith apples, peeled, cored, and julienned

Mango Vinaigrette

2   ripe mangos
¼   cup sherry vinegar
   Juice of 2 lemons
1   cup hazelnut oil
   Salt and pepper to taste

2   small cucumbers, peeled, seeded, and diced
   Fresh chervil for garnish

❖ **To cook the lobsters:** In a large stockpot or kettle (at least 16 inches in diameter) pour in 1½ inches of water and add the vinegar, peppercorns, onion, bay leaf, and dill. Set a rack or colander in the pot and bring to a boil over high heat. Add the lobsters and cover tightly to make sure no steam escapes. (If necessary, place a weight on the cover to hold securely.) Lower the heat and cook until done, about 15 minutes. Test the lobster by removing one of the little legs and tasting the meat. Remove the lobsters from the stockpot and chill.

❖ **To make the celery root and apple salad:** For the dressing, combine the mayonnaise, mustard, half the lemon juice, and parsley in a small bowl. Season to taste with salt and pepper.

❖ To prevent the celery root and apple from discoloring, as soon as the fruit is cut, toss with the remaining half of the lemon juice and a sprinkle of salt. Taste the celery root before completing the salad to make sure it doesn't taste salty. If it does, rinse under cold water and dry it. In a mixing bowl combine the celery root and apple and fold the mayonnaise dressing into the salad.

🖎 *To make the mango vinaigrette:* Peel the mangos, remove the pits, and coarsely chop. In the work bowl of a food processor fitted with a metal blade purée the mangos with the vinegar and lemon juice. With the motor running, slowly add the oil. Season to taste with salt and pepper.

🖎 *To serve:* Remove the lobsters from the refrigerator. Remove the claws, crack them, and pull out the meat in one piece. Cut through the head and tail lengthwise and pull out the tail meat in 2 whole pieces. Cut the tail meat into 8 medallions.

🖎 Arrange celery root and apple salad in the center of each serving plate and place lobster medallions on top of the salad. Position a claw in the middle. Drizzle the mango vinaigrette over and around the lobster meat and sprinkle the diced cucumbers around the plate. Garnish the top with fresh chervil.

SALADE NIÇOISE

Stephen Austin
HEDGEROSE HEIGHTS INN
ATLANTA, GEORGIA

SERVES 4

Vinaigrette

3	tablespoons balsamic vinegar
1	tablespoon sherry vinegar
1	teaspoon anchovy paste
¾	cup extra-virgin olive oil
	White pepper to taste

Niçoise Salad

2	ounces fresh fava beans, shelled
3	ounces haricots verts or small green beans
4	ounces red bliss potatoes, sliced
4	quail eggs

8	ounces sashimi-grade yellowfin tuna
1	tablespoon olive oil
	Coarse sea salt and white pepper to taste
4	sprigs fresh thyme, chopped
4	ounces mesclun salad greens
4	Roma tomatoes, peeled and seeded (see page 221)
1	red bell pepper, roasted (see page 217) and sliced into thin strips
4	anchovy fillets
2	tablespoons pitted black olives

To make the vinaigrette: In a small bowl whisk together the vinegars and anchovy paste. Beat in the oil by droplets to make a homogeneous sauce. You may find it easier to do this with a handheld electric mixer. Season to taste with white pepper.

To prepare the salad: Bring a large pot of lightly salted water to a boil over high heat. Cook the fava beans in the water just until they turn bright green, about 2 minutes. With a long-handled strainer remove the fava beans from the pot and plunge them into a bowl of ice water. Drain again and peel. Next, cook the haricots verts in the boiling water, about 2 minutes or until tender. Remove with a long-handled strainer to the ice water, cool, and drain. Finally, add the red bliss potatoes to the boiling water and cook about 10 minutes until tender. Remove to the ice bath, drain, and reserve.

In a small saucepan over high heat cook the quail eggs in lightly salted boiling water about 4 to 6 minutes until boiled. Peel and halve the eggs. Divide the fresh tuna into 2-ounce portions. Season with olive oil, coarse salt, white pepper, and fresh thyme. Heat a large nonstick sauté pan or skillet over high heat. Sear the tuna in the skillet about 30 seconds on each side. Remove from the pan and slice.

Line the serving plates with the mesclun salad greens, drizzle with the olive oil, and sprinkle with salt. Toss the fava beans in a mixing bowl with a little of the vinaigrette. In a separate bowl toss the haricots verts with a little of the vinaigrette. Cut the tomatoes into 4 pieces, and drizzle a small amount of the dressing over the tomatoes.

To serve: Place a portion of tuna in the center of each serving plate, and arrange the potatoes around the tuna. Mound the haricots verts at strategic points, interspersing with tomatoes, red pepper strips, and fava beans. Place the quail egg halves around the salad, and curl an anchovy fillet on top of each half. Spoon more vinaigrette over all. Scatter on the olives.

MOREL–CRUSTED TROUT SALAD WITH APPLE AND WALNUT VINAIGRETTE

Dean Mitchell
MORELS RESTAURANT
BANNER ELK, NORTH CAROLINA

SERVES 4

The quickness and ease with which you can prepare the trout makes this already delicious dish taste even better. But remember to start the night before to allow time for the trout to marinate.

Dressing

¼ cup walnut oil
1 teaspoon shallots, peeled and finely minced
¼ cup apple cider vinegar

Salad

½ cup coarsely chopped walnut pieces
2 small apples, peeled and diced
4 cups mixed lettuces (red leaf, oak leaf, Boston, arugula, mache)

Trout and Marinade

4 8- to 10-ounce whole brook trout, cleaned, washed, and dressed

2 cups heavy cream
½ tablespoon kosher salt
1 tablespoon black pepper
½ teaspoon Tabasco sauce

Morel Flour Mix

1 cup morel powder (see Note)
½ cup yellow cornmeal
¼ cup all-purpose flour
Salt and pepper to taste

1½ cups vegetable oil or clarified butter (see page 215) for frying
Walnut pieces for garnish

🐟 **To make the dressing:** In a small bowl combine the walnut oil, shallots, and vinegar. Beat with a whisk until well combined.

🐟 **To make the salad:** In a large bowl toss the walnut pieces, apples, and assorted lettuces.

🐟 **To prepare the trout:** Wash and dry the trout. Remove the head, gills, and viscera with kitchen shears. Cut off the fins close to the body. In a large shallow baking dish mix the heavy cream, salt, pepper, and Tabasco. Place the trout in the marinade and refrigerate overnight.

🐟 In a large bowl combine the morel powder, cornmeal, flour, salt, and pepper. Remove the trout from the marinade, dredge in the morel flour mix. In a large skillet heat the clarified butter or oil over medium heat. Sauté the trout slowly over medium heat, about 5 minutes per side. They are done when you can just separate flesh from bone at the ridge end of the back and there is no pink color near the bone when you look into the cavity. Remove the trout to the center of 4 serving plates.

🖝 *To serve:* Arrange the mixed greens around the trout and drizzle with dressing. Garnish with walnut pieces.

🖝 *Note:* Morel powder is available in specialty grocery stores, but if you can't locate morel powder you can make your own by grinding dried morels in an electric blender to a fine powder.

BAYONA CRISPY SMOKED QUAIL SALAD

Susan Spicer
BAYONA
NEW ORLEANS, LOUISIANA

SERVES 4

Marinade

1   tablespoon honey
1   teaspoon sweet soy (Indonesian Ketjap
      Manis)
1/2 cup peanut oil
1   tablespoon bourbon
1   quail, deboned

Dressing

1   pound quail or chicken bones
2   cups chicken stock
2   tablespoons molasses
2   tablespoons cider vinegar
1   ounce (2 tablespoons) walnut vinegar
1/4 cup peeled and minced shallots
1   cup olive oil
    Salt and pepper to taste
1   to 2 tablespoons bourbon

Spiced Pecans

1   tablespoon butter
1/2 cup pecans

1   teaspoon Lea & Perrins Worcestershire
      sauce
1/2 teaspoon salt
    Dash cayenne pepper
1   tablespoon sugar

Rice Flour Batter

1   cup rice flour
3/4 cup water
1/4 teaspoon salt
    Pinch pepper

4   cups vegetable oil for deep-frying

Salad

1/2 pound fresh spinach, trimmed, rinsed,
      and dried
1   pear, ripe
1/4 cup pickled red onion
1/2 cup celery hearts and leaves

❧ ***To make the marinade:*** In a small bowl whisk together the honey, sweet soy, peanut oil, and bourbon. Add the quail to the marinade ingredients and let the flavors combine for at least 1 hour. Drain the quail before proceeding to cold smoke.

❧ ***To smoke the quail:*** Prepare a cold smoker by placing the quail on a wire rack over a baking pan filled with ice cubes. Place this in the smoker (see Note below) and smoke at 75° for about 30 minutes. The quail should still be mostly raw.

❧ ***To make the dressing:*** Preheat the oven to 450°. Place the bones in a shallow roasting pan and roast for 30 minutes or until browned. Bring the chicken stock to a boil over high heat, add the bones to the stock, and reduce the heat to medium. When the stock comes back to a boil, skim frequently until the scum stops rising, and simmer uncovered until reduced to ½ cup of syrupy liquid. Remove the pan from the heat, and strain the stock through a fine mesh strainer into a small bowl. Discard the solids. Whisk in the molasses, vinegars, and shallots. Add the oil in a thin stream, whisking continually. Season to taste with salt and pepper, and stir in the bourbon.

❧ ***To make the spiced pecans:*** Preheat the oven to 350°. In a small saucepan melt the butter over medium-low heat. Pour the butter into a small bowl and toss with the pecans, Worcestershire, salt, cayenne pepper, and sugar. Spread the pecans out on a small baking sheet and roast in the preheated oven for 10 minutes or until lightly toasted. Remove from the oven and set aside until ready to use.

❧ ***To fry the quail:*** In a shallow bowl whisk together the rice flour, water, salt, and pepper. In a large saucepan heat the oil over medium-high heat to 375° or until a bread cube turns brown in 10 seconds. Dip the quail in the batter, shake off any excess, and cook the quail 1 or 2 at a time, for 3 to 4 minutes. With a slotted spoon, remove the quail from the pan and drain on paper towels. Let the quail cool slightly, then cut into quarters.

❧ ***To serve the salad:*** Toss the cleaned and dried spinach with the dressing and portion onto 4 plates. Core, peel, and cut the pear into ¼-inch slices. Top each serving with a whole quartered quail, 1 tablespoon of red onion, one fourth of the celery hearts and leaves, 2 tablespoons of pecans, and one-fourth of the pear slices.

❧ ***Note:*** If a commercially built smoker is not available, you may make a smoker by building a low fire in a kettle-type grill. Push the coals to the side, add a pan of soaked wood chips, and set the quail with the rack and ice cubes on the grill. Cover and smoke for about 30 minutes. Or place soaked wood chips in the bottom of a heavy wok, then place a rack or perforated pan over the wood chips. Set the quail with the rack and ice cubes on top. Cover and set the wok over low heat.

FRUITED COBB SALAD

Reimund Pitz
DISNEY-MGM STUDIO
LAKE BUENA VISTA, FLORIDA

SERVES 6

Dressing

1/4	cup water
	Pinch of sugar
	Dash of Worcestershire sauce
	Salt and pepper to taste
1	small clove garlic, peeled and minced
1/4	cup red wine vinegar
2	teaspoons lemon juice
1/2	teaspoon English mustard
3/4	cup vegetable oil
1/4	cup extra-virgin olive oil

Fruited Cobb Salad

1/2	head iceberg lettuce
1/2	head romaine lettuce

1	head Belgian endive
1	orange, peeled and sectioned, white pith removed
2	tablespoons peeled, finely diced fresh pineapple
4	strawberries, hulled and thinly sliced
2	tablespoons peeled, seeded, and finely diced honeydew melon
2	tablespoons peeled, seeded, and finely diced cantaloupe
1/4	bunch fresh watercress for garnish
1/4	radicchio head for garnish

❧ **To make the dressing:** In a medium mixing bowl whisk to combine the water, sugar, salt, pepper, Worcestershire sauce, garlic, vinegar, lemon juice, and mustard. Slowly add the oils in a steady stream, whisking continually in order to form an emulsion. Set aside.

❧ **To make the fruited cobb salad:** Wash and dry in a salad spinner or by hand with paper toweling the lettuces, endive, watercress, and radicchio. In a salad bowl combine the lettuces. Arrange the diced fruit on top, and toss with dressing as desired. Garnish with watercress and radicchio.

FISH & SEAFOOD

The waters of the southern region yield a wealth of riches, and ocean and fresh-water cookery in the South is as old as an Indian oyster roast. Oysters and shrimp are found in abundance in the salt waters of the coastal Carolinas, along both Florida coasts, and the Gulf coasts of Alabama and Mississippi. Some of the best crab in the world can be found in McClellanville, South Carolina, just south of Charleston, and finfish—snapper, grouper, flounder, shad, and trout—are widely available in the region. I've never had a better trout than one fished out of a cold brook in the North Carolina mountains, or eaten more eagerly than at a crawfish boil in a Louisiana roadhouse. Nor have I met anyone who left New Orleans without a tummy full of oysters from one of the legendary oyster bars, or who declined the fried catfish that had been fished out of the Atchafalaya swamp.

The astonishing selection and range of fish and shellfish that are available in the fresh and salt waters of the region have provided a grand and varied palette for the creations of these southern chefs. The diversity and range of recipes within this chapter are, in fact, another example of the eclecticism of southern cuisine. Nearly every style of southern cookery is exemplified here—a spicy Caribbean shrimp dish, a Low Country shad roe meal, catfish panéed Creole style or with an Oriental bent, and a French-inspired sole, to name a few. Any of these dishes would make an exceedingly good main course (as suggested here) or in smaller portions as second course in a banquet. Neither is it uncommon for Southerners to take their fish and seafood at breakfast.

PAN-SEARED SCALLOPS WITH ZUCCHINI AND SUMMER SQUASH, CHEDDAR GRITS SOUFFLÉ, AND SALMON ROE BUTTER SAUCE

Guillermo Thomas
THE HERMITAGE HOTEL
NASHVILLE, TENNESSEE

SERVES 4

White Cheddar Grits Soufflé

¼	cup (½ stick) unsalted butter
1	teaspoon minced garlic
1	tablespoon minced shallot
½	teaspoon chopped fresh rosemary
2	cups milk
1	cup chicken stock
½	teaspoon salt
¼	teaspoon freshly ground black pepper
1	cup stone-ground grits
1	egg yolk
1	cup grated sharp white Cheddar cheese
3	egg whites
¼	teaspoon cream of tartar
	Vegetable spray

Salmon Roe Butter Sauce

1	cup white wine
¼	cup champagne vinegar
1	sprig fresh thyme
1	sprig fresh tarragon
1	sprig fresh Italian parsley
1	tablespoon roughly chopped shallot
3	lemons, peeled, seeded, and roughly chopped

½	cup heavy cream
1	cup (2 sticks) very cold unsalted butter, cut into small pieces
¼	teaspoon salt
½	teaspoon freshly ground black pepper

Zucchini and Summer Squash Roses

4	6-inch squares aluminum foil
1	tablespoon unsalted butter
2	medium zucchini, sliced diagonally ⅛ inch thick
2	medium summer squash, sliced diagonally ⅛ inch thick
	Salt and pepper to taste
	Olive oil for drizzling

Scallops

1	pound sea scallops
1	tablespoon olive oil
1	teaspoon unsalted butter
	Salt and pepper to taste
2	ounces salmon roe
1	tablespoon fresh chives, chopped

🖎 **To cook the grits:** In a heavy-bottomed saucepan melt the butter over medium-high heat. Add the garlic, shallot, and rosemary, and sauté 1 minute. Add the milk, stock, salt, and pepper, and bring to a boil. Slowly pour in the grits, stirring constantly. Reduce the heat to low and continue to stir so the grits do not settle to the bottom and burn. In about 5 minutes the grits will plump up and become a thick mass. Continue to cook the grits for a total of about 12 minutes, stirring frequently. The grits should have absorbed all of the water and become soft. Transfer the grits to clean container and refrigerate for 1 hour.

❧ Preheat the oven to 350°. In an electric mixer fitted with a paddle, beat the grits at high speed about 8 minutes until light and fluffy. Add the egg yolk and cheese and continue to whip 1 minute.

❧ In a separate bowl of the electric mixer using a whip attachment, whip the egg whites and cream of tartar until stiff peaks form. Immediately fold the whites into the grits mixture. Liberally coat four 4-ounce soufflé dishes with vegetable spray. Pour the grits into the soufflé dishes. Place the soufflé dish in a baking pan and pour in warm water halfway up the sides of the soufflé cups. Bake in the preheated oven for 35 to 45 minutes or until the soufflés have risen and are slightly browned.

❧ *To make the salmon roe butter sauce:* In a small saucepan combine the wine, vinegar, herbs, shallot, and lemon, and bring to a boil over high heat. Boil until reduced by half. Add the cream, bring back to a boil, and reduce again by half. Over very low heat whisk in the butter, one piece at a time, completely incorporating each piece before adding the next. Season with salt and pepper. Remove the sauce from the heat and pour through a fine mesh strainer into a clean saucepan. Keep warm on the back of the stove.

❧ *To make zucchini and squash roses:* Preheat the broiler. Lightly butter four 6-inch squares of aluminum foil. Arrange the zucchini and summer squash on the foil in a circular pattern, overlapping each piece and alternating colors. Season with salt and pepper and drizzle with olive oil. Place under the broiler until vegetables are a light golden brown, about 3 minutes.

❧ *To cook the scallops and assemble the dish:* Place a large, dry, nonstick sauté pan or skillet over high heat for 3 minutes. Add the oil and butter and heat until very hot. Pat the scallops dry with paper towels, season with salt and pepper, and place in the pan, being careful not to overcrowd the pan. If necessary, cook the scallops in 2 batches. Sear the scallops on one side for about 2 minutes, then turn them with tongs and cook for 2 minutes on the other side. Remove the scallops from the pan and set aside.

❧ *To finish the dish:* Slide the zucchini/squash roses off the foil onto the center of the serving plates. Run a knife around the edges of the soufflés to loosen them from their molds, and remove by turning over onto the center of the dish. Add the salmon roe and 1½ tablespoons of the chives to the warm butter sauce, and spoon around the soufflé. Place the scallops on top of the sauce and garnish with the remaining chopped chives.

SEA SCALLOPS WITH MANGO AND JALAPEÑOS

Kathy Cary
LILLY'S
LOUISVILLE, KENTUCKY

SERVES 6 AS AN APPETIZER OR 4 AS AN ENTRÉE

Scallops

1	tablespoon Dijon mustard
½	teaspoon kosher salt
¼	teaspoon pepper
2	tablespoons fresh tarragon
1½	pounds sea scallops, cut in half horizontally
¼	cup (½ stick) butter

Sauce

¼	cup (½ stick) butter
¾	cup chopped shallots
1	jalapeño pepper, diced
¼	cup dry sherry

1½	tablespoons frozen orange juice concentrate
½	cup heavy cream
1	teaspoon fresh tarragon
½	teaspoon kosher salt
¼	teaspoon pepper

Potatoes

4	cups vegetable oil for deep-frying
2	potatoes, julienned

Garnish

6	ounces fresh spinach
1	mango, peeled and thinly sliced
	Fresh tarragon sprigs

☙ **To make the scallops:** In a medium bowl combine the mustard, kosher salt, pepper, and fresh tarragon. Add the cleaned and cut scallops and marinate in the refrigerator for 4 hours or overnight. Place a large, dry, nonstick sauté pan or skillet over high heat for 3 minutes. Add the butter and heat until melted. Pat the scallops dry with paper towels and place in the pan, being careful not to overcrowd the pan. If necessary, cook the scallops in 2 batches. Sear the scallops on one side for about 2 minutes, then turn them with tongs and cook for 2 minutes on the other side. Remove the scallops from the pan and set aside.

☙ **To make the sauce:** In the skillet used to cook the scallops melt the butter. Add the shallots and jalapeño. Sauté the shallots and jalapeño over medium heat 3 to 5 minutes until softened. Increase the heat to high and add the sherry, stirring with a wooden spoon to deglaze the pan. Add the orange juice, cream, tarragon, salt, and pepper, and cook until combined.

☙ **To make the potatoes:** In a separate skillet heat the oil to 375° or until a bread cube turns brown in 10 seconds. Add the potatoes and fry until brown and crisp. Remove them from the pan with a slotted spoon and drain on paper towels.

🍂 **To assemble:** Wash and dry the spinach leaves and divide evenly in the middle of the plates. Top with the thin strips of fried potatoes. Ladle the sauce around the sides of the plates, and place the seared scallops on top. Decorate each plate with slices of fresh mango and a sprig of fresh tarragon.

SPICY SHRIMP, SAUSAGE, AND TASSO GRAVY OVER WHITE GRITS

Donald Barickman

MAGNOLIA'S
CHARLESTON, SOUTH CAROLINA

SERVES 8

This very popular dish brings together all of the flavors of the Old South. The stone-ground grits are a must. It's a great Low Country dish that can be served year round and turns up on local tables morning, noon, and night.

Creamy White Grits

12   cups chicken broth
4½   cups coarse stone-ground grits
1   cup heavy cream
     Salt and white pepper to taste

Tasso Gravy

¼   cup (½ stick) butter
½   cup sliced tasso, cut into 1-inch strips
½   cup all-purpose flour
4   cups chicken broth
2   tablespoons finely chopped parsley

Salt and white pepper to taste

Shrimp and Sausage

½   pound spicy Italian sausage (¾ pound if raw)
1   tablespoon olive oil
2   pounds medium or large shrimp, peeled and deveined
2   cups chicken broth
1   recipe Tasso Gravy
2   tablespoons parsley, finely chopped

🍂 **To make the creamy white grits:** Bring the chicken broth to a boil in a heavy-bottomed saucepan. Slowly pour in the grits, stirring constantly. Reduce the heat to low and continue to stir so that the grits do not settle to the bottom and burn. In about 5 minutes the grits will plump up and become a thick mass.

🍂 Continue to cook the grits for about 20 to 25 minutes, stirring frequently. The grits should have absorbed all of the chicken stock and become soft. Stir in the heavy cream and cook for another 10 minutes, stirring frequently. The grits should now have a thick consistency and be creamy like oatmeal. Season to taste with salt and white pepper. Keep warm over low heat until ready to serve. If the grits become too thick, add warm chicken broth or water to thin them down.

To make the tasso gravy: In a heavy-bottomed saucepan melt the butter over low heat. Add the tasso and sauté for 1 minute. Make a roux by adding the flour and stirring until well combined. Continue to cook over low heat for 5 minutes, stirring frequently, until the roux develops a nutty aroma. Turn the heat up to medium and gradually add 2 cups of the chicken broth, stirring vigorously. Keep stirring until the broth begins to thicken and is smooth. Gradually add the remaining 2 cups of broth, stirring until the broth thickens into gravy. Reduce the heat and simmer over low heat for 15 minutes to cook out the starchy flavor. Add the parsley. Simmer for another 5 minutes. Season to taste with salt and white pepper.

To cook the shrimp and sausage: Preheat the oven to 400°. Place the Italian sausage on a baking sheet with raised sides. Place on the top rack of the preheated oven and bake for 10 to 15 minutes or until the sausage is firm and the juices run clear. Cool and cut into bite-size pieces.

In a heavy-bottomed frying pan heat the olive oil over medium heat. Add the sausage and sauté for 2 minutes to brown slightly. Add the shrimp and sauté until they begin to turn pink, about 1 minute. Add 1 cup of the chicken broth to deglaze the pan. Add the tasso gravy and 1 tablespoon of the parsley. Bring to a boil and let simmer 1 minute. The last cup of chicken stock is to be used to thin the gravy if needed.

To serve: Divide the hot grits between 8 warm bowls. Spoon the shrimp-sausage mixture over the grits. Sprinkle with the remaining tablespoon of parsley and serve immediately.

PECAN FLOUR–DUSTED SOFTSHELL CRAB WITH ROASTED GARLIC TOMATO BUTTER

John Currence

CITY GROCERY
OXFORD, MISSISSIPPI

SERVES 4

Roasted Garlic Tomatoes

4	tomatoes, halved, cored, and seeded
½	cup olive oil
4	garlic cloves, peeled and thinly sliced
2	tablespoons fresh thyme leaves
	Salt and black pepper to taste

Pecan Flour

2	cups pecan pieces, toasted
2	cups all-purpose flour
2	teaspoons garlic powder
2	teaspoons onion powder
2	teaspoons salt
1	tablespoon cracked black pepper

Garlic Olive Oil

9	cloves garlic, peeled
3	cups olive oil

Asparagus

1	pound fresh asparagus, peeled
½	cup olive oil
2	teaspoons fresh parsley, chopped
	Salt and pepper to taste

Crabs

4	jumbo softshell crabs
¾	cup plus 2 tablespoons Garlic Olive Oil
	Pecan Flour for dusting
2	tablespoons shallots, peeled and chopped
¼	cup white wine
½	cup chicken stock
10	tablespoons cold butter
¼	cup fresh parsley, chopped
¼	each green, red, and yellow bell pepper, seeded, deribbed, and minced

🌿 **To prepare the roasted garlic tomatoes:** Preheat the oven to 275°. On a baking sheet covered with aluminum foil place the tomato halves cut side up. Drizzle with the olive oil, sliced garlic, thyme, and salt and pepper. Roast in the oven 5 hours or until the tomatoes are shriveled, and have lost most but not all of their moisture. Transfer the tomatoes to a cutting board and coarsely chop.

🌿 **To make the pecan flour:** Preheat the oven to 350°. In a small shallow pan spread the pecans in a single layer and bake 5 to 8 minutes until the nuts are golden. Transfer the pecans to the work bowl of a food processor fitted with a metal blade and pulse until smooth. Add the flour, garlic and onion powders, salt, and pepper, and pulse to combine. Use a rubber spatula to push any pecans clinging to the side of the bowl into the center.

☙ **To make the garlic olive oil:** Place the garlic and oil in a saucepan set over very low heat and simmer until garlic is tender. Remove from the heat and allow to cool. Pour through a fine mesh strainer into a glass jar or bottle and cover. (Since the recipe makes more oil than you will need for this recipe, enjoy the leftovers spread on toast for what the chef calls a "monumental snack.")

☙ **To cook the asparagus:** Prepare a grill or preheat the oven to 500°. Remove the tough ends of the asparagus, and place in a medium bowl. Combine the olive oil, parsley, salt, and pepper, and pour over the asparagus. Toss the asparagus in the oil and transfer to the hot grill or place on a half-sheet pan and cook in the preheated oven. Cook, turning occasionally, about 5 to 7 minutes until tender.

☙ **To cook the softshell crabs:** If the crabs have not been cleaned by the fish monger, clean them by turning them on their backs and pulling off the triangular apron. Lift up the side flaps and pull out the spongy gills. With scissors, cut off the face just behind the eyes and gently press above the legs to pull out the bile sac. Rinse the crabs under cold running water.

☙ Dredge the crabs in the pecan flour, shaking off the excess. Heat ¾ cup of the garlic olive oil in a large sauté pan or skillet over high heat. Add the crabs top side down and cook for 2 to 3 minutes or until the crabs are crusty and brown. Gently turn the crabs with a slotted spatula and cook for 1 minute. Remove the crabs with the spatula and place them in a separate pan. Keep the crabs warm in a slightly warm oven while finishing the sauce.

☙ Return the crab-cooking pan to the stove, and heat 2 tablespoons of the garlic olive oil over medium-high heat. Being careful not to burn any of the pecan flour that may be remaining in the pan, add the chopped shallots and sauté 1 to 2 minutes until tender. Add the white wine, increase the heat to high, and bring to a boil. Cook until reduced to 1 tablespoon. Add the chicken stock and chopped roasted garlic tomatoes, and reduce to 2 tablespoons. Remove the pan from direct heat and add the butter, 1 tablespoon at a time, making sure each piece has been incorporated into the sauce before adding the next. If necessary, briefly return the pan to the heat to melt the butter. The finished sauce should be smooth and thick and glossy. Season with salt and pepper.

☙ **To serve:** For each serving, arrange a portion of asparagus on the plate and place 1 softshell crab in the center. Top with some of the roasted garlic tomato butter, chopped parsley, and minced bell peppers.

Roast Bahamian Lobster
with Chili, Saffron, Vanilla, and Rum

Allen Susser
CHEF ALLEN'S
MIAMI, FLORIDA

SERVES 6

Bahamian lobsters, unlike their kin hailing from northern waters, have no claws. Either type of lobster will work in this recipe, in which Caribbean cooking establishes a beachhead in South Florida.

Green Papaya Slaw

1   medium green papaya
1   medium red bell pepper, julienned
1   small carrot, julienned
1   small white onion, julienned
2   tablespoons julienned fresh ginger
     Juice of 1 large lime
2   tablespoons olive oil
2   teaspoons celery seeds
1   tablespoon kosher salt
1   teaspoon white pepper

Lobsters

6   Bahamian lobsters (or 6-ounce lobster
     tails)

1   teaspoon fresh thyme leaves
     Salt and freshly ground black pepper
        to taste
1/4 cup olive oil

Glaze

1   cup dry white wine
2   shallots, minced
1   vanilla bean, split lengthwise
1   teaspoon minced Scotch bonnet (habañero)
        chile
     Pinch of saffron
3   tablespoons Myers' dark rum

1   tablespoon Myers' dark rum

🍃 *To make the green papaya slaw:* With a small sharp knife, peel the skin from the papaya. Cut the flesh into quarters and discard the green seeds. Using a grater or mandolin, julienne the papaya pieces. In a medium bowl, combine all the ingredients and toss well. Let sit for 1 hour before serving to let the flavors blend.

🍃 *To prepare the lobsters:* Light a wood or charcoal fire in a grill. (The lobsters may also be broiled under a preheated broiler or baked in a 350° oven until the meat is opaque.) Kill the lobster by using the point of a large knife to make a small incision in the back of the shell where the chest and tail meet. Twist the body (head) and tail apart, and twist off the legs where they join the body. Reserve the legs to use for stock another time. With a large, heavy, sharp knife, cut through each tail shell on the top side, spread it open, and pull out the meat, leaving it attached to the shell at the tail end. Remove and discard the black strip.

Lay the meat on top of the shell and sprinkle with the thyme, salt, and pepper. Drizzle the olive oil over the lobster and set the lobster aside for 15 minutes.

☙ *To make the glaze:* Heat a medium sauté pan or skillet over high heat, add the wine and shallots, and cook to reduce for 1 minute. Add the vanilla bean, chile, saffron, and 3 tablespoons of the rum. Continue to cook over medium heat until the glaze is thick, syrupy, and reduced to $1/2$ cup, about 10 minutes.

☙ Preheat the oven to 350°. Place the lobsters meat side down on the grill and cook about 5 minutes until they are nicely charred and have absorbed some of the smoky flavor of the grill. Remove the lobsters to a heavy metal sizzle platter and brush with glaze. Place the pan in the oven and roast for 8 minutes. Brush the lobsters with the remaining glaze. Add 1 tablespoon of rum to the pan, warm it, and light it with a match. Shake the pan until the flames subside, then turn the lobsters in the pan to pick up the juices.

☙ *To serve:* Place a mound of papaya slaw in the center of each serving plate. Remove the lobster from each shell and lay the tail over the slaw on each plate. Brush with any remaining glaze and serve.

CREOLE SPINY LOBSTER

Mark Militello

MARK'S PLACE
MIAMI, FLORIDA

SERVES 6

In this wildly festive Caribbean dish, spiny lobsters are marinated in a lime-tinged Antilles marinade, sautéed, and served with a spicy mixture of island vegetables and a garnish of plantains, salt cod, and key limes.

Lobsters and Antilles Marinade

6	1½-pound fresh Caribbean spiny lobsters
½	cup extra-virgin olive oil
½	cup dry white wine

6	tablespoons fresh lime juice
3	tablespoons minced shallots
	Salt and freshly ground black pepper to taste

Sauce

2	tablespoons extra-virgin olive oil
2	tablespoons peeled and minced garlic
1/2	cup peeled and finely diced onion
1/2	cup fresh or frozen corn kernels
1/2	cup seeded and diced red bell pepper
1	Scotch bonnet (habañero) chile, seeded and minced
3	tablespoons dry sherry
1 1/2	tablespoons curry powder
2	large (8-ounce) tomatoes, peeled, seeded, and finely chopped
2	cups Lobster or Fish Stock (see page 219)
1/2	cup finely diced chayote
1/2	cup finely diced calabaza or acorn squash
1/2	cup peeled and finely diced yellow yam or sweet potato
1/2	cup cooked pigeon peas
2	tablespoons fresh thyme leaves
2	tablespoons chopped flat-leaf parsley
	Salt and freshly ground back pepper to taste

Garnish

3	unpeeled plantains
1	tablespoon olive oil
1	bunch calaloo or spinach, cleaned, stemmed, and roughly chopped
2	tomatoes, peeled, seeded, and cut into 1/4-inch cubes
1	garlic clove, minced
2	ounces salt cod, soaked in 4 changes of warm water for 15 minutes and rinsed each time, then drained and separated into flakes
	Salt and freshly ground pepper to taste
	Vegetable oil for frying
6	dal puri or flour tortillas, folded into quarters and grilled
	Lime wedges, preferably key limes

𝒮 To prepare the lobster: Separate the tails from the heads of the lobsters, then split the tails in half lengthwise, leaving the ends attached at the fins. Loosen the meat from the shell, but leave it slightly attached. Place the lobster tail halves shell side down in a shallow dish or non-aluminum pan. In a small bowl combine the olive oil, wine, lime juice, shallots, salt, and pepper. Spoon the marinade over the lobster. Let sit at room temperature for 15 minutes. (If it sits longer, the lime juice will begin to cook the lobster meat.) Reserve the heads and bodies for another use, such as stock.

𝒮 To make the sauce: In a 12-inch sauté pan or skillet heat the olive oil over medium-high heat. Add the garlic and onion, then add the corn, pepper, chile, 2 tablespoons of the sherry, and the curry powder, and sauté for 2 to 3 minutes. Add the tomatoes and stock and bring to a boil. Reduce the heat and simmer for 15 minutes. Pass the sauce through a fine food mill or a fine-mesh sieve and return the sauce to the pan. Add the chayote, calabaza, yam, peas, thyme, parsley, salt, and pepper. Simmer the mixture over low heat for 15 minutes or until the vegetables are tender.

𝒮 To make the vegetable garnish: In a small saucepan boil the plantains in lightly salted water over high heat about 15 minutes or until tender. Peel the plantains and cut 2 of them into 1/4-inch thick slices. Reserve the other plantain. Place the olive oil in a sauté pan or skillet over high heat, sauté the calaloo or spinach, tomatoes, garlic, and salt cod flakes until the vegetables are tender, 3 to 5 minutes. Add the plantain slices and stir until they are heated through. Add salt and pepper. Set aside and keep warm.

    Slice the remaining plantain into very thin lengthwise slices. In a sauté pan or skillet, heat 1 inch of vegetable oil to 350°. Deep-fry the plantain slices until crisp. Pat the lobsters dry with paper towels. In a large sauté pan or skillet over medium-high heat, heat the oil and sear the lobsters, cut side down, until lightly colored, about 2½ minutes, then turn and cook on the shell side for 1 minute. Make sure the heat is not too high or the lobster meat will become tough. Drain the oil from the pan, return the pan to the heat, and add the remaining 1 tablespoon of sherry. Ladle the sauce over the lobsters and place the pan in the oven for 7 to 8 minutes to finish cooking.

    To serve: Remove the meat completely from the shell and dip the meat briefly into the sauce. Return it to the shells for presentation. Place some of the vegetable garnish in the center of each plate and add 1 split lobster tail to each plate. Spoon the sauce over the lobster and onto the plate. Serve with the grilled dal puri and the lime wedges, and place a fried plantain slice in the center of each dish.

SMOKED SCOTCH BONNET JERK SPICE MAHIMAHI STUFFED WITH CHRISTOPHENE, CARROT, AND PEPPER WITH MOFONGO BROTH

Marty Blitz
MISE EN PLACE
TAMPA, FLORIDA

SERVES 4

Jerk Spice Barbecue

3	Scotch bonnet (habañero) chilies, smoked
1	teaspoon allspice
1	tablespoon peeled and chopped shallots
1	teaspoon peeled and grated fresh ginger
	Juice and grated zest of 1 orange
¼	cup vinegar
¼	cup olive oil
1	tablespoon fresh thyme
1	teaspoon sugar
½	teaspoon salt

Mofongo Broth

2	cups vegetable oil for frying
2	green plantains, peeled and quartered
8	slices bacon, diced
2	tablespoons peeled and chopped garlic
4	cups chicken stock
	Salt and pepper to taste

Fried Plantain Strips

2   firm-ripe plantains
2   cups vegetable oil for deep frying

4 8-ounce fillets mahimahi, butterflied

Vegetables

1   christophene squash, julienned
1   carrot, peeled, julienned, and blanched in
      boiling water for 1 minute

1   red bell pepper, julienned
1   red onion, peeled and julienned

Garnish

    Zest of 1 lime
2   tablespoons chopped cilantro
1   tomato, peeled, seeded, and diced

To make the jerk spice barbecue paste: In the work bowl of a food processor fitted with a metal blade, blend the chilies, allspice, shallots, ginger, orange juice, orange zest, vinegar, olive oil, thyme, sugar, and salt until a paste is formed. Remove the paste to a medium bowl.

To make the mofongo broth: In a medium saucepan over medium-high heat, heat the oil until 375° or until a cube of bread turns brown in 10 seconds. Add the plantain slices and fry about 3 to 4 minutes or until golden brown. Remove with a long-handled strainer and let drain on paper towels.

In a medium skillet sauté the bacon over medium heat until crisp. Add the garlic and cooked plantains and sauté together about 1 minute. Remove this mixture to the work bowl of a food processor fitted with a metal blade and purée until smooth. Remove to a medium saucepan. Add the chicken stock and set over medium-high heat. Bring the mixture to a simmer and continue to cook about 10 minutes or until slightly reduced. Adjust the seasoning to taste.

To make the fried plantain strips: In a medium saucepan heat the oil to 375° over medium-high heat. Meanwhile, peel the plantains, cut off the ends, and then cut lengthwise into thin slices. Place a few slices in the hot vegetable oil and fry just until golden, 1 to 2 minutes. Drain on paper towels and salt lightly. Continue frying in small batches until all the fruit is fried.

To cook the fish: Place the mahimahi fillets in the jerk paste and marinate for 30 minutes.

Preheat the oven to 400°. Remove the fish from the marinade and place on the counter. In a medium mixing bowl combine the vegetables. Divide this mixture into 4 portions. In the center of each fillet, place 1 portion of the vegetable mixture. Gently roll up the fish, enclosing the vegetables. Place the fillets in a small roasting pan, and roast in the preheated oven about 10 minutes or until just done. Remove the fish from the oven and proceed with the final assembly.

🐚 *To assemble the dish:* Place ⅔ cup of broth in each of 4 soup bowls. Place the cooked mahimahi in the center of the bowl. Garnish with lime zest, fresh cilantro, diced tomato, and crisp fried plantain strips. Serve immediately.

YELLOWTAIL SNAPPER ENCRUSTED IN YUCA WITH ROASTED PEPPER-ORANGE SALSA AND SIZZLING BLACK BEANS

Dawn Sieber

CHEECA LODGE
ISLAMORADA, FLORIDA

SERVES 4

At Cheeca Lodge this dish is more frequently referred to as the "President's Snapper," as the chef prepared it for President Bush during his visit. You are certain to relish the fresh and lively flavor combinations as much as the President did. Here's a great chance to share a meal with a president!

Roasted Pepper-Orange Salsa

½ cup extra-virgin olive oil
¼ cup black beans
4 oranges, peeled, pith and seeds removed, separated into sections
1 red bell pepper, roasted, peeled (see page 217), and diced
Juice of 2 key limes
½ bunch cilantro, chopped
Salt and pepper to taste

2 pounds (about 4 medium) yuca
4 7- to 8-ounce yellowtail (or other type) snapper fillets, skin on
Salt and pepper to taste
½ cup extra-virgin olive oil

1 eggplant, sliced into eight ½-inch thick rounds

🐚 *To make the salsa:* Wash and dry the black beans. In a small skillet heat ¼ cup of olive oil over high heat until nearly smoking. Add the beans and cook about 5 minutes or until beans begin to sputter and are slightly softened.

🐚 In a large bowl combine the orange sections, red pepper, lime juice, cilantro, ¼ cup of olive oil, salt, and pepper, and mix well. This will keep about 4 days, covered and refrigerated. Just before serving toss in the cooked black beans.

✍ **To prepare the snapper:** Preheat the oven to 450°. Cut the yuca crosswise into 3-inch pieces and peel with a paring knife. Finely grate the yuca. Season with salt and pepper.

✍ Rinse the snapper fillets and pat dry. Season the fish on both sides with salt and pepper. Place the grated yuca on a plate and place the fillets on the yuca skin side down. Firmly press the yuca into the fillets. Heat a cast-iron skillet over medium-high heat, add ¼ cup of the olive oil, and starting with the yuca coated side down, sear the fillets a minute or two on each side, turning carefully. Remove the skillet to the preheated oven, and finish cooking the fillets until just done. The fish will be done when just springy to the touch, and there is no red color when you peer inside the fish cavity, about 4 to 5 minutes.

✍ **To cook the eggplant:** Prepare a grill. Over a medium-hot fire, grill the eggplant about 3 to 4 minutes per side until golden brown. Alternately, clean and reheat the skillet used in the fish frying. Add ¼ cup of olive oil, heat until nearly smoking, and brown the eggplant in the oil, turning, about 2 to 3 minutes per side.

✍ **To serve:** Place 2 eggplant slices on each of 4 serving dishes. Top with a snapper fillet, yuca side up, and garnish with the salsa.

HERB-CRUSTED RED SNAPPER WITH PINE NUT-HERB SAUCE

Anoosh Shariat

SHARIAT'S
LOUISVILLE, KENTUCKY

SERVES 4

Sauce

2	tablespoons pine nuts
1	red bell pepper
¼	cup fresh stemmed and chopped cilantro
¼	cup fresh stemmed and chopped thyme
2	tablespoons stemmed and chopped parsley
2	tablespoons chopped fresh dill
2	tablespoons chopped fresh chives
2	tablespoons olive oil
1	tablespoon peeled and minced shallots
1	tablespoon minced garlic
¼	cup white wine
2	tablespooons capers
¼	cup Fish Stock (see page 219) or bottled clam juice
2	tablespoons key lime juice
	Salt and pepper to taste

Vegetables

¼	cup olive oil
	Salt and pepper to taste
½	cup peeled and julienned turnips (¼-inch julienne)
1	cup green asparagus tips
½	cup purple asparagus tips
2	tablespoons stemmed and chopped fresh tarragon
½	cup dry white wine

For the Fish

4	6-ounce red snapper fillets, skin on, scales removed
2	tablespoons olive oil
	Salt to taste
½	teaspoon paprika
1	teaspoon angelica (see Note)
	Reserved fresh herbs

☛ *To make the sauce:* Preheat the oven to 300°. In a small heatproof dish toast the pine nuts until just browned. Remove and reserve. Prepare a grill or heat the broiler. Roast the pepper over the grill or on a pan under the broiler, turning from side to side until the skin is blackened and blistered.

☛ Transfer the pepper to a small bowl and cover with plastic wrap. After 10 minutes, remove the pepper from the bowl cut in half, remove the stems and seeds, and peel off the skin. Cut the flesh into narrow ¼-inch strips. Combine the fresh herbs, portion in two, and reserve half to be used later for the fish cooking.

☛ In a medium saucepan heat the olive oil over medium-high heat. Add the shallots and garlic, and cook for 1 to 2 minutes or until the garlic just begins to brown, being careful not to burn the garlic. Deglaze the pan with the white wine. Add the roasted pepper strips, pine nuts, and capers. Pour in the fish stock or clam juice and key lime juice. Boil down the juices to reduce slightly and thicken. Add the half portion of fresh herbs. Season to taste with salt and pepper. Reserve.

To make the vegetables: In a large sauté pan or skillet heat the olive oil over medium-high heat. Add the julienned turnips, season with salt and pepper, and cook 2 minutes or until slightly softened. Add the green and purple asparagus tips, toss to combine, and cook 1 minute. Add the chopped tarragon and continue to cook another 3 to 4 minutes or until the vegetables are tender and the flavors have blended. If the pan gets too dry during the final cooking, add some or all of the white wine.

To cook the fish: Preheat the oven to 450°. Rub the fillets with the olive oil, and season with salt, paprika, and the angelica. Use the remaining half of the herbs to rub both sides of the fillets. Heat a cast-iron skillet over medium-high heat, add the olive oil, and sear the fillets 1 or 2 minutes on each side, turning carefully. Remove the skillet to the oven and finish cooking the fillets about 4 to 5 minutes or until just done. The fish will be done when just springy to the touch and there is no red color when you peer inside the fish cavity.

To assemble: Heap a couple of tablespoons of the vegetables in the center of each plate. Crown with a snapper fillet, and spoon the pine nut sauce on top. Garnish with fresh garlic chives and fresh thyme.

Note: Angelica, often referred to as the sweet "herb of the angels" is a member of the parsley family. Grown extensively in Europe, it has pale green, celerylike stalks, and is often used in the production of liqueurs.

GRILLED YELLOWFIN TUNA WITH RATATOUILLE, RISOTTO, GRILLED SHALLOTS, AND RED WINE–MOREL SAUCE

Wally Joe
KC'S RESTAURANT
CLEVELAND, MISSISSIPPI

SERVES 4

Tuna

4	#1 Sashimi grade yellowfin tuna loin fillets (about 7 ounces)
	Sea salt and pepper to taste
1	cup red wine
12	whole shallots, peeled
1	tablespoon olive oil

Ratatouille

2	tablespoons extra-virgin olive oil
2	tablespoons 1/4-inch diced onions
1/2	cup 1/4-inch diced yellow squash
1/2	cup 1/4-inch diced zucchini
1/2	cup 1/4-inch diced eggplant
1	tablespoon Roasted Garlic Purée (see page 218)
	Salt and pepper to taste
1	teaspoon chopped fresh rosemary
1	teaspoon chopped fresh thyme
1/2	cup peeled, seeded, and 1/4-inch diced Roma tomatoes

Risotto

1	quart Chicken Stock (see page 218)
2	tablespoons olive oil
2	tablespoons finely chopped onion
2	cups Arborio rice
1/2	cup dry white wine
1	tablespoon tomato paste

Red Wine-Morel Sauce

3	tablespoons butter
1	small shallot, finely chopped
16	fresh morels (or dried morels soaked in boiling water 15 minutes)
1	cup good quality dry red wine
1/2	teaspoon fresh thyme leaves
1	cup Veal Stock (see page 219)

❧ **To prepare the tuna:** Season the tuna with salt and pepper and marinate in the red wine. While the tuna is marinating, prepare the ratatouille.

❧ **To make the ratatouille:** In a large sauté pan or skillet heat the oil over high heat and sauté the onion 2 minutes. Add the squash, zucchini, eggplant, garlic, salt, pepper, and herbs, and sauté for 5 minutes or until the vegetables are just tender. Transfer the mixture to a bowl and let cool. Add the diced tomato.

❧ **To make the risotto:** In a deep saucepan bring the stock to a slow, steady simmer. In a medium skillet heat the oil over medium heat and sauté the onion until translucent. Add the rice and stir until it is well coated. Add the wine and sauté 2 minutes or until the wine has evaporated. Add ½ cup of the simmering broth. Stir while cooking until the rice absorbs the liquid. When the rice dries out, add another ½ cup of simmering broth and continue to stir, cook, and wait for the rice to dry out before adding another ladleful of the simmering stock. Continue cooking the rice in this fashion, reducing the additions of stock to ¼ cup at a time after about 15 minutes of cooking to insure that you do not flood the rice with the liquid. The rice is done when it is tender but firm to the bite. When the rice reaches the proper consistency, taste for seasoning. Turn off the heat and mix in the tomato paste and the ratatouille.

ℒ *To make the red wine-morel sauce:* In a medium saucepan melt the butter over medium heat, add the chopped shallots, and cook 1 minute until softened. If using dried morels, remove them from their soaking liquid with a slotted spoon. Add the morels to the pan and cook until soft. Add the red wine, bring to a boil, and cook until reduced to ¼ cup. Add the veal stock and reduce again until the sauce is thickened and can coat the back of a spoon. Pour through a fine mesh strainer into a clean saucepan. Reserve the morels in a separate container. When ready to serve, reheat the sauce over low heat.

ℒ *To cook the tuna and assemble the dish:* Prepare a charcoal grill or heat a large non-stick sauté pan or skillet over high heat. Season the shallots with salt and pepper, and brush with some of the olive oil. Grill the shallots until soft, or roast in a preheated 400° oven about 17 minutes.

ℒ Brush the tuna fillets with the remaining olive oil. Sear the tuna on a very hot grill or in the prepared skillet about 2 minutes on each side.

ℒ *To serve:* In the center of each serving plate mound the risotto. Slice each tuna fillet in half on the diagonal, and arrange the halves on top of the risotto. Pour the sauce around the tuna and rice, and arrange the shallots and reserved morels around the edge of the plate.

GRILLED BARBECUED TUNA

Frank Lee

SLIGHTLY NORTH OF BROAD
CHARLESTON, SOUTH CAROLINA

SERVES 4

Mustard Barbecue Sauce

1¼   cups cider vinegar
1¼   cups prepared mustard (French's is
        suggested)
¼   cup ketchup
½   cup honey
½   cup water
1   tablespoon Worcestershire sauce
1   tablespoon Tabasco hot sauce

Country Ham Green Onion Butter

1   cup Chicken Stock (see page 218)
4   ounces country ham, julienned

½   cup (1 stick) unsalted butter
½   cup chopped scallions

Tuna and Oysters

24   oysters
2   cups cornmeal
4   cups vegetable oil
4   5-ounce portions tuna loin
2   tablespoons olive oil
¼   cup cracked pepper
2   tablespoons vegetable oil

¼   cup chopped scallions, for garnish

🐚 **To make the mustard barbecue sauce:** In a medium nonreactive saucepan combine the cider vinegar, mustard, ketchup, honey, water, Worcestershire sauce, and Tabasco. Bring to a boil over medium-high heat. Reduce the heat to low and simmer for 15 minutes. Set aside, and allow the sauce to cool before using.

🐚 **To make the country ham green onion butter:** In a small saucepan heat the stock over medium-high heat. Add the country ham and cook until stock is thickened and reduced by half. Whisk in the butter, add the green onions, and cook over medium heat for 1 minute. Remove from the heat and set aside to cool.

🐚 **To prepare the tuna and oysters:** Dredge the oysters in the cornmeal. Heat the oil to 375° or until a bread cube turns brown in 10 seconds. Add the oysters and fry until lightly brown and golden. Remove them from the pan with a slotted spoon and drain on a rack. Keep the oysters warm by covering loosely with aluminum foil.

🐚 Rinse the tuna portions and pat dry with paper towels. Lightly brush the tuna with the olive oil and coat with the cracked pepper. Place a large sauté pan or skillet over high heat for 3 minutes. Add the oil and place the tuna portions in the pan. Sear the tuna on one side for 2 minutes, then turn with tongs and cook for approximately 2 minutes on the other side, or until just medium rare. Reduce the heat to medium and add ¼ cup of the mustard barbecue sauce to the pan. Cook just until the tuna is glazed with sauce. Immediately remove the tuna from the pan and set aside.

🐟 *To assemble:* Place 2 tablespoons of barbecue sauce in the center of each plate. Place the tuna on the sauce and top with 6 oysters. Divide the country ham green onion butter into equal portions, and place on top of the oysters. Garnish with a tablespoon of chopped green onion.

GROUPER PIBIL

Johnny Earles
CRIOLLA'S RESTAURANT
GRAYTON BEACH, FLORIDA

SERVES 4

The name "callaloo," which the chef uses for his spicy coconut broth, usually refers to a thick, spicy soup that is made with a leafy spinach-like vegetable that Caribbean locals call callaloo. On Guadeloupe, the French descendants say that "the Creole cuisine is superb, and callaloo with crab is the king." We think you will find this combination no less royal.

Jerk Oil

1	tablespoon jerk spices (available at specialty stores)
⅔	cup peanut oil

Calabaza Stew

½	cup olive oil
1	cup diced sweet onions
2	tablespoons minced garlic
1	cup diced calabaza
1	cup diced zucchini
	Juice of 3 limes
2	Scotch bonnet (habañero) chilies, seeded and minced
1	cup Chicken Stock (see page 218)
1	cup peeled, seeded, and diced tomato
12	opal basil leaves
	Salt and pepper to taste

Callaloo Broth

1	cup dry unsweetened coconut
3	cups coconut milk
3	cups Chicken Stock (see page 218)
1	Scotch bonnet (habañero) chile, seeded and minced
1	tablespoon minced garlic
1	tablespoon minced ginger
3	ounces fresh lime juice
1	sprig fresh basil, crushed
6	fresh cilantro sprigs
24	littleneck clams
2	cups chopped spinach

Grouper

4	10 x 10-inch banana leaves (or 10-inch squares of aluminum foil)
4	6-ounce grouper fillets
	Salt and pepper to taste

❧ **To make the jerk oil:** In a small saucepan combine the jerk spices and peanut oil and heat over medium-high heat until simmering. Remove from the heat, strain through a fine mesh strainer into a clean container, and let the flavors macerate 1 hour before using.

❧ **To make the calabaza stew:** In a large sauté pan or skillet heat the oil over medium-high heat and cook the onion and garlic until softened. Add the calabaza, zucchini, lime juice, chilies, and chicken stock and simmer about 20 minutes, stirring occasionally, until the vegetables are tender. Stir in the tomato, basil, salt, and pepper, and remove the pan from the heat.

❧ **To make the callaloo broth:** In a large nonreactive pot combine the coconut, coconut milk, chicken stock, chile, garlic, ginger, lime juice, basil, and cilantro over high heat. Bring to a boil, reduce the heat to medium, and simmer 20 minutes. Pour through a fine mesh strainer into a clean large skillet. Set the skillet over medium-high heat and steam the littlenecks in the broth until they open. Toss in the spinach, stir just long enough for the spinach to wilt, and remove from the heat.

❧ **To cook the grouper and assemble the dish:** Form the "banana boat" by tying the ends of the banana leaf, or aluminum foil square. Spoon one-fourth of the calabaza stew into the boat and place a fillet on top. Season with salt and pepper, and place in a bamboo steamer that has been set over a pan of simmering water. Steam for 10 minutes or until the flesh is opaque, but still moist. Remove the fish from the steamer to large, warm serving bowls. Place 3 steamed clams on each side of the boat. Pour one-fourth of the callaloo broth over each portion of fish and drizzle with the jerk-flavored oil.

Horseradish-crusted Sea Bass with Roast Shiitake Mushrooms and Miso

Clifford Harrison
BACCHANALIA
ATLANTA, GEORGIA

SERVES 4

2	tablespoons miso paste	4	pea shoots
1	cup water	1	ounce enoki mushrooms
4	6-ounce Chilean sea bass fillets, skin removed	4	large shiitake mushrooms, trimmed
2	tablespoons olive oil	1	lemon
	Salt and pepper to taste	3	tablespoons yuza sauce (available in specialty shops or mix together 1 tablespoon lemon juice, 1 tablespoon soy sauce, and 1 tablespoon honey)
6	ounces fresh horseradish root, peeled and grated		
2	tablespoons white wine vinegar		
¼	cup fresh breadcrumbs, toasted		

To prepare the sea bass: In a small saucepan dissolve the miso paste in the water. Set the pan over medium-high heat and bring to a simmer. Immediately remove the pan from the heat, strain through a fine mesh strainer and return to the saucepan. Set the pan over very low heat to keep warm while preparing the sea bass fillets.

Preheat the oven to 400°. Brush the sea bass fillets with 1 tablespoon of the olive oil, season on both sides with salt and pepper. Combine the horseradish and white wine vinegar. Spread the sea bass fillets with the horseradish mixture, and top with a tablespoon of breadcrumbs. Place the sea bass fillets upside down on a sheet pan that has been coated with 1 tablespoon of the olive oil. Add the shiitake mushrooms to the pan and roast in the preheated oven for 5 to 8 minutes or until the fish is mostly opaque but still slightly translucent in the center. Remove from the oven. Remove the shiitake mushrooms from the pan to a cutting board and slice into julienne. Preheat the broiler, turn the fish right side up, and heat under the broiler for 1 minute or until lightly browned.

To serve: Place one-fourth of the miso mixture in each of 4 large bowls. Place a sea bass fillet in the center of each bowl, and top with a garnish of 1 pea shoot, ½ tablespoon of the enoki, and julienned shiitake mushrooms. Squeeze the juice from the lemon over the fillet. Finish with 2 teaspoons of the yuza sauce or the lemon, soy, and honey mixture. Serve immediately.

NAGE OF DOVER SOLE RIVERIA

Jean Banchet

RIVERIA RESTAURANT
ATLANTA, GEORGIA

SERVES 4

Mussel Stock

1	tablespoon chopped parsley
1	pound fresh mussels
2	tablespoons butter
1	tablespoon peeled and chopped shallots
1/4	cup Fish Stock (see page 219)
1/4	cup dry white wine
1/4	cup dry vermouth
1	teaspoon saffron

Sole

1/4	cup olive oil
2	fennel bulbs, trimmed and cut into 1/16-inch julienne
2	fresh 18-ounce Dover sole, boned and filleted
	Salt and pepper to taste

Sauce

1/4	cup heavy cream
1/4	cup olive oil
	Salt and pepper to taste

Pasta

8	ounces fresh or dried black linguini pasta
1/2	cup (1 stick) butter
	Salt and pepper to taste

Garnish

8	outer leaves from fennel bulbs
8	medium mushroom caps
2	medium tomatoes, peeled, seeded, and diced

❧ **To make the mussel stock:** Carefully pick through the mussels, discarding any that do not smell sweet. Scrape off the beards. In a medium saucepan melt the butter over medium heat, stir in the shallots, and cook slowly until limp. Then add the parsley, mussels, fish stock, white wine, vermouth, and saffron. Cover the pan and shake to mix together the ingredients. Raise the heat to high, cover the pan, and let the mussels steam 3 to 4 minutes or just until the mussels open. Remove the pan from the heat, and strain the mussel stock into another pan. Reserve the mussels separately.

❧ **To prepare sole:** In a medium sauté pan heat the olive oil over medium heat, add the fennel, and cook slowly for 2 to 3 minutes or until the fennel is tender and wilted. Set aside.

❧ Preheat the oven to 400°. Pat the fish dry with paper towels and season with salt and pepper. Lightly butter a flameproof baking dish that will just hold the fish. Place the fillets in the baking dish, sprinkle with the julienned fennel, and roll up the fillets. Fasten with a toothpick.

🍢 Pour in enough of the mussel stock to come two-thirds of the way up the fillets. Lay buttered waxed paper or parchment paper over the fish and set the dish over medium heat just until the liquid starts to bubble. Place in the preheated oven and cook 8 to 10 minutes or until the skin has turned an opaque white. Remove the pan from the oven, drain the fish cooking juices into a saucepan, and keep the fish warm while finishing the sauce.

🍢 **To make the sauce:** Set the pan with the fish cooking juices over medium-high heat, and reduce by three-fourths. Add the cream and bring to a boil. Simmer until reduced by half. Remove from the heat and pour into a blender. Add the olive oil, salt, and pepper, and blend well.

🍢 **To prepare the pasta:** Bring a large pot of salted water to a boil over high heat. Add the pasta and cook about 5 minutes until al dente. Drain and return the pasta to the warm saucepan. Add the butter, salt, and pepper and mix well.

🍢 **To prepare the garnishes:** Remove 8 of the large outer leaves from the fennel bulbs. Trim and clean the mushroom caps. Place a medium saucepan over high heat, fill with salted water, and bring to a boil. Add the fennel leaves, and cook until softened. Remove the leaves from the water with a long-handled strainer. Add the mushroom caps to the water and cook 1 to 2 minutes or until softened.

🍢 **To serve:** Remove the mussels from their shells. Place the pasta in the center of 4 serving dishes. Arrange 2 fennel leaves around the pasta and put 1 sole fillet in each leaf. Garnish each plate with the mussels and spoon the sauce over the mussels and sole. Top each sole fillet with a mushroom cap and 1 tablespoon of the diced tomatoes.

PANÉED CATFISH WITH CRAYFISH STUFFING IN AN HERB BUTTER SAUCE

Nick Apostle

NICK'S
JACKSON, MISSISSIPPI

SERVES 6

Since most of the components of this recipe can be prepared ahead of time, it makes a terrific entrée for guests. Serve it with chunky garlic, fresh boiled potatoes flavored with parsley, and simply prepared fresh asparagus or broccoli.

Seasoning Mix

1	teaspoon salt
½	teaspoon white pepper
¼	teaspoon cayenne pepper
½	teaspoon onion powder
¼	teaspoon dried thyme leaves
⅛	teaspoon dried oregano leaves

Crayfish Stuffing

½	cup (1 stick) margarine
1	cup finely chopped onions
½	cup finely chopped celery
½	cup finely chopped green bell pepper
½	cup chopped green onions
1	teaspoon minced garlic
1	pound peeled crayfish tails with fat, coarsely chopped
1	cup very fine dry breadcrumbs
¼	cup (½ stick) unsalted butter
2	eggs, beaten
3	tablespoons finely grated Parmesan cheese

Herb Butter Sauce

1	tablespoon clarified butter
2	shallots, minced
2	garlic cloves, minced
2	tablespoons chopped fresh thyme
1	tablespoon chopped fresh oregano
2	bay leaves
¾	cup dry white wine
1¼	cups Fish Stock (see page 219) or bottled clam juice
½	tablespoon lemon juice
¼	cup heavy cream
2	cups (4 sticks) butter, cut into small pieces

Milk Wash for Fillets

½	teaspoon salt
½	teaspoon white pepper
1½	cups milk
12	2- to 4-ounce fillets catfish (or Tilapia, rainbow trout, salmon, or any other freshwater fish)

Seasoned Flour

3	cups all-purpose flour
1	teaspoon white pepper
3	teaspoons onion powder
1	teaspoon cayenne pepper
1½	teaspoons garlic powder
1½	teaspoons dried thyme leaves
¾	teaspoon dried oregano leaves
	Clarified butter for pan frying

✐ **To make the seasoning mix:** In a small bowl combine the salt, white pepper, cayenne, onion powder, thyme, and oregano, and set aside.

✐ **To make the stuffing:** Melt $\frac{1}{2}$ cup of margarine in a skillet over medium-high heat. Add the onions, celery, and bell pepper, and sauté 5 to 7 minutes or until lightly browned and softened. Add the seasoning mix, green onions, and garlic, and cook about 3 minutes, stirring to combine. Add the crayfish and cook for 3 to 4 minutes, stirring occasionally. Add $\frac{1}{2}$ cup of the breadcrumbs and stir well. Continue to cook without stirring until the mixture sticks, about 1 minute. Stir and scrape the bottom of the pan well to prevent burning. Add the butter and continue cooking until the butter melts, constantly stirring and scraping the pan bottom. Stir in the remaining $\frac{1}{2}$ cup of breadcrumbs and remove the pan from the heat. Reserve and let cool slightly.

✐ In a small bowl combine the beaten eggs with the Parmesan. Add to the stuffing mixture in the skillet, mix well to combine, and transfer to a shallow pan. Refrigerate until needed.

✐ **To make the herb butter sauce:** In a small skillet melt the clarified butter over medium-high heat. Add the shallots, garlic, thyme, oregano, and bay leaves, and cook 1 to 2 minutes or until the shallots are softened. Add the white wine and stock and bring to a boil. Continue to boil until the liquids have been reduced to a glaze. Reduce the heat to very low and add the heavy cream. Blend in the lemon juice. Over very low heat add the butter, piece by piece, making sure it is completely incorporated into the sauce before the next piece is added. Do not let the mixture come to a boil. If necessary, remove the sauce from the heat while adding the butter. Strain the sauce through a fine mesh strainer into a warmed thermos or a mixing bowl set over a pan of simmering water.

✐ **To cook the fish fillets:** Preheat the oven to 400°. In a shallow bowl whisk together the salt, pepper, and milk. Sprinkle the fish fillets with salt and pepper. In a large skillet heat enough clarified butter over medium heat to sauté the fillets. Dip the fillets first in the milk wash, and then dredge in the seasoned flour, coating evenly and shaking off any excess. Sauté the fillets in the hot butter until light golden, about 2 minutes per side. Remove the fillets from the pan and place half on a work surface and half on a baking sheet. Spoon about 3 ounces of the stuffing mixture onto the fillets in the baking pan. Lay the remaining fillets over the stuffing. Bake in the preheated oven for 5 minutes or until the stuffing is heated through.

✐ Using a large spatula, transfer the stuffed catfish fillets to serving plates. Ladle the butter sauce around the fillets.

WHOLE SIZZLING CATFISH WITH CHILE-BLACK BEAN SAUCE

Thomas Catherall
TOM TOM
ATLANTA, GEORGIA

SERVES 4

This dish makes a spectacular presentation. The deep-frying stiffens the fish, making it possible for it to stand up on the platter, staring at its consumer.

2	*whole catfish (1½ to 2 pounds each)*
½	*cup peeled and thinly sliced fresh ginger*
	Vegetable oil for deep-frying
1	*cup rice flour*

Sauce

1	*tablespoon olive oil*
1	*teaspoon sesame oil*
1	*teaspoon chopped garlic*
1	*teaspoon minced ginger*

¼	*cup Chinese fermented black beans*
1	*teaspoon garlic chile paste (available in Oriental markets)*
¼	*cup dry sherry*
½	*cup soy sauce*

Garnish

¼	*cup chopped green onions*
¼	*cup seeded and diced tomatoes, peeled*
¼	*cup pickled ginger*

✒ Make 5 incisions on each side of the whole catfish by slicing on the diagonal to bone. Stuff the slits with the fresh ginger slices.

✒ In a large heavy pot or deep fryer heat 6 inches of oil to 350°. Dredge the fish in the rice flour, coating evenly, and shake off any excess flour. One at a time, drop the fish in the hot oil and fry until golden brown, about 5 to 8 minutes. Using a pair of slotted spoons, lift out the fish and drain on paper towels.

✒ In a small saucepan heat the olive and sesame oils over medium-high heat and sauté the garlic, ginger, and black beans for 1 minute. Add the chile paste, sherry, and soy, and reduce by half. Pour over the cooked fish and garnish with the green onions, tomatoes, and pickled ginger.

PANFRIED MOUNTAIN RAINBOW TROUT WITH GREEN TOMATO AND LIME BUTTER SALSA ON SWEET POTATO, ARTICHOKE, AND CRAYFISH HASH

Ben Barker

MAGNOLIA GRILL
DURHAM, NORTH CAROLINA

SERVES 4

Salsa

¼ cup chopped tomatillo, cut into ½-inch cubes

3 ounces green-ripening tomatoes, peeled, seeded, and cut into ½-inch cubes

1 to 2 red or green serranos, seeded and cut into fine slivers

1 pasilla or poblano chile, roasted, peeled, and julienned

1 tablespoon peeled and minced garlic

4 ounces cooked crawfish tail meat, split lengthwise

⅓ cup baby artichokes, marinated in olive oil and cut into eighths, or artichoke bottoms cut into wedges

Salt and black pepper to taste

¼ cup chopped mixed Italian parsley, cilantro, and oregano

Hash

½ cup olive oil

1 pound sweet potatoes, peeled and cut into ½-inch cubes

⅔ cup chopped, peeled onion, cut into ½-inch cubes

⅓ cup seeded, chopped red bell pepper, cut into ½-inch cubes

⅓ cup seeded, chopped yellow bell pepper, cut into ½-inch cubes

Trout

¼ cup olive oil

½ cup chopped mixed Italian parsley, cilantro, and oregano

4 10-ounce butterflied rainbow trout

Salt and black pepper to taste

6 tablespoons unsalted butter, cut into 3 to 4 pieces

¼ cup freshly squeezed lime juice

4 garlic cloves, poached in 3 changes of water until tender, peeled, and thinly sliced

To make the salsa: In a medium mixing bowl combine the diced tomatillo, green tomatoes, slivered serrano, and julienned pasilla or poblano chile. Stir to combine and set aside at room temperature until ready to serve.

To make the hash: In a large sauté pan or skillet heat the oil over medium-high heat. Add the raw sweet potatoes and sauté 2 minutes or until the potatoes start to caramelize and soften. Add the onion and peppers and cook 1 minute. Add the garlic and cook 30 seconds. Add the crawfish tails and artichokes and warm through. Season generously with salt and pepper, and toss with herbs. Divide among 4 warm serving platters.

🗫 **To make the trout:** Preheat the oven to 350°. In one or two large ovenproof sauté pans heat the olive oil over medium-high heat. Divide half of the herbs into fourths, and sprinkle the cavities of the trout. Season the cavities liberally with salt and fresh black pepper. Place the trout on one side in the sauté pan(s), reduce the heat to medium, and cook 3 minutes. Turn the trout and place the pan(s) in the oven. Cook for 3 to 4 minutes or until the flesh is just firm at the backbone. Remove the trout from the oven and season with salt, pepper, and the remaining herbs.

🗫 In an 8-inch sauté pan melt the butter over high heat until past the foaming point. It will begin to brown lightly and will smell nutty. Caution: The butter will sizzle and splatter! Add lime juice, poached garlic, and salsa, and toss to warm.

🗫 **To assemble:** Divide the hash equally among the 4 plates. Set the trout alongside, and pour 2 tablespoons of the hot salsa over each serving.

RICE PAPER–WRAPPED TUNA LOIN WITH GINGER SAUCE

Cory Mattson
THE FEARRINGTON HOUSE
PITTSBORO, NORTH CAROLINA

SERVES 4

Steamed Rice

1	tablespoon salt
2	cups uncovered long-grain rice

Vegetable Garnish

1	tablespoon olive oil
1	small onion, peeled and diced
1/2	red bell pepper, deribbed, seeded, and diced
1	carrot, cleaned and diced
1	small zucchini, cleaned and diced
1	small yellow squash, cleaned and diced

Ginger Sauce

1	cup white wine
1	tablespoon honey
1/2	cup soy sauce

	Juice of 2 lemons
1	teaspoon dried red pepper flakes
1	tablespoon fresh gingerroot, grated
1	small garlic clove, thinly sliced
	Pinch of salt
1	to 2 tablespoons cornstarch dissolved in 1/4 cup apple juice
4	6-ounce fresh yellowfin tuna steaks, trimmed
8	sheets rice paper
1	egg, beaten
	Salt and pepper to taste
	Vegetable oil for deep-frying
1	large leek, cleaned and julienned
1	tablespoon cornstarch

ASPARAGUS CHARLOTTE

GNOCCHI STUFFED WITH FONDUTA
IN PARMESAN CHEESE-CREAM SAUCE

BARBECUED SPICED OYSTERS
ON CREAMY SUCCOTASH

Shrimp and Plantain Torte

Yuca-stuffed Shrimp with a Sour Orange Mojo and Scotch Bonnet Tartar Salsa

MAINE LOBSTER WITH CELERY ROOT AND APPLE SALAD

SALAD NIÇOISE

Nage of Dover Sole Riviera

Horseradish-crusted Sea Bass
with Roast Shiitake Mushrooms
and Miso

WHOLE SIZZLING CATFISH WITH CHILE-BLACK BEAN SAUCE

ROASTED CHICKEN
WITH COLLARDS, RED ONION,
AND SWEET POTATO CHIPS

COQ AU VIN

GUINEA HEN "SOUVA ROFF" MODERN
with FOIE GRAS, TRUFFLES,
AND MORELS

BARBECUED DUCK WITH WILTED GREENS

BARBECUED BREAST OF DUCK
WITH CRUSHED PEPPER, PLUMS,
AND PLUM WINE

GRILLED AND BRAISED RABBIT
WITH MOLASSES, BOURBON, SLAB BACON,
AND STONE-GROUND GRITS

PORK TENDERLOIN "AU POIVRE"

CUBAN FRENCH TOAST

PRALINE MOUSSE SERVED WITH CHOCOLATE MERINGUE

LEMON PARFAIT WITH FRUITS AND SAUCES

BERRY COBBLER

STRAWBERRY NAPOLEON

Havana Bananas with Rum, Chilies, and Chocolate Sauce

Frozen Lime Ganache Parfait with Chocolate Tuiles

🔊 **To make the rice:** In a large saucepan over high heat, bring 5 quarts water to a boil with the salt. Sprinkle in the rice, stirring until the water returns to a boil, and boil vigorously for 10 minutes. Drain the rice in a large colander and rinse with cold water. Bring a large saucepan of water to a boil over high heat. Reduce the heat to low and set the colander with the rice over the simmering water. Cover the rice with a kitchen towel and the lid, and steam for 15 minutes or until it is fluffy and dry.

🔊 **To make the vegetable garnish:** In a medium sauté pan or skillet heat the olive oil over medium-high heat. Add the onion, pepper, and carrot and cook about 5 minutes until softened. Add the zucchini and yellow squash and cook just until tender, about another 2 minutes. Remove from heat and reserve.

🔊 **To make the ginger sauce:** In a small saucepan combine the white wine, honey, soy sauce, lemon juice, red pepper flakes, and grated ginger, and bring to a simmer over medium-high heat. In a mortar with a pestle, crush the garlic with the salt to make a paste. Add the garlic paste to the saucepan, stir to combine, and then whisk in the cornstarch that has been dissolved in the apple juice. Continue to cook, stirring until the cornstarch is dissolved and the sauce is clear. Keep warm on the back of the stove.

🔊 **To make the rice paper-wrapped tuna:** Cut each steak nearly in half vertically, leaving about ¼-inch thickness on the bottom. Fold the two sections on top of each other and set aside. Dip the sheets of rice paper into lukewarm water for a few seconds until they are softened and pliable, and place them on the work surface. Position one sheet of rice paper on the diagonal. Place a second sheet on and at the top of the first sheet. The bottom corner of the second sheet should be positioned over the top corner of the first sheet. The two sheets should have the appearance of intersecting diamonds. Brush the sheets with the beaten egg. Season the tuna with salt and pepper to taste. Place a tuna steak in the center of the first rice paper sheet and roll toward you, folding the bottom of the wrapper over the tuna. Fold in the sides of the wrapper over the filling. Roll up tightly, pressing to seal the edges. Use additional egg wash if needed to seal edges. The finished product should resemble a large egg roll. Repeat with the remaining wrappers and tuna steaks. (Can be made 6 hours ahead. Cover and chill.)

🔊 In a large heavy pot pour oil to a depth of 3 inches. Heat to 350°. Working in batches, add the rolls to the oil and deep-fry about 4 to 5 minutes until golden brown. Remove with a slotted spoon and drain on paper towels. Using a serrated knife, cut each roll into diagonal slices. Keep the oil on the hot burner to fry the leeks.

🔊 In a small bowl toss the julienned leek with the cornstarch, and deep-fry in the hot oil about 30 seconds. Remove with a slotted strainer, and drain on paper towels.

🔊 **To serve:** For each serving fill a cup with the steamed rice, and unmold onto the center of the serving plates. Surround the rice with the vegetables, and spoon the sauce on the vegetables and around the plate. Place the tuna slices around the rice and top with the fried leeks.

BACON-WRAPPED TROUT STUFFED WITH CRAWFISH

John Heer

THE INN AT BLACKBERRY FARM
WALLAND, TENNESSEE

SERVES 8

An equally tasty but low-fat alternative to the bacon wrapped trout is to wrap the trout in large leek leaves. To do so, simply cook the leek leaves in boiling water until softened, and cool quickly in an ice bath. Pat the leaves dry with paper towels and proceed with the recipe using the method described with the bacon.

Crawfish Stuffing

3/4	cup (1 1/2 sticks) unsalted butter
1	cup peeled and diced onions
1	cup diced celery
1/2	cup diced red bell pepper
1/2	cup peeled and minced garlic
1	pound crawfish tails

1/4	cup white wine
8	10-ounce whole trout, boned and skinned
	Salt and pepper to taste
12	ounces smoked slab bacon, thinly sliced into 8 pieces
2	tablespoons clarified butter

🖎 **To make the crawfish stuffing:** In a medium skillet or sauté pan melt 1/4 cup of butter over medium heat. Add the onion, celery, pepper, and garlic, and cook until softened. Stir in the crawfish tails and pour in the wine. Cook just until the wine begins to bubble, stir well, and add the remaining 1/2 cup of butter. When the butter is incorporated, remove the pan from the heat. Let cool.

🖎 **To make the trout:** Clean the fish, dry, and remove the heads, gills, and viscera. With shears, cut the fins close to the body and trim off a bit from the tails. Sprinkle a little salt and pepper inside each cavity.

🖎 Preheat the oven to 350°. Lay out 2 bacon slices on a work surface, overlapping slightly lengthwise. Place one-eighth of the stuffing in the trout cavity, close the cavity, and wrap the bacon around the trout. Repeat with the remaining fish. In a skillet large enough to contain the trout in a single layer or 2 skillets melt a tablespoon of clarified butter over high heat. Add the trout and sear just until the bacon has crisped slightly. Remove the skillet(s) to the oven and continue cooking about 8 minutes or until the fish is just beginning to exude some of its juices.

SHAD STUFFED WITH SHAD ROE

Elizabeth Terry
ELIZABETH'S ON 37TH
SAVANNAH, GEORGIA

SERVES 6

Shad is a local and favorite tradition in the Low Country, and Elizabeth loves to serve it with a simple accompaniment of perfectly boiled new potatoes and sautéed zucchini.

Stuffing

6	tablespoons (¾ stick) butter
½	cup peeled and minced onion
10	to 12 ounces shad roe, large central vein removed, cut into 1-inch cubes
2	hard-boiled eggs, finely grated
2	slices whole wheat bread, finely shredded
¼	cup minced chervil (or minced Italian parsley)
2	tablespoons minced fresh tarragon
½	teaspoon salt

Fish and Marinade

3	tablespoons extra-virgin olive oil
¼	cup white wine or vermouth
3	tablespoons garlic, peeled and minced
1	teaspoon black pepper
¼	cup minced chervil (or minced Italian parsley)
6	6-ounce boneless shad fillets, skin left on
2	tablespoons minced fresh tarragon
1	tablespoon butter, at room temperature
1	lemon, very thinly sliced, ends and seeds discarded

To prepare the stuffing: In a medium sauté pan melt the butter over medium heat and add the onion. Sauté about 2 minutes or until translucent. Add the roe and sauté, stirring constantly, until the roe begins to change color but still remains pink. Stir in the eggs, breadcrumbs, chervil, tarragon, and salt, and remove to a plate to cool.

To prepare the fish: Preheat the oven to 425°. In a small bowl combine the oil, wine, garlic, black pepper, chervil, and tarragon. Set aside.

Divide and stuff the roe stuffing mixture between the flaps of the shad fillets. Be careful not to cover the flesh with the stuffing as the fish will not cook evenly. Spread the butter on a nonreactive baking pan and place the stuffed fish fillets on the pan. Spoon the marinade over the fillets, and top each with a lemon slice. Tent the pan with aluminum foil, and tightly close on all four sides so that no steam escapes during the roasting. Roast for 20 minutes until cooked through.

SALMON SOUTH BY SOUTHWEST

Debra Paquette
BOUND'RY RESTAURANT
NASHVILLE, TENNESSEE

SERVES 6

White Bean Filling

2	cups white beans, rinsed and picked over
1	medium onion, peeled and diced
1	poblano, seeded and diced
2	tablespoons cumin seed, roasted
1	tablespoon salt
1	teaspoon black pepper
2	tablespoons olive oil
1/2	bunch cilantro (save half for garnish)

Tamales

7	to 8 corn husks, soaked in water
5	to 6 medium sweet potatoes
1/2	cup cornmeal or masa harina
1/2	cup pecans, roasted
10	garlic cloves, peeled and chopped
2	teaspoons salt
1	teaspoon black pepper
1	egg

Cilantro Oil

2	cloves garlic, peeled
1/4	cup cilantro leaves
	Pinch of kosher salt
3/4	cup olive oil

Fried Chili Pepper Pasta

1/4	pound chili pepper pasta
2	cups vegetable oil for deep-frying

Pepper Glaze

1	quart water
2	cups sugar

1	cinnamon stick
1/2	teaspoon whole cloves
1	teaspoon ground cardamom
1/2	teaspoon salt
1	teaspoon diced lavender (optional)
	Juice and zest of 1 orange
1	small chipotle pepper, seeded and minced
1	small jalapeño pepper, seeded and minced
1/2	pint fresh blackberries

Vanilla Vidalia Onions

1/2	cup canola oil
6	medium Vidalia onions, peeled and sliced 1/4-inch thick or less
1/2	vanilla bean
	Salt and pepper to taste

Salmon

1	cup rice or cake flour
1/2	cup cornmeal
6	6-ounce salmon fillets
	Salt and pepper to taste
2	eggs, lightly beaten
1/4	cup canola oil
1/2	teaspoon ground cardamom
1/2	teaspoon ground coriander
1/2	teaspoon ground ginger

Garnishes

1/4	cup fresh cilantro
1	red bell pepper, seeded and thinly sliced
3/4	cup cilantro infused oil

To prepare the white bean filling: In a large heavy pot soak the beans in cold water to cover by at least 3 inches for not less than 4 hours or overnight. Drain the beans in a colander, rinse, and return to the cooking pot with 2 quarts of water. Bring to a boil over high heat. Skim off any foam that rises to the surface. Reduce the heat and gently simmer the beans for 20 minutes. Add the onion, poblano, cumin, salt, and pepper, and continue to cook uncovered, stirring occasionally, 45 minutes to 1 hour or until tender and the water is absorbed. Add the olive oil and half of the cilantro. Drain the beans in a colander. Cover and refrigerate for up to 3 days.

To make the tamales: Place the corn husks in a large bowl with cold water to cover. Let soak about 2 hours or until soft. Preheat the oven to 400°.

Prick the sweet potatoes with a fork and roast in a 400° oven for 1 hour or until tender. Cool the potatoes slightly until they can be handled, and scoop out flesh. In a rice mill or food processor purée the sweet potato until smooth. Add the cornmeal, pecans, garlic, salt, pepper, and egg to the potatoes and mix well. Refrigerate until ready to use.

Tear 8 strips ⅙-inch wide from 1 or 2 of the husks for tying the tamales. Divide the sweet potatoes evenly among the 6 remaining husks, and spread in the center, leaving 1 inch at each end uncovered. Repeat this procedure for the white bean filling, mounding a heaping tablespoon on top of the sweet potato filling. Roll the corn husks so that the dough is completely enclosed. Twist and tie each end with the reserved strips. Place the tamales in a small roasting pan and bake in the preheated oven for 10 to 12 minutes. The tamales are done when the filling comes away easily from the husk. Allow the tamales to cool slightly before serving.

To make the cilantro oil: In a blender or food processor combine the garlic, cilantro, and salt and purée. With the machine running, add the olive oil in a thin stream. Strain through a fine mesh sieve and pour into a squeeze bottle.

To make the fried pasta: In a large saucepan or deep-fryer heat the oil to 350° or until a noodle dropped in the oil puffs and comes to the surface. Add the chili pepper pasta to the oil in small batches and fry until completely browned, about 15 seconds. Remove the noodles from the oil with a slotted spatula and drain on paper towels.

To make the pepper glaze: In a medium saucepan combine the water, sugar, cinnamon stick, cloves, cardamom, salt, lavender, orange juice, orange zest, and peppers, and bring to a simmer over medium heat. Simmer for 1 hour or until a syrupy consistency has been achieved, stirring from time to time. Strain the glaze through a fine mesh sieve over a bowl and discard the solids.

To make the Vidalia onions: In a large sauté pan or skillet, heat the canola oil over high heat. Add the onions and cook, stirring constantly to prevent burning, until the onions begin to brown. At this point reduce the heat to medium and cook until the onions are well browned and have taken on a shiny mahogany color. Split the vanilla bean in half lengthwise with the tip of a paring knife and scrape the seeds from half of the bean only into the onions. Season with salt and plenty of black pepper. Keep warm over very low heat or remove from the heat and rewarm when needed.

To prepare the salmon: Preheat the oven to 400°. Set aside ½ cup of the rice or cake flour. In a medium mixing bowl combine the remaining ½ cup of rice or cake flour, corn-meal, cardamom, coriander, and ginger. Season the salmon with salt and pepper. Dredge in the flour mixture, then in the eggs, and finally in the flour mixture. Shake off any excess. In a large sauté pan or skillet heat the canola oil over medium-high heat and cook the fillets on each side for 3 minutes or until lightly browned. Place in the preheated oven and cook for 6 minutes or until the fish flakes easily.

To serve: Place one tamale in the center of each dinner plate. Place one-sixth of the onions around the tamale and one salmon fillet on top of the tamale. Stir the berries into the pepper glaze and pour around the plate. Garnish with a handful of fried chili pepper pasta, a few sprigs of the cilantro leaves, and some red pepper slices. Drizzle with 2 table-spoons of cilantro oil. Repeat with the remaining plates.

MEATS & POULTRY

*P*erhaps *because he often hunts himself (or would like to), a Southerner takes his meat and game seriously. Visitors through this section will see much evidence of the infatuation of today's southern chefs with duck and game birds. It is no accident that Southerners are dark-meat eaters. Historically, game was not only available in the region, but was tasty, and as John Egerton tells us, "Even after pork, beef, mutton, and chicken had made farm-raised meats a commonplace feature of American cookery, wild animals and birds still retained visibility and importance at the table."*

Chicken continues to be a staple of the southern diet. Although references to southern food commonly conjure up images of fried chicken, today's innovative young southern chefs are turning this traditional staple into some exotic and delicious dishes. Gregory Gammage's recipe for Roasted Chicken with Collards, Red Onion, and Sweet Potato Chips and Frank Stitt's Pork Tenderloin au Poivre are two fine examples of how southern chefs are brightening up traditional recipes with indigenous ingredients and serious imagination.

Because city regulations normally forbid selling game in restaurants,* wild ducks and game meats are normally consumed in private homes and at outdoor dinners hosted by such associations as Ducks Unlimited and the Sure Short Rabbit Hunters Association.

* In 1988 my husband, Louis Osteen, was arrested at his Georgetown County, South Carolina restaurant—the Pawleys Island Inn—for selling venison that had been domestically raised and was purchased from a commercial supplier in the Midwest. Although his sentence was later probated and ultimately expunged, such prohibitions continue.

ROASTED CHICKEN WITH COLLARDS, RED ONION, AND SWEET POTATO CHIPS

Gregory Gammage
BONES
ATLANTA, GEORGIA

SERVES 4

This quick and easy dish is an elegant answer to last-minute dinner guests. They will agree that the flavor components are very complementary!

Garlic Olive Oil

3   garlic cloves, peeled
1   cup olive oil

Collards

2½   cups collard greens
3   cups Chicken Stock (see page 218)

Red Onions

2   tablespoons garlic oil (recipe follows)
2   cups red onions, peeled and cut into ¼-inch thick julienne

Sweet Potato Chips

¼   cup Garlic Olive Oil
    Salt and freshly ground black pepper to taste
2   sweet potatoes (about 1½ pounds), peeled

Molasses Sauce

3   tablespoons molasses
½   cup Chicken Stock (see page 218)
½   cup Veal Stock (see page 219)
½   teaspoon red pepper flakes
⅛   teaspoon salt
⅛   teaspoon white pepper

Chicken

2   whole free-range chicken breasts with wings attached
1   tablespoon Garlic Olive Oil
    Salt and pepper to taste

3   tablespoons butter

🖙 **To make the garlic olive oil:** In a small saucepan place the garlic oil over very low heat, and simmer until the garlic is tender. Remove the pan from the heat, cool, and pour through a fine mesh strainer into a glass jar or bottle. Cover.

🖙 **To cook the collards:** Remove and discard the coarse stems from the collards. Wash the leaves thoroughly and drain well. The easiest way to chop the collards is to stack the leaves and cut crosswise, and then cut lengthwise into ½-inch pieces. In a medium saucepan bring the chicken stock to a boil over high heat. Cook the greens about 6 minutes or just until tender. Drain thoroughly.

✍ To cook the red onions: In a large skillet heat the garlic oil over medium-low heat. Add the onions, salt, and pepper, and stir 1 minute. Cook about 15 minutes until the onions are tender, stirring occasionally. Add the collards to the pan, stir to combine, and keep warm over very low heat.

✍ To make the sweet potato chips: Preheat the oven to 450°. In a small bowl whisk together the oil and salt and pepper to taste. Arrange the potato slices, not touching, in rows on an oiled baking sheet, brush with the oil mixture, and roast in the upper third of the preheated oven for 18 to 22 minutes or until they are golden and crisp, turning once with a spatula. Transfer the potatoes to paper towels to drain, sprinkle them with additional salt and pepper to taste, and serve them warm.

✍ To make molasses sauce: In a small mixing bowl combine the molasses, chicken stock, veal stock, red pepper flakes, salt, and white pepper.

✍ To cook the chicken: Preheat the oven to 400°. Brush the chicken with 1 tablespoon garlic oil, salt, and pepper. In a large nonstick skillet heat another tablespoon of oil over medium-high heat. Add the chicken to the skillet and cook about 4 minutes until golden. Turn the chicken over and transfer to the preheated oven. Bake about 11 minutes until the chicken is cooked through. Remove the chicken from the skillet, drain off any excess fat, and slice on the diagonal. (There should be 4 slices per chicken breast half.)

✍ Meanwhile, heat the same skillet over medium-high heat. Add the sauce mixture to the hot skillet, bring to a boil, and cook until the sauce is reduced by half. Remove from the heat and add the butter, 1 tablespoon at a time, making sure the butter is completely incorporated before adding the next piece.

✍ To serve: Place one-fourth of the collard mixture in a mound in the center of each serving plate. Fan 3 sweet potato chips next to the collards, and arrange the chicken pieces in a fan over the collards. Drizzle the sauce over the chicken and around the base of the plate.

COQ AU VIN

Robert Holley
BRASSERIE LE COZE
ATLANTA, GEORGIA

SERVES 4

1   5-pound free-range chicken

Marinade

1   onion, peeled and quartered
1   carrot, peeled and cut into 1-inch pieces
1   celery rib, cut into 1-inch pieces
5   garlic cloves, peeled and crushed
1   24-ounce bottle red wine, preferably
       Cabernet Sauvignon or French
       Bordeaux
       Bouquet garni: 1 bay leaf, 1/4 teaspoon dry
       thyme, and 1 sprig fresh parsley
       wrapped in cheesecloth

4   strips bacon, blanched (see Note)
1/4   cup olive oil
1/2   cup Cognac
2   cups Veal Stock (see page 219)

Mushrooms and Onions

1/2   pound small pearl onions, peeled
4   tablespoons butter

       Pinch of sugar
1/2   pound fresh mushrooms, trimmed and
       quartered
       Salt and pepper

Vegetable Accompaniments

6   boiling potatoes, peeled, washed, and
       shaped into olives
2   tablespoons clarified butter
2   tablespoons peeled and minced garlic
1   leek, the tender part cleaned, washed, and
       cut into 1/2-inch dice
1   cup white onion, peeled and cut into
       1/2-inch dice
3/4   cup carrot, peeled and cut into 1/2-inch dice
1/2   cup tender celery stalks, trimmed, washed,
       and cut into 1/2-inch dice
1   cup Veal Stock (see page 219)
1   bay leaf

       Sprig of fresh thyme

🐚 **To marinate the chicken:** Thoroughly wash and dry the chicken. Remove the chicken legs and thighs, and separate the thighs from the legs at the ball joint. Cut off the wings. Remove the breast in one piece, leaving the bone intact. Cut the breast into 4 pieces.

🐚 In a deep, nonreactive dish combine the chicken, onion, carrot, celery, and garlic. Pour the wine over the chicken and vegetables, and add the bouquet garni. Cover and marinate in the refrigerator overnight. Remove the chicken and pat dry with paper towels. Strain the marinade and reserve the vegetables and strained liquid.

🐚 **To prepare the mushrooms and onions:** In a medium sauté pan or skillet place the pearl onions with enough water to barely cover over high heat. Add 2 tablespoons of the butter, the sugar, and a pinch of salt. Bring to a boil and continue boiling until all the water has evaporated, shaking the pan often to ensure even cooking. Reduce the heat to medium low and caramelize the onions in the dry pan. Shake and stir them until they become golden brown. Remove to a mixing bowl.

☞ In a separate large sauté pan melt the remaining 2 tablespoons of butter over medium-high heat. Add the mushrooms, season with salt and pepper, and sauté about 3 minutes until well browned. Combine the mushrooms with the onions, and set aside until needed.

☞ **To cook the chicken:** Preheat the oven to 300°. In a heavy-bottomed 12-inch frying pan or 2-inch deep casserole cook the bacon over medium-high heat about 2 minutes until browned and crisp. With a slotted spoon, remove the bacon to paper towels and set aside. Pour off all but 2 to 3 tablespoons of the bacon fat from the pan. Add ¼ cup of olive oil and heat until nearly smoking. Season the chicken with salt and pepper, and return to the pan. Cook the chicken over moderately high heat about 3 minutes or until lightly browned. Remove the chicken to a side dish and set aside.

☞ Remove all but 2 tablespoons of fat from the chicken cooking pan. Add the vegetables from the marinade, reduce the heat to medium, and cook about 5 minutes until softened. Add the Cognac and flame. Pour in the reserved liquid from the marinade, increase the heat to high, and boil until reduced by half.

☞ Return the chicken and bacon to the vegetables and reduced liquid. Add the veal stock and bring to a simmer. Cover and place in the preheated oven. After about 20 minutes, check the white meat for doneness and if done, remove from the casserole while the dark meat finishes cooking, another 10 to 15 minutes. Five minutes before the cooking time is up, add the mushrooms and onions to the casserole. Remove the casserole from the oven, remove the chicken, and set aside. Remove the mushrooms and onions from the casserole and set aside in a separate dish. Strain and degrease the sauce, discarding the onion, carrot, and celery. Pour the strained sauce into a medium saucepan and set aside until service.

☞ **To make the vegetable accompaniments:** Fill a large saucepan one-third full with salted water and bring to a simmer. Line a steamer with a double thickness of cheesecloth, place the potatoes on the cheesecloth, and fold the cheesecloth over the potatoes. Set the steamer over the water, making sure that the water level is just below the steamer and not touching the potatoes. Cover and let the potatoes cook about 25 to 30 minutes or until tender.

☞ In a large nonstick sauté pan melt the clarified butter over medium-low heat. Add the garlic, diced leek, onion, carrots, celery, and bay leaf, and cook slowly about 5 minutes or until tender. Gradually ladle in the rich veal stock about ⅓ cup at a time. Increase the heat to medium-high and allow the stock to reduce by half after each addition. Continue cooking until all the veal stock is used. Remove the pan from the heat and set aside.

☙ *To serve:* Portion the chicken pieces among the 4 serving plates. Return the strained sauce to a medium heat, add the diced vegetables, and rewarm. Using a slotted spoon, spoon the diced vegetables around the chicken. Add the mushroom-onion mixture and potatoes to the sauce and rewarm slightly. Strew the mushrooms, onions, and potatoes over the chicken, with some extra sauce. Garnish with a sprig of fresh thyme.

☙ *Note:* In order to remove its smoky flavor, the bacon is blanched before browning. To do this, drop the bacon into a small saucepan of cold water to cover by 2 to 3 inches. Bring to a boil and simmer 5 to 8 minutes. Remove from the saucepan and drain, rinse under cold water, and remove to paper towels to dry before proceeding.

ROASTED GAME HEN WITH GOAT CHEESE AND SPINACH

Steven Schaefer

THE RITZ CARLTON AMELIA ISLAND
AMELIA ISLAND, FLORIDA

SERVES 4

Confit is an old-fashioned alternative to roasting goose or duck legs. Here the frugal chef makes good use of the legs and thighs of the game hen to prepare a delicious confit that adds flavor and texture to the filling. Although the procedure is simple, there is a long baking time, so begin early.

Goat Cheese Filling

1	teaspoon olive oil
1	tablespoon peeled and minced shallots
1	garlic clove, peeled and minced
3	ounces spinach, washed, cleaned, and dried
4	ounces goat cheese
4	ounces Game Hen Confit

Game Hen Confit

	Legs and thighs from the game hens
1	garlic clove, peeled
2	sprigs fresh thyme
	Cracked pepper to taste
3	cups (or enough to cover hen parts by 1/2 inch) duck fat and/or olive oil

Stewed Vidalia Onions

3   tablespoons olive oil
6   cups thinly sliced Vidalia onions
1   tablespoon red wine vinegar
3   tablespoons sugar
½   teaspoon salt
1   teaspoon chopped fresh thyme
    Cracked black pepper to taste

Apple Cider Vinaigrette

½   cup apple cider
2   tablespoons (about 1 small lemon) freshly
      squeezed lemon juice
1   tablespoon peeled and finely diced Granny
      Smith apple
1   tablespoon peeled and finely diced Red
      Delicious apple
1   tablespoon peeled and minced red onion
6   tablespoons olive oil
    Salt and pepper to taste

Apple Ginger Pecan Butter

4   cups peeled and diced Granny Smith
      apples

½   cup apple cider
½   cup brown sugar
1   teaspoon minced fresh ginger
½   teaspoon ground cinnamon
¼   teaspoon grated nutmeg
¼   cup chopped pecans

Cherry Tomato Garnish

1   tablespoon olive oil
½   cup (about 2-ounce weight) stemmed and
      halved cherry tomatoes
3   tablespoons peeled and chopped red onion
1   teaspoon chopped fresh thyme
2   fresh basil leaves, thinly sliced
2   tablespoons chopped fresh parsley

4   whole game hens, breasts, legs, and thighs
      removed, breasts boned except for wing
      bone
½   cup Chicken Stock (see page 218)
¼   cup olive oil
¼   cup Apple Cider Vinaigrette
½   cup Cherry Tomato Garnish

🐦 **To make the goat cheese filling:** In a large sauté pan heat the olive oil over medium-high heat and sauté the shallots and garlic about 1 minute, just until softened, being careful not to burn the garlic. Add the spinach and cook about 1 minute, just until the spinach begins to wilt. Immediately remove the pan from the heat and transfer to a medium mixing bowl. When the spinach has cooled, fold in the goat cheese and game hen confit.

🐦 **To make the game hen confit:** Preheat the oven to 200°. Season the legs and thighs with the garlic, thyme, and cracked pepper and place in a roasting pan with enough fat and or fresh oil to cover by ½ inch. Cover the pan and continue cooking until the meat is tender when pressed. The skin should be crisp and evenly colored, but the fat should not turn more than a deep yellow. Remove the hen pieces from the fat and drain on paper towels. When cool enough to handle, remove the skin and shred the meat. If desired, strain the cooking oil and reserve for another use.

🐦 **To stew the Vidalia onions:** In a large sauté pan heat the olive oil over medium-high heat. Add the onions and stir 1 minute. Cover and cook about 15 minutes or until the onions are tender, stirring occasionally. Uncover and add the red wine vinegar, sugar, and salt. Increase the heat to high and boil about 5 minutes or until the liquids have evaporated and the onions are deep golden and caramelized. Season with chopped thyme and pepper. Remove the pan from the heat and keep at room temperature.

To make the apple cider vinaigrette: In a small mixing bowl combine the apple cider, lemon juice, apples, and onion. Add the oil in a thin stream, whisking constantly. Season to taste with salt and pepper.

To make the apple ginger pecan butter: In a medium saucepan combine the apples, cider, brown sugar, ginger, cinnamon, and nutmeg. Cook over medium-high heat, stirring occasionally, until most of the liquid has evaporated. Transfer the mixture to the work bowl of a food processor fitted with a metal blade and pulse two or three times. The mixture should be slightly lumpy rather than smooth and puréed. Fold in the chopped pecans.

To make the cherry tomato garnish: In a small sauté pan heat the olive oil over medium-high heat. Add the tomatoes and onion and cook until the onion is tender, about 5 minutes. Remove the pan from the heat and add the fresh herbs.

To cook the hens: Preheat the oven to 400°. Stuff the boned breasts by loosening them from their skin, but keeping attached to the wing as follows. Lay the game hen breasts skin side down on the work surface. Being careful to leave the skin whole, pull the breast meat from the skin and spoon a tablespoon of the stuffing on the skin. Bend the meat back down onto the stuffing, and fold the skin around to partially enclose it. Lightly season with salt and pepper. Place the breasts skin side up in a roasting pan. Add the chicken stock and brush with the olive oil. Roast in the oven about 10 minutes or until the juices just begin to run clear. Remove from the oven and reserve the cooking juices.

To serve: Place 2 tablespoons of the stewed onions on each of the four serving plates. Add 2 tablespoons of the apple butter on one side of the onions, and place a hen breast on top. Drizzle 1 tablespoon each of the roasting juices and apple cider vinaigrette over the game hens. Finish with 1 tablespoon of the seasoned cherry tomatoes.

GUINEA HEN "SOUVA ROFF" MODERN
WITH FOIE GRAS, TRUFFLES, AND MORELS

Paul Albrecht

PANO'S AND PAUL'S
ATLANTA, GEORGIA

SERVES 4

Guinea Hens

2   2-pound guinea hens
     Salt and freshly ground pepper
¼   cup Clarified Butter (see page 215)

Foie Gras

     Salt and freshly ground pepper
     2-ounce pieces foie gras
2   tablespoons butter

Sauce

¼   cup olive oil
2   shallots, peeled and finely chopped
16   medium morels

     Salt and freshly ground pepper
½   cup white wine
2   cups brown guinea stock or chicken stock
¼   cup Madeira
¼   cup brandy
2   large black truffles, diced into small cubes
2   tablespoons unsalted butter, cut into 1-inch
     cubes, at room temperature

"Souva Roff" Cover

16   12-inch sheets frozen phyllo dough, thawed
2   eggs mixed with 2 teaspoons water (egg
     wash)
2   tablespoons lightly salted butter, melted

🍃 **To prepare the guinea hens:** Remove the backbones and wings from the guinea hens and reserve to make a brown stock as described on page 219. Cut each hen into breast and thigh quarters, reserving any trimmings for the stock. Salt and pepper the breasts and thighs. In a large sauté pan or skillet set over high heat melt the butter and add the breast and thigh pieces skin side down. Sauté quickly, about 2 to 3 minutes per side or until the skin has browned. Divide the meat between two 2-inch deep round ovenproof dishes.

🍃 **To prepare the foie gras:** Salt and pepper the foie gras. Preheat a dry skillet over high heat. Melt the butter. Cook the foie gras for about 15 seconds on each side or until lightly browned. Immediately remove the foie gras to a cutting board, and slice into ½-inch thick pieces. Divide the sliced foie gras into 2 equal portions, and add to the dishes containing the guinea hens.

🍃 **To make the sauce:** Return the pan in which the foie gras was cooked to the heat and reduce the heat to medium-high. Add 2 tablespoons of olive oil and sauté the shallots about 2 to 3 minutes until softened. Add the fresh morels and cook the morels 2 to 3 minutes. Season to taste with salt and pepper. Add the white wine and bring to a boil. Cook, stirring another 1 to 2 minutes or until the alcohol has cooked off and the flavors are combined. Remove the morels to a plate.

🖎   Strain the liquid remaining in the pan through a fine mesh strainer into a medium saucepan. Return the morels to the saucepan containing the strained liquid. Pour the guinea hen stock, Madeira, and brandy into the pan containing the morels. Add the diced black truffles and bring the mixture to a boil over high heat. Cook to reduce by half, stirring occasionally. The sauce should achieve a rich dark glaze. Adjust the salt and pepper to taste and remove from the heat. Add the butter one piece at a time, stirring after each addition. Let the sauce cool to room temperature and pour over the hens.

🖎   *To cover and bake the "souva roff":* Preheat the oven to 350°. Place 1 sheet of phyllo dough on a large cutting board. Keep the remaining dough covered with a towel to keep it moist. Lightly brush the phyllo sheet with melted butter, and top with another sheet. Brush again with the melted butter. Repeat again with a third and fourth sheet. You now have 4 sheets of phyllo stacked. Cut the dough into a circle 1½ inches larger than the dish in which the hens will cook. Brush the rim of the pastry circle with the egg wash, and cover the baking dish with the pastry. Press the dough firmly onto the dish to seal tightly. Repeat this process one more time to make the pastry cover for the second baking dish. Cut the remaining sheets of puff pastry into 3-inch circles, and cut the circles into decorative half moon and crescent shapes. Brush the shapes with egg wash and affix to the pastry cover, brushing the tops and sealing with egg wash. Bake in the preheated oven 8 to 10 minutes or until the pastry is puffed and browned.

🖎   *To serve:* Open each "souva roff" at the table so guests can enjoy the wonderful brandy, truffle, and Madeira aromas.

BARBECUED DUCK WITH WILTED GREENS

Roger Kaplan
CITY GRILL
ATLANTA, GEORGIA

SERVES 4

The chef begins the preparation of the ducks by smoking them first, giving the dish an added flavor dimension that enhances the barbecue sauce and greens.

2	whole ducks
1	tablespoon salt
2	tablespoons black pepper
6	ounces hickory chips

Carolina Barbecue Sauce

2	tablespoons vegetable oil
1	onion, peeled and roughly chopped
1	tablespoon minced garlic
1	ancho chili, seeded and soaked in warm water for 15 minutes
5	tablespoons brown sugar
1½	cups champagne vinegar
3	tablespoons ketchup
2	tablespoons whole-grain mustard
2	tablespoons black pepper
½	teaspoon cayenne pepper
4	cups water
	Salt and black pepper to taste

Corn Sauce

3	ears fresh yellow corn
1	tablespoon canola oil
¼	Vidalia onion, peeled and roughly chopped
1	shallot, peeled and chopped
1	tablespoon seeded and diced yellow bell pepper
1	cup water
	Salt and pepper to taste
⅛	teaspoon Dijon mustard

Greens

2	cups fresh seasonal greens (combination of collards, spinach, and red Swiss chard)
	Salt and pepper to taste
1	tablespoon olive oil
1	tablespoon butter
4	fresh thyme sprigs

🖝 **To cold-smoke the ducks:** Prepare the duck for smoking. Pull all the loose fat from the cavity, and remove the wishbone from inside the neck cavity. Cut through the ball joints of the wings and chop off the wings at the elbows. Cut through the ball joints of the thighs to remove the leg and thigh in one piece. Cut the breast in half between the breastbone, and remove the breast halves with the attached wings from the backbone. (The wingtips and backbones may be reserved for making duck stock for another recipe.)

🖝 Season the duck pieces with salt and pepper and place the legs (with thighs still attached) on one rack. Place the breasts on a separate rack. Heat the smoker to 300°, and place the hickory wood chips (the chips should not be soaked) in the chamber. Place the racks with the duck pieces in the smoker and cook for 30 minutes. Remove the breasts and let the legs remain in the smoker for another 1 hour and 30 minutes or until the meat is very tender. When the duck pieces have sufficiently cooled, remove the duck breast meat from the bone, and scrape the skin back from the duck to remove the fat, leaving the skin attached to the breast meat. Pull the meat from the duck legs in shreds. Discard the skin from the legs.

To make the barbecue sauce: In a large saucepan combine the vegetable oil, onion, garlic, ancho chili, brown sugar, champagne vinegar, ketchup, mustard, black pepper, cayenne pepper, water, salt, and pepper and bring to a simmer over medium-high heat. Reduce the heat and cook the sauce for 1 hour or until the flavors are well combined. Transfer the sauce to the work bowl of a food processor and blend well. Adjust the salt and pepper to taste.

To make the corn sauce: Using a sharp knife, remove the corn kernels from the cob. Then using the back of the knife, scrape along the cob to remove any remaining pulp. Put the scraped corn through a juicer. (Note: If you do not have a juicer, proceed with the recipe adding the scraped corn kernels and corn pulp. The result will be nearly as successful.)

In a medium sauté pan heat the canola oil over medium-high heat and sauté the Vidalia onion, shallot, and yellow bell pepper until tender. Reduce the heat to medium low and add the corn juice and water, stirring constantly. Simmer until the sauce is thickened, about 8 to 9 minutes. If the sauce becomes too thick, you may thin it out by adding additional water. Season the sauce with salt, pepper, and mustard. Pour into the container of a blender or the work bowl of a food processor and purée the sauce. Strain through a fine mesh strainer into a small saucepan. Keep the sauce warm over very low heat. If reheated, the corn will become starchy again.

To cook the greens: Remove and discard the coarse stems from the greens. Wash the leaves thoroughly and drain well. The easiest way to chop the greens is to stack the leaves and cut crosswise, and then cut lengthwise into ½-inch pieces. Bring a large pot of lightly salted water to a boil over high heat. Add the greens and cook about 1 to 5 minutes or just until tender. The younger the greens the less cooking time required. Drain thoroughly.

To cook the duck breasts and finish the dish: Film a cast-iron skillet with the olive oil and place over medium heat. When the skillet is hot, add the duck breasts skin side down. Reduce the heat to low and cook for about 10 minutes, allowing the skin to crisp. The slow cooking process will render any excess fat remaining in the duck breast. Increase the heat to high and turn the duck breasts, searing the skin for about 1 minute. Slice the breast on the bias into ¼-inch thick slices.

In a saucepan warm the smoked duck leg meat with the Carolina BBQ over medium heat. In a large skillet melt the butter over medium-high heat. Add the greens and toss to coat. Season with salt and pepper and place in the center of the serving plates. Place the duck leg meat on top of the greens, and top with more greens. Fan the duck breast slices over the greens and finish with a sprig of fresh thyme. Ladle the warm corn sauce around the duck.

BARBECUED BREAST OF DUCK
WITH CRUSHED PEPPER, PLUMS, AND PLUM WINE

Jonathan Eismann

PACIFIC TIME
MIAMI BEACH, FLORIDA

SERVES 8

Marinade

½   cup Galliano liqueur
¼   cup ground cinnamon
½   cup coarsely ground pink pepper
¼   cup ground black pepper

Duck Breasts

8   boneless Long Island duck breasts, 7 to 8
       ounces each
¼   cup peanut or other vegetable oil

Plum Sauce

8   large, ripe, dark-skinned plums, halved and
       pitted
3   cups plum wine (chef recommends Takara
       brand)
½   cup fresh or frozen huckleberries, elder-
       berries, or black currants (optional)
1¼ cups sugar

¾   cup water
2½ cups rice vinegar, unseasoned

Pancakes

½   cup all-purpose flour
¼   cup milk
¼   cup water
1   tablespoon dry Sake
1   large egg
1   egg yolk
1½ tablespoons peanut oil
       Pinch of salt
1   teaspoon peeled and minced fresh ginger
1   tablespoon minced green scallion
½   teaspoon red pepper (the chef suggests the
       Japanese red pepper, Sashimi tagarshi)
2   to 4 tablespoons butter

8   scallion bulbs for garnish

❧ **To make the marinade:** Pour half of the Galliano liqueur evenly over the bottom of a cookie pan or sheet pan with sides. Combine the cinnamon and peppers, divide in half, and sprinkle one-half of the spices evenly over the liqueur. Arrange the duck breasts on the pan skin side up. Brush the remaining liqueur over the skins of the duck breasts, sprinkle with the remaining spice mixture, and refrigerate for 24 hours.

❧ **To make the sauce:** In a medium saucepan combine the plums, plum wine, and optional berries, and bring to a boil over medium-high heat. Stir to prevent scorching, reduce the heat, and simmer for 10 minutes. Be careful not to overcook as this will cause the fruit to lose its color. After 10 minutes cover and remove the pot from the heat. Let the fruit remain in the pan for 30 minutes. Strain the sauce through a fine mesh strainer or chinoise, making sure to push through all of the fruit and liquid. Discard the skins and pits. Return the sauce to the saucepan and reserve at room temperature until needed.

In a clean, small, heavy saucepan combine the sugar and water and bring to a boil over high heat. Boil until a light golden brown caramel forms. Be careful not to overcook. If it is too dark, the sauce will be bitter and too thick. Remove the pan from the heat and reserve.

In a medium saucepot reduce the rice vinegar over medium-high heat to one-third its original volume, or slightly less than a cup. Reheat the plum sauce to a full boil over medium-high heat, and add the rice vinegar. Slowly drizzle in the hot caramel and reduce to a simmer, stirring constantly and vigorously for 3 to 5 minutes until the sauce is smooth. Strain the sauce through a fine mesh strainer or chinoise and reserve.

To make the crêpe batter: In a blender or food processor blend the flour, milk, water, Sake, egg and egg yolk, peanut oil, and salt for 5 seconds. Turn off the motor and scrape down the sides of the container with a rubber spatula. Blend the batter for 20 seconds more to make a perfectly smooth blend. Transfer the batter to a bowl. Stir in the ginger, scallion, and red pepper. Cover, and let the batter stand for 1 hour. The batter may be made 1 day in advance and kept covered and chilled.

To cook the crêpes: Heat a 6- to 7-inch crêpe pan or nonstick skillet over moderate heat until hot. Brush the pan lightly with butter and heat it until it is hot but not smoking. Pour ¼ cup of pancake batter into the center of the hot pan and tilt it in all directions. The batter should cover the pan with a light coating; pour out any excess. Cook about 30 seconds until the bottom of the pancake is lightly brown. To turn the pancake, shake the pan by its handle to dislodge, then turn it over with your fingers or a spatula. Cook another 15 to 20 seconds. If using immediately, heat the oven to 200°, transfer the crêpes to a pan, and place in the oven to keep warm. If using later, transfer the crêpes to a rack and when thoroughly cool, stack them, place in a plastic bag, and refrigerate for up to 2 days and rewarm when needed in a 300° oven.

To cook the duck breasts: Preheat the oven to 400°. Heat a 10-inch skillet over high heat until hot but not smoking. Add 1 tablespoon of peanut oil and in batches (up to 3 at a time) cook the duck breasts skin side down. Sear the duck breasts about 2 minutes or until nicely browned. Turn and sear the other side, another 2 minutes. Add more oil to the pan as needed. As the breasts are seared, remove to a large heavy-bottomed sheet pan or cookie pan.

Place the duck breasts in the preheated oven for 12 to 16 minutes. This should result in a medium-rare duck breast. Adjust the timing to achieve the preferred doneness. Remove the breasts from the oven and let rest 5 minutes before slicing.

To serve: Make scallion brushes by cutting off the bulb ends and tops and making long lengthwise slits in the scallions two-thirds of the way down. Slice the duck breasts into thin slices at an angle. Ladle 2 tablespoons of the plum sauce on each plate. Arrange the duck slices in the sauce. Fold the pancakes into triangles, and slide a scallion brush inside the pancake. Place the pancake on the plate and serve.

PRESSED DUCK

Jamie Shannon
COMMANDER'S PALACE
NEW ORLEANS, LOUISIANA

SERVES 4

4	small wild ducks	1½	tablespoons minced garlic
	Salt and pepper to taste	6	tablespoons (about) clarified butter for
½	cup chopped carrots, cut into ½-inch cubes		sautéing (see page 215
½	cup chopped celery stalks, cut into ½-inch	3	tablespoons chopped shallots
	cubes	3	tablespoons brandy
6	tablespoons chopped onions, cut into ½-	1½	cups red wine
	inch cubes	2½	cups water
2	tablespoons chopped leeks, cut into ½-inch		
	cubes		

🖝 Pull all the loose fat out of the duck's cavity, wipe the duck dry, and rub all over the outside and inside of the cavity with salt and pepper. In a small mixing bowl combine the diced carrots, celery, onions, and leeks, and stuff the cavities of the ducks with half of this mixture. Add a teaspoon of the minced garlic to each of the duck cavities.

🖝 In a cast-iron skillet heat 1 tablespoon of the clarified butter over high heat until very hot but not smoking. One at a time, sear the whole ducks on all sides, turning to evenly brown. Add more clarified butter to the pan as needed. Remove the ducks to a clean cutting board. Cut through the ball joints of the thighs to remove the leg and thigh in one piece. Cut the breasts in half between the breastbone, and remove the breast halves from the backbone. Reserve the duck pieces and carcasses at room temperature.

🖝 Meanwhile, in the pan used to cook the ducks heat 1 tablespoon of clarified butter and sauté the rest of the diced vegetables and minced garlic over medium-high heat. Cook 1 to 2 minutes until softened. Increase the heat to high, add the red wine and enough water to cover, and stir with a wooden spoon. Bring the liquid to a boil and add the duck leg quarters only. (The duck breast meat will cook later.) Reduce the heat so that the liquid is just at a simmer, cover the pan, and cook until the legs and thighs are tender and the meat is nearly falling off the bone. This will take about 2 hours. If needed, add more water during the cooking time. When the leg quarters are cooked, remove from the liquid to a clean platter. Strain the braising liquid through a fine mesh strainer into a cool saucepan and let cool to room temperature.

🐦 While the legs are cooking, remove the mirepoix from the cavities of the duck carcasses, and cut the carcasses in half. Chop up one carcass and press it slowly and evenly in the duck press. Chop the next carcass, place it in the duck press on top of the first carcass, and press. Repeat with the remaining carcasses until about ½ cup of duck blood has been extracted.

🐦 Add a small amount of the room temperature braising liquid from the duck legs to the extracted duck blood. Pour this mixture into the remaining braising liquid, and rewarm very slowly over very low heat, stirring constantly. Make sure the liquid does not come to a simmer and does not exceed 140°, or the blood will congeal.

🐦 To finish cooking the duck breasts, heat 1 tablespoon of the clarified butter in a skillet until very hot but not smoking. Sauté the duck breasts a minute or two on each side, or only until the meat is lightly springy when pressed. Remove the duck breasts to a cutting board, and thinly slice. Arrange the duck breast meat on the serving plates and spoon the sauce over the meat. You may also place a duck leg quarter on each plate, or do as the chef prefers—serve the duck legs as a second course with some wild rice.

GRILLED AND BRAISED RABBIT WITH MOLASSES, BOURBON, SLAB BACON, AND STONE-GROUND GRITS

Frank Stitt

HIGHLANDS BAR & GRILL
BIRMINGHAM, ALABAMA

SERVES 4

The chef tells us that "fresh rabbit is a wonderful change from chicken, but free-range chicken could be prepared in a similar fashion. [At Highland's] we bone the rabbit so that we have a boneless loin, a hindquarter, fore quarter, flank, and the resulting bones from the loin. The loin and liver are well suited for grilling at the last moment, for they take only a very few minutes to cook. A simple but flavorful marinade is a welcome addition. Juniper, bourbon, garlic, rosemary, and olive oil as well as molasses are flavors that come to mind."

Marinade

2   teaspoons minced fresh rosemary leaves
2   tablespoons coarsely chopped fresh parsley
       leaves
12   juniper berries
2   garlic cloves, minced
       Salt and pepper to taste
1/2 cup bourbon
1   tablespoon olive oil

Stone-ground Grits

5   cups water
       Salt to taste
1   cup stone-ground yellow grits
3   tablespoons butter
       Pepper to taste
1/4 cup freshly grated Parmigiano-Reggiano
       cheese

1/2 cup heavy cream

Rabbit

2   rabbits, cut into serving pieces
       Salt and pepper to taste
2   tablespoons molasses
2   thick slices bacon, hickory or apple
       smoked, cut into 1/2-inch thick pieces
1   onion, peeled and chopped
1   carrot, chopped
1   celery stalk, chopped
       Sprig of fresh thyme
2   bay leaves
1/2 cup bourbon
2   cups red wine
3   to 4 cups Chicken Stock (see page 218)

To make the marinade: In a mortar combine the rosemary, parsley, juniper berries, garlic, salt, and pepper. Work with a pestle until the seasonings are blended. Whisk in the bourbon and oil, and transfer the mixture to a large shallow bowl. Add the rabbit pieces to the marinade and refrigerate overnight or for as long as 2 days.

To cook the grits: Bring the water to a boil in a heavy-bottomed saucepan. Add the salt, and slowly pour in the grits, stirring constantly. Reduce the heat to low and continue to stir so the grits do not settle to the bottom and burn. In about 5 minutes, the grits will plump up and become a thick mass. Continue to cook the grits for a total of about 12 minutes, stirring frequently. The grits should have absorbed all of the water and become soft. Stir in the butter, pepper, Parmesan, and cream, and whip until combined. The grits should now have a thick consistency and be creamy like oatmeal. Season to taste with additional salt and pepper, if needed.

To cook the rabbit: Preheat the oven to 325°, and prepare a grill. Season the rabbit hind and fore quarters with salt and pepper and drizzle with the molasses. In a heavy skillet fry the bacon over moderately high heat until the pieces are lightly browned. Remove the bacon pieces from the pan and reserve. Add the rabbit skin side down and brown in batches, transferring each piece to a platter. Reduce the heat and add the vegetables to the skillet. Sauté the vegetables, stirring occasionally, until softened but not browned.

Increase the heat to high and add the thyme, bay leaves, and bourbon. Bring to a boil and reduce by half. Add the wine and reduce by half again. Pour in the stock and bring to a simmer. Add the rabbit, cover, and cook in the preheated oven 45 minutes to 1 hour or until tender, depending on the age of the rabbit. Remove the rabbit from the cooking liquids to a serving plate, and strain the juices through a fine mesh sieve into a medium saucepan. Set the pan with the juices over high heat, bring to a boil, and reduce by half.

❧ Just before the cooking time is up, season the loin and liver pieces and transfer to the prepared grill. Grill the loin about 2 to 3 minutes just until browned but the meat remains pink. Add the liver and cook 1 to 2 minutes.

❧ *To serve:* Arrange the grits in the center of a large serving plate. Top with the rabbit legs and shoulder. Slice the loin and liver in half, and place in the center. Scatter the bacon pieces over the meat and nap with sauce. Finish with the fresh thyme.

BEEF TENDERLOIN STUFFED WITH HERB CREAM CHEESE, WITH SAUCE BORDELAISE

Susan Spicer

BAYONA
NEW ORLEANS, LOUISIANA

SERVES 4

Herb Cream Cheese Stuffing

4	ounces cream cheese, at room temperature
1/2	teaspoon peeled and minced garlic
2	teaspoons assorted fresh herbs, chopped (the chef uses thyme, tarragon, chives, and parsley)
	Pinch of salt and freshly ground black pepper
4	6- to 8-ounce centercut beef tenderloin steaks

Bordelaise Sauce

1	cup Cabernet Sauvignon or Bordeaux wine
1	teaspoon fresh thyme leaves, or 1/2 teaspoon dried thyme
2	tablespoons peeled and finely chopped shallots
1	cup Veal Stock (see page 219)
2	tablespoons butter, cut into 1-inch pieces, at room temperature
1	tablespoon olive or canola oil

To stuff the steaks: In a medium mixing bowl combine the cream cheese, garlic, herbs, salt, and pepper. Cover and chill until firm.

Cut an "x" in the top of each fillet almost but not quite all the way through. Open the "x" and stuff with 2 tablespoons of the cheese mixture, pushing the cheese in well until level with the top of the steaks. Cover and chill 15 minutes.

To make the Bordelaise sauce: Combine the wine, thyme, and shallots in a medium saucepan and bring to a boil over medium-high heat. Reduce the heat and simmer until reduced to 1/4 cup. Add the veal stock and continue to simmer until reduced by half. Remove the pan from the heat and reserve.

To cook the steaks: Preheat the oven to 400°, and remove the steaks from the refrigerator. Place a large sauté pan over medium-high heat, add the olive oil, and heat until almost smoking. Add the steaks cut side down to the hot pan. Sear 1 to 2 minutes on each side, turning carefully with a large metal spatula. Make sure to scrape up the cheese crust with the steak when turning. Remove the steaks from the sauté pan to a sheet pan and place in the preheated oven to finish. Cook to the desired temperature, about 6 to 8 minutes for medium-rare steaks.

While the steaks are finishing in the oven, finish the sauce. Return the sauce to a low heat, and gradually add the butter, piece by piece, until the sauce is glossy. Surround the steaks with the sauce and serve immediately.

PORK TENDERLOIN "AU POIVRE"

Frank Stitt

HIGHLANDS BAR & GRILL
BIRMINGHAM, ALABAMA

SERVES 8

2	1-pound pork tenderloins, cut into 4-ounce fillets

Marinade

2   garlic cloves, peeled and crushed
4   sprigs fresh thyme
1/2   sprig fresh rosemary
1   tablespoon molasses
1   tablespoon bourbon
1   tablespoon olive oil

Sweet Potatoes

4   sweet potatoes (about 2½ pounds)
2   thick strips apple-smoked bacon, cut into ¼-inch pieces
2   sweet onions, Vidalia if available, chopped
2   tablespoons olive oil
3   to 5 tablespoons butter, at room temperature
2   to 4 tablespoons hot Chicken Stock (see page 218)
    Salt and pepper to taste

Fried Onions and Sweet Potatoes

6   cups peanut or canola oil for frying
2   sweet onions, peeled and cut into ½-inch thick slices
1½   cups buttermilk
1   cup breadcrumbs
    Salt and pepper to taste
    Cayenne pepper to taste
1   sweet potato, peeled and shaved into thin strips with a vegetable peeler

Pork Tenderloin

2   tablespoons olive oil
3   tablespoons coarsely cracked black peppercorns
1   teaspoon juniper berries, toasted and ground
¼   cup peeled and minced shallots
6   tablespoons bourbon
1   cup Beef, Veal, or Chicken Stock (see pages 218 and 219)
2   tablespoons butter, at room temperature, cut into ½-inch pieces

    Fresh watercress

🍃 **To marinate the pork tenderloin:** Rub the garlic and herbs into the tenderloin pieces. In a small bowl combine the molasses, bourbon, and olive oil and brush the fillets with this mixture. Cover the fillets and allow to marinate overnight in the refrigerator or 2 hours at room temperature.

🍃 **To cook the sweet potatoes:** Preheat the oven to 400°. Wash and dry the potatoes, prick in several places with the tines of a fork, and place on a cookie pan lined with aluminum foil. Roast in center of the preheated oven for 1 hour or until tender.

❧ Meanwhile, cook the bacon and onions. In a medium heavy-bottomed skillet sauté the bacon over medium heat until firm but not crisp. Remove the bacon from the pan, reserving the rendered bacon fat, and drain on paper towels. Add the olive oil to the pan, heat, and cook the onions, until they are well caramelized and have turned a nutty brown. Return the bacon to the pan with the onions.

❧ When the potatoes are done, cut in half, scoop the flesh into a ricer or food mill, and purée into a heavy saucepan. Set the saucepan over low heat and one tablespoon at a time beat in 3 tablespoons of the butter and 2 tablespoons of the stock. Add the reserved bacon and onion, taste, and add salt and pepper as needed. To keep the potatoes warm, set in another pan of hot but not simmering water and cover the potatoes loosely. At serving time, bring the water to the simmer, beating the potatoes with a spoon. If the potatoes have thickened, add more soft butter or hot stock to lighten.

❧ *To fry the onions and sweet potatoes:* In a medium saucepan heat the oil over high heat to 350°. Dip the onions into the buttermilk and then into the breadcrumbs. Place on a rack until ready to fry. In small batches, deep-fry the onions about 3 minutes, turning, until crisp and golden brown. With a long-handled strainer or slotted spoon, remove to paper towels to drain. Season with salt, pepper, and cayenne to taste. Reheat the oil to 350°. Drop the sweet potato strips into the hot oil and fry until golden. Remove to paper towels to drain and reserve until service.

❧ *To cook the pork tenderloin:* Heat a heavy cast-iron skillet over medium-high heat. Add the olive oil and heat until nearly smoking. Combine the black pepper and juniper berries, and rub this mixture into the fillets, pressing with the heel of your hand to adhere. Season with salt and sear about 4 minutes on each side until medium rare. Remove the fillets to a cake rack to cool. Pour out all the remaining fat in the skillet, return to low heat, and add the shallots. Stir for 1 minute or until softened. Add the bourbon to the same pan, increase the heat to high, and cook 2 to 3 minutes, stirring, or until the liquid is reduced to a glaze. Add the stock and cook over high heat until the liquid thickens and is reduced by two-thirds. Off heat, gradually swirl in the butter one piece at a time until the sauce is smooth and glossy. Season to taste with salt and pepper.

❧ *To serve:* Place ½ cup of the mashed sweet potatoes in the center of each plate and top with one of the tenderloin fillets. Spoon 2 tablespoons of sauce over the pork, and place two onion rings on top. Add a few sprigs of watercress and scatter a few of the fried sweet potato chips over all.

GREENHOUSE GRILL RACK OF LAMB

Danny Mellman

GREENHOUSE GRILL
SANIBEL, FLORIDA

SERVES 4

Lamb Stock

4	pounds lamb bones and trimmings
3	quarts cold water
1	onion, chopped
1	carrot, peeled and chopped
1	celery stalk, chopped
5	tablespoons tomato paste
1/4	cup Burgundy wine
1/2	garlic clove, minced
1/2	bay leaf
1/4	teaspoon dried thyme
1/2	teaspoon whole black peppercorns
3	whole cloves
2	fresh parsley stems
2	8-bone lamb racks, approximately 2 pounds each
	Salt and pepper to taste

Lamb Coating

	Salt and freshly ground black pepper
2	garlic cloves, minced
2	sprigs fresh rosemary, minced
1	sprig fresh thyme, minced
1/2	pound goat cheese
3	tablespoons strong Dijon mustard

Rosemary Demi-glace

2	cups lamb stock
1	large sprig rosemary
1	tablespoon butter, at room temperature
	Salt and pepper to taste

Garlic

5	bulbs colossal Gilroy garlic
1/4	cup olive oil
1/4	cup Chicken Stock (see page 218)

French Fries

4	cups vegetable oil for frying
2	large unpeeled Idaho potatoes, washed and julienned

Smashed Potatoes

3	large Idaho potatoes
1	bulb roasted garlic
2	tablespoons sour cream
2	tablespoons butter
2	tablespoons heavy cream
	Salt and white pepper to taste

🖎 **To make the lamb stock:** Preheat the oven to 375°. Place the lamb bones and trimmings in a large shallow roasting pan and bake in the preheated oven, turning them occasionally, for 30 minutes or until evenly browned. Transfer the bones and trimmings to a large stockpot, reserving the roasting pan. Add the water to the stockpot and bring to a boil over high heat. Reduce the heat to a simmer and skim the scum that rises to the surface for the first 10 to 15 minutes. Simmer for 3 hours uncovered.

➧ While the bones are simmering, place the roasting pan over medium-high heat and add the onion, carrot, celery, and tomato paste. Cook the vegetables, stirring occasionally, about 8 to 10 minutes until they are golden and caramelized. When the vegetables are browned, add the wine to the pan and cook, stirring to scrape up the browned bits from the bottom of the pan. Set aside. When the bones have simmered for 3 hours, add the browned vegetables and the remaining stock ingredients to the stockpot. Pour the water into the stockpot and continue to simmer for an additional 3 hours. Remove the stock from the heat and strain through a fine mesh sieve. Chill well, and then discard the layer of fat that congealed on the top.

➧ **To prepare the lamb:** Salt and pepper the lamb racks. Place a large dry nonstick sauté pan or skillet over high heat for 3 to 5 minutes, until the pan is smoking. Place the lamb racks in the pan and sear for 1 minute on each side. Remove to a plate and chill the racks in the refrigerator for 2 hours.

➧ While the lamb is chilling, in an electric mixer blend the garlic, rosemary, thyme, and goat cheese until smooth. Remove the racks from the refrigerator and trim off all fat. French the bones by cutting and scraping off the meat about $1\frac{1}{2}$ inches from the ends of the ribs. (This allows the diners to hold the end of each chop more neatly.) Brush the lamb with the mustard, then evenly coat with the cheese mixture. Return the lamb to the refrigerator and chill at least 2 hours.

➧ Preheat the oven to 500°. Remove the racks from the refrigerator and cut each rack into 2 even pieces. Place the racks in a foil-lined roasting pan in the preheated oven and roast approximately 12 minutes or until medium rare. Remove the roasting pan from the oven and let the racks rest 8 to 10 minutes before cutting and serving.

➧ **To make the rosemary demi-glace:** In a medium saucepan bring the stock to a boil over medium-high heat. Add 1 sprig of rosemary and simmer about 30 to 45 minutes until reduced by half. Whisk in the butter, add salt and pepper to taste, and remove from the heat.

➧ **To roast the garlic:** Preheat the oven to 400°. Cut $\frac{1}{2}$ inch off the top of the garlic bulbs. Drizzle the garlic with the olive oil and place the bulbs in a small roasting pan. Add the chicken stock to the pan and loosely cover with foil. Roast the garlic in the preheated oven for 35 minutes or until softened and lightly colored.

➧ **To prepare the French fries:** Heat the oil to 375° or until a bread cube turns brown in 10 seconds. Add the potatoes and fry until brown and crisp. Remove them from the pan with a slotted spoon and drain on paper towels.

➧ **To prepare the smashed potatoes:** Peel and quarter the potatoes, and place them in a large pot. Add lightly salted water to cover by 1 inch. Bring the water to a boil over high heat. Reduce the heat to a simmer and cook the potatoes uncovered for 12 to 15 minutes or until barely fork tender.

  🌿 Drain the potatoes in a colander and return them to the saucepan. Remove the paper from the roasted garlic bulb, and add the garlic to the potatoes. Place the pan over very low heat and coarsely mash the potatoes and garlic with a potato masher or 2 large meat forks or force them through a ricer into a bowl. Do not use a whisk or an electric mixer or the potatoes will become gummy. Slowly add the sour cream, butter, and heavy cream. Stir in the salt and pepper to taste. Serve immediately.

  🌿 *To assemble:* Place a scoop of mashed potatoes in the center of each plate. Ladle 2 tablespoons demi-glace around the potatoes. Remove the garlic bulbs from their paper, and place one bulb on each plate at 3 o'clock. Stand a small portion of the fries in the center of the smashed potatoes. Slice the lamb between the bones and, using four chops per serving, arrange in a half circle around the perimeter of the plate.

  🌿 *Note:* The lamb stock may be made up to 3 days in advance and refrigerated or frozen for up to 3 months.

DESSERTS

Who doesn't like desserts? Certainly not a Southerner. The discovery that dessert can please all the senses remains the final achievement of all these great chefs. To complete a grand meal without dessert would certainly end it on a wrong, if not disappointing, note. Despite any health concerns, Southerners remain passionate about their sweets. So it is most appropriate that the dessert section is the largest in the book.

Contained in this chapter are all the great traditional recipes of the South—flaky berry cobblers, unctuous custards, melt-in-your-mouth beignets, and tangy key lime pie. There are also decadent, complex tortes, tarts, and French-inspired desserts like crème brûlée. As in all the region's cooking, desserts were often dependent on the season. So if the recipes for fresh fruit cobblers suggest midsummer's blackberries, adventurous cooks should feel free to substitute apples in the fall or pears in the winter.

Every one of these desserts merits a place on the southern table, and every one will put you in mind of a long-held childhood memory and clouds of beautiful smells from a baking oven somewhere in the South.

BRIOCHE PAIN PERDU WITH ORANGE-BALSAMIC SYRUP

Allen Susser

CHEF ALLEN'S
MIAMI BEACH, FLORIDA

SERVES 8

Pain perdu is "lost," or stale, bread that has been saved by using it to make what Americans know as French toast. In this sublime dessert, the custard mixture is enlivened with fresh ginger, the syrup is a reduction of balsamic vinegar and orange juice, and the dish is garnished with mango and chocolate sorbet.

Orange-Balsamic Syrup

1   28-ounce bottle balsamic vinegar
4   cups fresh orange juice

Pain Perdu

8   ¾-inch slices brioche (preferably orange
      brioche loaf; challah can be substituted)
2   large eggs
1   cup milk

1   teaspoon vanilla extract
½   teaspoon ground cinnamon
½   teaspoon minced fresh ginger
      Pinch of salt
6   tablespoons unsalted butter

Garnish

      Candied Orange Zest (recipe follows)
      Mango and chocolate sorbets (optional)

To make the syrup: In a medium saucepan combine the vinegar and juice and cook over medium heat about 30 to 40 minutes until reduced to 1½ cups. This can be made up to 2 weeks in advance and stored in an airtight jar in the refrigerator.

To make the pain perdu: Trim the crusts from the brioche. Cut each slice in half on the diagonal, and set the slices aside for 10 to 15 minutes. In a large shallow bowl whisk together the eggs, milk, vanilla, cinnamon, fresh ginger, and salt. Place the brioche slices in the milk mixture, turn to coat both sides, and allow them to absorb the liquid for 2 to 3 minutes. In a large skillet melt 2 tablespoons of the butter over medium heat. When it foams, add as many bread slices as will fit comfortably in the pan. Brown until golden, turning once, a total of about 2 to 3 minutes per side. Remove with a slotted metal spatula and drain on a paper towel. Repeat with the remaining butter and bread. Serve warm.

To make the Candied Orange Zest: Using a vegetable peeler, remove the zest from 8 scrubbed navel oranges; you should have about 1 cup. Trim the edges of each piece of zest and cut each piece into fine julienne. In a medium sauté pan or skillet over medium to high heat, combine ⅓ cup of sugar and the zest and toss the mixture, shaking the pan constantly, about 5 to 7 minutes or until the sugar caramelizes onto the zest. Transfer to a tray to dry for about 3 to 4 hours. Store in an airtight jar. Makes 1 cup.

To serve: Place 2 pieces of pain perdu on each serving plate, overlapping them slightly. Sprinkle a little candied orange zest over each plate and add a small scoop of each sorbet. Drizzle the syrup over and around the bread toast.

CUBAN FRENCH TOAST

Guillermo Veloso
YUCA RESTAURANT
MIAMI BEACH, FLORIDA

SERVES 6

This unusual version of French toast has its derivatives in Spain, and is really a scrumptious dessert. The "turron" referred to in the recipe is the Spanish word for the candy more familiarly known as nougat.

Spiced Honey

¾   cup honey
    Zest of 1 lemon
    Zest of 1 orange
    Zest of 1 lime
5   whole cloves
1   cinnamon stick
3   star anise
1   chipotle pepper

Cheese Filling

8   ounces mascarpone cheese
8   ounces cream cheese
3   tablespoons Frangelico
½   teaspoon black cherry extract (optional)
1½   teaspoons sugar

Turron Ice Cream

1   cup skim milk
2   cups heavy cream
½   vanilla bean
3½   ounces nougat
6   egg yolks
2   tablespoons sugar

French Toast

1   loaf brioche (or challah bread)
3   eggs
¼   cup heavy cream
2   tablespoons orange liqueur (or Frangelico or Amaretto)
½   teaspoon ground cinnamon
½   teaspoon grated nutmeg
½   teaspoon vanilla extract
2   tablespoons butter

To make the spiced honey: In a small saucepan combine the honey, lemon, orange, lime, cloves, cinnamon stick, star anise, and chipotle pepper and cook over low heat, stirring occasionally, for 10 minutes. Remove the pan from the heat, strain, and let cool. The honey is best prepared a day in advance, allowing the flavors to develop. When ready to serve, reheat over very low heat.

To make the cheese filling: In the bowl of an electric mixer fitted with a wire whip or with a stainless steel bowl and wooden spoon, combine the mascarpone cheese, cream cheese, Frangelico, black cherry extract, and sugar. Beat until smooth and fluffy.

To make the ice cream: In a large saucepan combine the milk, heavy cream, vanilla bean, and turron and bring just to a boil over medium-high heat. Remove the pan from the heat, cover, and let rest 15 to 20 minutes. In the bowl of an electric mixer fitted with a balloon whisk, whisk the egg yolks with the sugar until it forms a ribbon. In a steady stream, gradually whisk the cream mixture into the egg mixture (adding no more than ⅓ of the hot cream at a time). Return this mixture to the saucepan and cook over medium-low heat, stirring constantly with a wooden spoon, for about 5 minutes or until the custard thickens enough to coat the back of a spoon (180° on a candy thermometer). Do not let the custard boil. Strain the custard through a fine mesh strainer into a metal bowl. Cover and refrigerate, stirring occasionally, until cold. Pour into the canister of an ice cream maker and freeze according to the manufacturer's directions.

To make the French toast: Make a lengthwise horizontal opening in the brioche loaf, using the handle end of a wooden spoon to help hollow out the loaf's center. Spoon the cheese filling into a pastry bag fitted with a metal tip and pipe the filling into the pocket in the brioche. Cut the filled brioche into 6 equal portions.

In a flat-bottomed dish just large enough to hold the bread slices in one layer whisk together the eggs, cream, liqueur, cinnamon, nutmeg, and vanilla extract. Add the stuffed bread slices and soak, turning once or twice, until the custard is partially absorbed. In a 9- to 10-inch nonstick skillet heat the butter over moderate heat until the foam subsides, and cook the stuffed brioche pieces 5 to 7 minutes on each side or until golden and crisp. Transfer the French toast with a slotted spatula to paper towels to drain briefly. Serve hot with the ice cream and warmed spiced honey.

Aunt Irma's Banana-Pecan Beignets

Larry Gober
CRIOLLA'S RESTAURANT
GRAYTON BEACH, FLORIDA

SERVES 6

This delicious dessert might be the ultimate comfort food.

Goat Milk Lime Dipping Sauce

3	cups sugar
½	teaspoon cream of tartar
1	cup water
3	cups goat's milk (or substitute whole milk)
	Juice of 3 limes

Beignets

3	cups all-purpose flour
1½	tablespoons baking powder
6	tablespoons sugar

1	cup whole milk
2	tablespoons vanilla extract
6	large eggs
½	cup pecans, chopped and roasted
6	bananas
4	cups vegetable oil for deep-frying
2	cups confectioners' sugar

	Sprigs of fresh mint
½	cup blackberries

☙ **To prepare the goat milk lime dipping sauce:** In a large saucepan combine the sugar and cream of tartar. Add the water and bring to a boil over medium-high heat, occasionally scraping the sides with a rubber spatula to prevent the sugar from crystallizing. When the sugar begins to caramelize, remove the pan from the heat and allow the retained heat to turn the sugar to a golden brown. Quickly and carefully whisk in the milk (the milk will steam, causing the caramel to tighten, so be careful not to burn yourself). Add the lime juice. Strain into a clean bowl and cool.

☙ **To prepare the beignets:** In a medium mixing bowl whisk together the flour, baking powder, and sugar. Add the milk, vanilla, and eggs, and whisk until the batter is smooth and no lumps remain. Stir in the pecans. Slice bananas into ¾-inch slices. Dip the bananas into the batter, making sure they are well coated. Heat 4 cups of vegetable oil in a saucepan over medium-high heat until the temperature reaches 350°. Fry the bananas, keeping them submerged in the oil (if necessary, place a fry basket or another pan over the bananas) about 90 seconds or until golden brown. Remove to paper towels to drain. Sprinkle with confectioners' sugar. Since the frying will cause the bananas to soften to almost a pastry cream consistency, they are best eaten immediately.

☙ **To assemble:** Spoon the goat's milk lime dipping sauce into a bowl. Gently place the beignets on top of the sauce. Garnish with a sprig of fresh mint and fresh blackberries.

GALLIANO CRÊPES WITH SEASONAL BERRIES

Frank Caputo
THE KIAWAH ISLAND CLUB
CHARLESTON, SOUTH CAROLINA

SERVES 4

Crêpes (makes 15 to 20)

1	cup all-purpose flour
¾	cup milk
½	cup water
2	large eggs
2	egg yolks
	Pinch of salt
2	tablespoons confectioners' sugar
3	tablespoons melted butter
2	tablespoons brandy

Vegetable cooking spray or additional
butter for cooking crêpes

Pastry Cream

6	egg yolks
½	cup sugar
¼	cup cake flour
¼	cup cornstarch
2	cups milk
1	vanilla bean, split and scraped
2	tablespoons unsalted butter

Sauce

¼	cup sugar
¼	cup (½ stick) unsalted butter
¼	cup Galliano liqueur
6	tablespoons freshly squeezed orange juice
2	cups fresh berries
4	sprigs of mint for garnish

✒ **To make the crêpe batter:** In a clean bowl place the flour, then slowly whisk in the milk and water until a smooth blend is achieved. If any lumps remain after the liquids are added, pour the mixture through a fine mesh strainer to remove the lumps. Whisk in the eggs, egg yolks, salt, and sugar. Stir in the melted butter. Let the mixture rest for 1 hour, and add the brandy.

✒ **To make the pastry cream:** In the clean bowl of an electric mixer fitted with a whisk, beat the egg yolks with the sugar on high speed until thick and pale yellow. In a separate bowl sift the flour and cornstarch together. Whisk the dry ingredients into the egg yolk mixture. In a noncorrosive saucepan scald the milk with the vanilla bean. Remove the pan from the heat and pour about one-fourth of the hot milk into the egg yolk mixture, whisking constantly. Return this mixture to the saucepan, and the saucepan to the heat, whisking constantly until the mixture thickens, reaching a puddinglike consistency. Remove the pan from the heat and blend in the butter. Strain into a bowl and cover with film wrap, pressing down on the surface of the cream so that a skin will not form. Cool. Refrigerate until needed.

To make the crêpes: Heat a crêpe pan until nearly smoking and then coat with vegetable spray or butter. In the center of the pan pour a thin layer of the crêpe batter (approximately ¼ cup), tilting the pan in all directions to completely coat the pan with the batter. Cook approximately 30 seconds or until the bottom of the crêpe is lightly browned. Turn the crêpe over using a spatula or your fingers, and cook 15 to 20 seconds more or until the crêpe is set and spotty brown. Remove to a rack to cool, and refrigerate in plastic bags until needed.

To make the sauce: In a sauté pan melt the sugar and butter. Add the Galliano and orange juice and stir until completely dissolved. Add the berries to the sauce just to warm slightly.

To assemble: Remove the crêpes from the refrigerator and bring to room temperature. For each dessert fold two crêpes in half darker side up, and fill each with ¼ cup of pastry cream. Place the crêpes in opposite directions in the center of a warm plate and spoon ¼ cup of sauce and ½ cup of berries over the entire plate. Garnish with a sprig of fresh mint.

CHOCOLATE CRÈME BRÛLÉE
WITH A SWEET BASIL VANILLA SAUCE

Peter deJong
THE BEAUFORT INN
BEAUFORT, SOUTH CAROLINA

SERVES 4

Chocolate Crème Brûlée

5   ounces bitter chocolate
½   cup heavy cream
3   large eggs
¾   cup sugar
1½ cups milk

Sweet Basil Vanilla Sauce

½   cup milk
1   cup basil leaves

¼   cup sugar
1   cup heavy cream
1   vanilla bean

Dark and White Chocolate Triangles

4   ounces white chocolate
4   ounces semisweet chocolate

¼   cup firmly packed light brown sugar
½   cup fresh raspberries

To prepare the crème brûlée: Preheat the oven to 300°. Place the chocolate in a small metal bowl. In a heavy saucepan heat the cream over moderately high heat until it just comes to a boil and pour over the chocolate. Let the chocolate stand until softened and whisk the mixture until smooth. In a separate bowl whisk together the eggs and sugar. Whisk in the chocolate mixture. In a saucepan heat the milk just to a boil. Add the milk to the egg mixture in a stream, whisking. Skim off any froth. Divide the custard among four ½-cup flameproof ramekins set in a roasting pan. Add enough hot water to the pan to reach halfway up the sides of the ramekins. Bake the custards in the middle of the oven about 60 minutes until they are just set but still tremble slightly. Remove the ramekins.

To prepare the basil vanilla sauce: In the bowl of a food processor combine the milk, basil, and sugar, and purée until smooth. In a small heavy saucepan bring the puréed mixture just to a boil with the cream and vanilla bean. Remove the pan from the heat. Scrape the seeds from the vanilla bean with a knife into the pan, reserving the pod for another use. Cover and refrigerate for at least 2 hours.

To prepare the chocolate triangles: Line a 10 x 15-inch cookie sheet with parchment paper. Temper the white chocolate: In the bottom of a double boiler heat 1 inch of water over medium heat. Place 4 ounces of white chocolate in the top of the double boiler and heat, stirring constantly, for about 3 minutes or until the chocolate has melted. Transfer the melted chocolate to a stainless steel bowl and continue stirring until the mixture is cooled.

Temper the dark chocolate using the same procedure as for the white chocolate. Pour the white and dark chocolate side by side on the parchment paper. Use a rubber spatula to evenly spread the chocolates (making sure to keep the chocolates separate). Place the baking sheet in the refrigerator until the chocolate has set, about 10 minutes. Remove from the refrigerator and invert the chocolate onto a cutting board. Cut the chocolates into triangles.

To assemble: Set broiler rack so that custards will be 2 to 3 inches from heat and preheat broiler. Sift brown sugar evenly over custards and broil custards until sugar is melted and caramelized, about 2 minutes. (Alternately, raw sugar may be sprinkled over the custards and caramelized with a blowtorch.) Place brûlées on individual dessert plates and surround with the sauce, a white and dark chocolate triangle, and fresh raspberries.

FEARRINGTON HOUSE CHOCOLATE REFRESH-MINT

Heather Mendenhall

FEARRINGTON HOUSE
PITTSBORO, NORTH CAROLINA

SERVES 8

Chocolate Cake

2	whole eggs
2	egg yolks
1/2	cup sugar
1/3	cup cake flour
1/4	teaspoon baking powder
	Pinch of salt
1/4	cup melted butter
1/4	cup cocoa powder

Minted Chocolate Mousse

1/4	cup water
1/2	cup sugar
2	egg whites
1 1/2	cups sour cream
1	cup heavy cream
6	ounces bittersweet chocolate
1/4	cup bourbon
2	tablespoons mint extract

Mint Julep Simple Syrup

1/2	cup sugar
1	cup water
1/2	cup fresh mint, chopped
1/4	cup bourbon

Chocolate Ganache Glaze

4	ounces bittersweet chocolate
1	cup sour cream
2	tablespoons light corn syrup
1/4	cup bourbon

Garnish

10	sprigs fresh mint, finely chopped

To make the chocolate cake: Preheat the oven to 350°. Line the bottom of a greased 10½-inch springform pan with waxed paper, grease the paper, and dust the pan with flour, knocking out the excess. In the large bowl of an electric mixer beat the eggs and yolks with the sugar on high speed for 5 minutes or until the mixture is pale yellow and forms a ribbon when the beaters are lifted. In a separate bowl sift the flour, baking powder, and salt together. Fold the dry ingredients into the egg mixture until the batter is just combined. In a small saucepan set over low heat melt the butter and cocoa together. Fold the chocolate-butter mixture gently but thoroughly into the flour mixture. Pour the batter into the pan, smoothing the top. Bake the cake in the middle of the oven for 20 minutes or until a tester comes out clean. Transfer the cake to a rack, run a sharp knife around the edge, and remove the side of the pan. Invert the cake onto another rack and remove the waxed paper. Reinvert the cake onto the rack and let it cool completely. Clean the springform pan; it will be needed later to assemble the Refresh-Mint.

𝒮 *To make the minted chocolate mousse:* In a small saucepan combine the water and sugar and bring to a boil over medium heat. Continue cooking until the syrup has thickened and has large bubbles. In the well chilled bowl of an electric mixer fitted with a balloon whisk, beat the egg whites at medium speed until soft peaks begin to form. Switch the speed to high and add the simple syrup. Whip until cool and stiff peaks have formed, about 5 minutes. Remove the meringue to a clean mixing bowl.

𝒮 In a separate bowl combine the sour cream with the heavy cream and beat until soft peaks form. Place the chocolate in the top of a double boiler over hot water. Stir the chocolate until melted. Add the bourbon and mint extract to the chocolate, and let cool slightly. Fold into the cream mixture. Gently but thoroughly fold the chocolate mixture into the meringue.

𝒮 *To make the mint julep simple syrup:* In a medium, heavy-bottomed saucepan bring the sugar, water, chopped mint, and bourbon to a boil over medium-high heat. As soon as the mixture has come to a boil, remove the pan from the heat. Strain through a fine mesh strainer and reserve.

𝒮 *To make the chocolate ganache:* Finely chop the chocolate and place in a clean mixing bowl. In a heavy-bottomed saucepan bring the sour cream, corn syrup, and bourbon to a boil over medium heat. Stir to combine. Pour this mixture over the chocolate and allow to rest 2 to 3 minutes before stirring. This will allow the chocolate to melt. With a rubber spatula, stir gently to combine.

𝒮 *To assemble:* Cut the top of the cake to level it, and cut horizontally into 2 even layers. Place one layer of the cake into the cleaned springform pan and sprinkle with ½ cup of mint julep simple syrup. Once the syrup is absorbed, spread the cake layer with chocolate mousse until it reaches halfway up the pan. Top with second layer and sprinkle with syrup as before. Top with the remaining chocolate mousse, smoothing with a rubber spatula. Freeze the mousse cake for 1 hour. Remove from the freezer and spread chocolate ganache on top. Garnish with finely chopped fresh mint leaves. To remove from the pan, wrap a damp, hot towel around the pan for 1 minute, and release the sides. Smooth the sides of the cake with a rubber spatula.

CHOCOLATE SOUFFLÉ

James Burns
BISTRO
MT. PLEASANT, SOUTH CAROLINA

SERVES 6

Chocolate Soufflé

½ cup sugar
¼ cup all-purpose flour
¼ cup cocoa powder
2 cups cream
1 egg
1 egg yolk
1 tablespoon butter, at room temperature
6 egg whites

Chocolate Sauce

2 cups heavy cream
1 cup (2 sticks) butter

1 cup firmly packed brown sugar
1 cup sugar
1½ cups cocoa powder
1 tablespoon bourbon
1 tablespoon vanilla extract

Chantilly Cream

1¾ cup heavy cream
¼ cup sugar
1 teaspoon vanilla extract

½ pint fresh raspberries for garnish

🖐 **To make the chocolate soufflé:** Preheat the oven to 375°. Butter 6 individual soufflé dishes and coat with a light dusting of sugar, knocking out the excess sugar.

🖐 In a bowl whisk together the flour and cocoa powder. In a heavy saucepan combine the cream and sugar and heat until it comes to a boil. Add the flour and cocoa, whisking briefly until smooth. Transfer the mixture to the bowl of an electric mixer fitted with a paddle attachment and beat until smooth. With the machine running add the whole egg, then the egg yolk. In a heavy saucepan heat the butter over low heat until melted. Cool. Add the butter to the mixing bowl, beating for an additional minute.

🖐 In the well-chilled bowl of an electric mixer fitted with a balloon whip, beat the egg whites with a pinch of sugar until the meringue just holds stiff peaks. Stir one-fourth of the meringue into the custard to lighten. Fold in the remaining meringue gently but thoroughly. Spoon the mixture into the prepared dishes. The soufflé may be prepared up to this point 1 hour ahead and chilled, covered with a paper towel and plastic wrap. Do not let the paper towel touch the surface of the soufflé. Place the cold soufflé in a preheated oven. Bake the soufflé dishes in the middle of the oven (make sure the rack is low enough to allow soufflé to rise about 2 inches) about 16 to 20 minutes or until firm and set in the center.

♨ To make the chocolate sauce: In a small heavy saucepan cook the cream, butter, and sugars over medium heat, stirring constantly, until sugar is dissolved and mixture is no longer grainy. Remove the pan from the heat, add the cocoa, and stir until melted. Stir in the bourbon and vanilla, strain, and set aside to cool. If made in advance, the sauce may be reheated gently over low heat.

♨ To make the chantilly cream: Place the whipping cream in the well-chilled bowl of an electric mixer fitted with a well-chilled balloon whip. Whip on low speed until the cream is frothy. In a steady stream add the sugar and whip, gradually increasing the mixer's speed until the cream begins to form peaks. Add the vanilla and whip until soft peaks form.

♨ To present: Place individual soufflé cups on plates and accompany with chantilly cream, fresh raspberries, and a pitcher of warm chocolate sauce.

BAKED CREAMS WITH ORANGE CUSTARD SAUCE

Norma Naparlo
MAGNOLIA'S RESTAURANT
CHARLESTON, SOUTH CAROLINA

SERVES 4

The creamy custard with a slightly tart orange custard sauce is a soothing completion to a dinner at home with friends.

Baked Creams

2   cups milk
3/4 cup sugar
1/4 vanilla bean, split (or 1/2 teaspoon pure vanilla extract)
     Rind of 1/2 orange, roughly chopped
3   large eggs
2   egg yolks

Orange Custard Sauce

1/4 cup sugar
1   cup heavy cream

     Rind of 1/4 orange (or 1/2 to 1 tablespoon grated rind)
1/2 teaspoon pure vanilla extract
2   egg yolks
1   vanilla bean

16   orange segments
8   fresh strawberries, halved
4   sprigs fresh mint

To make the baked creams: Preheat the oven to 300°. In a heavy-bottomed saucepan combine the milk, half the sugar, the vanilla bean or extract, and orange rind over medium heat. Slowly bring this mixture to a boil. Remove the pan from the heat and strain through a fine mesh strainer. Scrape the vanilla bean into the hot milk. Discard the vanilla bean and the orange rind. In a mixing bowl beat together the eggs, egg yolks, and remaining sugar until well combined. In a slow stream add the warm milk, whisking constantly. After half of the milk is incorporated into the egg mixture, slowly pour the mix back into the pan of hot milk, whisking constantly. Divide the mixture into four 6-ounce ovenproof ramekins, and place them in a roasting pan. Place the pan on the middle shelf of the preheated oven, and add enough hot water to the pan to come halfway up the sides of the ramekins, being careful not to get any water into the creams. Bake for 1 hour and 15 minutes or until the creams are firm to the touch. (A cake tester inserted into the center should come out clean without any milky residue.) Remove from the oven and cool. Chill the cream 4 hours or overnight.

To make the orange custard sauce: In a heavy-bottomed saucepan set over medium heat, place half the sugar, the heavy cream, orange rind, and vanilla, and stir until dissolved. Slowly bring the cream to a simmer, stirring to prevent scorching. In a clean mixing bowl whisk the egg yolks with the remaining sugar until well combined. Slowly stream in ½ cup of the hot cream, whisking constantly. Return the mixture to the pan. Place the pan over low heat and cook, stirring with a wooden spoon, until the custard is thick enough to coat the back of the spoon. Remove the pan from the heat and strain through a fine mesh strainer into a nonmetal container. Scrape the inside of the vanilla bean into the sauce. Discard the vanilla bean and the orange rind. Cool the custard at room temperature for 15 minutes, stirring occasionally. Pour the custard sauce into a container and refrigerate until cool. Once the custard has cooled, cover it with a lid.

To serve: Pour ½ cup of orange custard sauce around individual dessert plates. Unmold the custard and place on the edge of the plates. Garnish with 4 orange segments, 4 fresh strawberry halves, and a sprig of mint.

Coffee Cup with Sabayon

Shane Gorringe
ZOE'S BAKERY
COVINGTON, LOUISIANA

SERVES 8

This is a spectacular dessert to serve for a very special occasion. But if time is a consideration, substituting your favorite brand of coffee or espresso ice cream for the mousse is an equally delicious option!

Bailey Sabayon

5	large egg yolks
½	cup sugar
¼	cup champagne
¼	cup Bailey's Irish Cream
1¼	cups heavy cream

Coffee Cup Tulip Cookies

1¼	cups all-purpose flour
1	cup confectioners' sugar
¼	cup (1 stick) unsalted butter, melted
3	tablespoons heavy cream
½	teaspoon pure vanilla extract
4	large egg whites
	Pinch of salt
1	tablespoon vegetable oil
1	tablespoon cocoa powder (optional)

Meringue Sugar Cubes

½	cup egg whites (about 5 to 6)
¾	cup sugar
1	cup water

Chocolate Coffee Mousse

4	egg yolks
10	ounces semisweet chocolate, broken into small pieces
½	cup Kahlua
¼	cup espresso or strong coffee
1½	cups heavy cream
4	egg whites
¼	cup sugar

To make the sabayon: In the top half of a double boiler over simmering water whisk together the egg yolks, sugar, champagne, and Bailey's. Continue whisking the mixture vigorously until the yolks are light and frothy and the mixture has begun to thicken, about 10 minutes. Immediately transfer the mixture to a large mixing bowl and whisk until cooled.

Place the cream in a deep bowl and whip until stiff peaks form. Fold the whipped cream into the sabayon. Transfer to a covered bowl and refrigerate for up to 2 days.

To make the coffee cup tulip cookies: Preheat the oven to 400°. In a large mixing bowl sift the flour and sugar together. Gradually stir in the melted butter. Add the cream, vanilla, egg whites, and salt and stir to blend. The cookie dough will be used for making the coffee cups, decorations, handles, and spoons.

To make the coffee cups: Grease a large baking sheet with vegetable oil and dust with flour, shaking out any excess. Take a thin, flat piece of cardboard, and make a template by cutting out a rectangular hole the size of a coffee cup. Place the rectangle onto the baking sheet and, using a rubber spatula, evenly spread some of the cookie mix into the hole. Remove the template and repeat 7 more times. To make a design on the coffee cup, take a small amount of the cookie mix and place it in a mixing bowl. Stir in 1 tablespoon of cocoa powder to color. Place this colored battered into a piping bag and pipe a design onto the rectangles. Bake the "coffee cups" in the oven until golden, 10 to 12 minutes.

Open the oven door and set the baking sheet on it. This will help keep the cookies flexible while you are unmolding. Using a large, flexible spatula, lift the cookies off the baking sheet by sliding the spatula underneath and onto a rolling pin or another object the width of your coffee cup. Quickly shape the baked tulips to form the cup. Work rapidly to prevent the cookies from crisping—at which time they would no longer be pliable enough to make the cup mold. Close the oven door and allow the oven to return to 400°.

To make the spoons: Prepare a baking sheet as before. Fill a pastry bag with cookie mix and pipe the shape of a spoon onto the sheet. Bake until golden, about 5 minutes.

For the cup handles: Prepare another baking sheet. Pipe a line of the cookie mix about 2½ to 3 inches long onto the baking sheet. Place in the oven and bake 3 to 4 minutes or until golden. Remove from the oven and quickly bend the strips into the shape of a handle and press the ends together. It is important to do this while the dough is still warm and malleable. Although the cookie shapes may be stored in a covered container for up to 2 days, they will lose their crispness in a humid environment.

To make the meringue sugar cubes: In the metal bowl of an electric mixer whip the egg whites until they begin to foam. With the machine still running, slowly add the sugar and continue whipping until firm peaks form. In a medium saucepan bring 1 cup of water to a simmer over medium-high heat. Reduce the heat to low and, ¼ cup at a time, scoop the meringue into the water. Cook the meringue about 1 minute on each side, turning until firm. Be careful not to let the liquid come to a boil. Remove the meringue from the liquid and place on a wire rack to cool. Once the meringue has cooled, cut into sugar cubes.

To make the chocolate coffee mousse: In a medium mixing bowl beat the egg yolks with a whisk until frothy and slightly thickened. Place the chocolate in the top of a double boiler set over hot water, and stir the chocolate until melted. Remove ¼ cup of the melted chocolate to a separate container and reserve to use later in assembling the dessert. Add Kahlua and coffee to the chocolate, and let cool slightly. Fold into the egg yolks.

Place the heavy cream in the well-chilled bowl of an electric mixer fitted with a chilled balloon whip and beat on high speed about 1 minute until peaks form. Fold the whipped cream into the chocolate.

✍ In a separate bowl of the electric mixer fitted with a balloon whip, whisk the egg whites on high speed until soft peaks form. In a steady stream add the sugar and continue beating over high speed about 3 to 5 minutes until stiff. When the peaks are shiny, use a rubber spatula to fold the egg whites into the chocolate mixture. Cover and refrigerate until ready to use.

✍ ***To assemble:*** Spoon a little sabayon into the center of a plate. Attach the handle to the coffee cup by brushing with a little of the melted chocolate. Place the coffee cup in the center of the sayabon, fill the cup halfway with the mousse, and fill to the top with the sabayon. Stand the spoon against the side of the coffee cup and place 2 meringue sugar cubes in front of the cup.

CRÈME BRÛLÉE NAPOLEON WITH BOURBON CRÈME ANGLAISE

Wally Joe
KC'S RESTAURANT
CLEVELAND, MISSISSIPPI

SERVES 6

Custard

6	egg yolks
½	cup sugar
2¼	cups heavy cream
1	vanilla bean, split

Bourbon Crème Anglaise

5	egg yolks
2	cups milk
¾	cup sugar
1	vanilla bean, split
2	tablespoons bourbon

Phyllo Squares

2	sheets phyllo dough
2	tablespoons butter, melted
	Confectioners' sugar

To make the custard: Preheat the oven to 325°. In the metal bowl of an electric mixer fitted with a balloon whip, combine the egg yolks and sugar and beat lightly. Add the cream and scrape the seeds from the vanilla bean into the eggs with the tip of a knife. Continue to beat until thickened. Pour this mixture through a fine mesh strainer into a shallow pan that has been lined with plastic wrap. Place the pan containing the custard into a larger pan. Fill the bottom pan halfway with water, being careful not to wet the custard, and set in the preheated oven to bake for 25 to 30 minutes or until the custard is set and firm to the touch. (A cake tester inserted into the center should come out clean without any milky residue.) Remove from the oven and refrigerate until cool. Place in the freezer for 20 minutes.

Preheat the broiler or ready a blow torch. Invert the custard onto the back of a sheet pan, and cut into 2-inch squares. Sprinkle the squares liberally with sugar and brown under the broiler or with a blowtorch.

To prepare the phyllo pastry: Preheat the oven to 350°. Line an inverted baking sheet with parchment paper or aluminum foil. Place 1 sheet of phyllo dough on the baking sheet. (Keep the remaining dough covered with a towel to keep it moist.) Lightly brush the phyllo sheet with melted butter, sprinkle with the confectioners' sugar, and top with another sheet of phyllo. Brush again with the melted butter and sprinkle with more sugar. Place a second sheet pan on top and weight it down with a cast-iron skillet or any heavy ovenproof object. Bake in the preheated oven until golden brown.

❧ **To make the bourbon crème Anglaise:** In a medium heavy saucepan whisk the egg yolks over low heat until they are pale in color. Whisk in the sugar 1 tablespoon at a time, then continue to whisk until the mixture reaches the consistency of cake batter. Whisk in the milk and vanilla bean, if using, then stir continuously with a wooden spoon until the custard coats the spoon and a line drawn down the back of the spoon remains visible. Remove the pan from the heat and stir in the bourbon, and remove the vanilla bean pods.

❧ If the custard is to be chilled, press a sheet of plastic wrap directly onto the surface to prevent a skin from forming, or dot the top with bits of optional butter. Chill the custard for up to 2 days.

❧ **To assemble the napoleon:** In the center of each serving plate place a square of crème brûlée (custard) and top with a phyllo square. Repeat the procedure until the napoleons are stacked 4 layers high. Ladle the crème Anglaise around the napoleons and garnish with fresh berries and mint sprigs.

PRALINE MOUSSE SERVED WITH CHOCOLATE MERINGUE

Frederick Monti

BRASSERIE LE COZE
ATLANTA, GEORGIA

SERVES 6

Simple Syrup

1 cup sugar
1 cup water

Praline

1 cup sugar
1 cup pecan halves

Praline Mousse

4 egg yolks
1/4 cup Simple Syrup
3 1/2 ounces white chocolate
1 3/4 cups whipped cream
8 ounces praline

Chocolate Meringue

8 egg whites
2 cups sugar
3/4 cup unsweetened cocoa powder

Chocolate Sauce

6 tablespoons heavy cream
1/2 cup Simple Syrup
6 ounces bittersweet chocolate, finely chopped
2 tablespoons Grand Marnier

❧ To make the simple syrup: In a small saucepan combine the sugar and water over high heat. Bring the mixture to a boil, and boil 1 minute. Remove the pan from the heat and reserve until ready to use.

❧ To make the praline: Brush a baking sheet lightly with oil. In a heavy-bottomed saucepan heat the sugar over high heat, stirring constantly with a wooden spoon. The sugar will form lumps at first, then as it begins to melt, the lumps will dissolve. When the sugar begins to take on a light color, lower the heat slightly and continue to cook, stirring until the sugar turns a light caramel color. At this point you may add the nuts all at once, and stir with the spoon to make sure they are all coated with caramel. Boil and stir 30 seconds more or until the nuts have separated. Turn the caramelized nuts onto the oiled baking sheet and set aside to cool and harden.

❧ When the praline has hardened, break it into pieces, transfer to the work bowl of a food processor fitted with a metal blade, and process until chopped fine. The praline can be made up to a week in advance and stored in an airtight container.

❧ To make the praline mousse: In a double boiler over simmering water melt the chocolate, stirring until smooth. Remove the pan from the heat. In the same double boiler heat the egg yolks with the simple syrup and whisk constantly for about 6 minutes or until thick ribbons form when the whisk is lifted and a thermometer inserted into the mixture registers 160°. Let cool slightly. Fold in the chocolate. Place the heavy cream in the well-chilled bowl of an electric mixer fitted with a chilled balloon whip and beat on high speed about 1 minute until peaks form. With the mixer on low speed add the chocolate and continue mixing until the chocolate is completely incorporated. Fold in the praline. Chill this mixture 2 hours or overnight.

❧ To make the chocolate meringue: Preheat the oven to 250°. In a large bowl beat the egg whites with an electric mixer until they just hold soft peaks. Add the sugar in a stream and beat until stiff peaks form. When the peaks are shiny, use a rubber spatula to fold the cocoa into the meringue, one-third at a time. Spoon the meringue mixture into a pastry bag and pipe 3- to 4-inch circles onto a cookie sheet that has been lined with parchment paper. Continue to spiral each circle upward to about 2 inches, leaving the center hollow, and filling only the bottom completely. Next make the meringue decorations. Pipe 2 long thin strips of meringue lengthwise across the sheet pan. Place the meringues in the preheated oven and bake 1 hour and 30 minutes until dry. Remove the meringues from the oven and cool on parchment paper. Lift them off the paper and store in an airtight container until ready to use. Can be stored in a cool dry place for at least one week.

❧ To make the chocolate sauce: In a heatproof bowl over a saucepan of simmering water heat the heavy cream with the simple syrup. Add the chocolate to the bowl and stir until the mixture is smooth. Stir in the Grand Marnier. Remove the bowl from the heat, transfer to a clean container, and cool. The sauce may be made 1 week in advance, kept covered and chilled, and reheated slowly over low heat.

🍂 **To present:** Spoon chocolate sauce onto individual dessert plates. Place a meringue cup on each plate, and spoon in the praline mousse. Break the meringue strips into pieces of varying length, and place vertically into the mousse so the meringue sticks resemble spikes.

TROPICAL TIRAMISU

Pascal Oudin
THE GRAND BAY HOTEL
MIAMI, FLORIDA

SERVES 4

The chef's tiramisu is a composition of three distinctly flavored fruit sauces, which he refers to as tiramisus. The same cooking method is employed to make each tiramisu, but they are made separately. If you cannot locate the exotic fruit naranjilla, any slightly tart fruit can be substituted.

Naranjilla "Lulo" Fruit Tiramisu

8   ounces Naranjilla "Lulo" Purée, (see Fruit Purées, page 216)
8   ounces mascarpone cheese
3   tablespoons confectioners' sugar
1   cup heavy cream

Passion Fruit Tiramisu

8   ounces Passion Fruit Purée (see Fruit Purées, page 216)
8   ounces mascarpone cheese
3   tablespoons confectioners' sugar
1   cup heavy cream

Coconut Tiramisu

6   tablespoons Coco Lopez
8   ounces mascarpone cheese

2   tablespoons confectioners' sugar
1   cup heavy cream

Swiss Meringue Garnish

8   ounces egg whites
    Pinch of cream of tartar
2   tablespoons sugar
4   ounces pecans, finely ground to a powder

Garnish

¼   cup chocolate, melted
¼   cup Apricot Purée (see Fruit Purées, page 216)
½   cup Raspberry Purée (see Fruit Purées, page 216)

To make the tiramisus: In separate small saucepans reduce the naranjilla and passion fruit purées over medium heat by two-thirds. There should be approximately 3 ounces (6 tablespoons) of each flavored fruit reduction. Watch carefully during the reducing; as the liquid evaporates, the fruit pulp is subject to burning. Remove the reduction to a small bowl and allow to cool completely.

In separate bowls combine the naranjilla and passion fruit reductions with mascarpone cheese and sugar, and beat with an electric mixer fitted with a paddle at low speed until smooth. With the machine running, slowly add the heavy cream, scraping the sides of the bowl with a rubber spatula. Increase the speed to medium-high and continue beating until thickened.

For the coconut tiramisu, in another bowl combine the mascarpone cheese and sugar and beat until smooth.Slowly add the heavy cream and Coco Lopez, scraping the sides of the bowl with a rubber spatula. Increase the speed to medium-high and continue beating until thickened.

Transfer each mixture to a pastry bag fitted with a plain round tip, and pipe a layer of each flavored tiramisu into a 9-inch springform pan with removable sides. Place the mold in the refrigerator for 3 to 4 hours, or until the tiramisu is completely set up.

To make the meringue: Preheat the oven to 225°. In a metal bowl combine the egg whites, cream of tartar, and sugar. Set the bowl over a saucepan of hot but not simmering water, and stir the mixture until the sugar is dissolved. Transfer the mixture to a mixer fitted with a whip attachment or, using a hand-held electric mixer, beat the meringue for 5 minutes or until it holds glossy stiff peaks. Spread a thin layer of the meringue on the tiramisu, and return the tiramisu to the refrigerator. Transfer the remainder of the meringue to a pastry bag fitted with a small round tip, and on a cookie sheet lined with parchment paper, pipe twelve 4-inch long straight lines the diameter of a finger. Sprinkle the lines with the pecan dust. Bake the meringue fingers in the preheated oven for 10 to 15 minutes or until completely dry. Reserve the rest of the meringue to finish the tiramisu.

To assemble the tropical tiramisu: On a 10-inch plate make a grid with the melted chocolate, then place dots of alternating apricot and raspberry fruit purée evenly throughout the squares. Remove the tiramisu from the refrigerator and, using as blowtorch, flame the top of the mold until the meringue is lightly browned. Alternately, heat the broiler and brown the tiramisu quickly under the broiler. Remove the ring from the tiramisu, and place in the middle of the plate. Garnish with the meringue fingers, and spread the rest of the meringue around the edge of the tiramisu.

LEMON SOUFFLÉ

Hallman Woods
LE ROSIER
NEW IBERIA, LOUISIANA

SERVES 6

Raspberry Sauce

2	cups raspberries
1	to 1½ tablespoons sugar
1	teaspoon kirsch
1	tablespoon lemon juice

Lemon Soufflé

½	cup sugar

¼	cup (½ stick) unsalted butter
⅓	cup fresh lemon juice
4	large egg yolks
1	tablespoon finely grated lemon zest
8	large egg whites, at room temperature
	Confectioners' sugar for dusting

Fresh berries and mint for garnish

To make the raspberry sauce: In the bowl of a food processor, combine the raspberries, sugar, kirsch, and lemon juice. Blend until liquid, and refrigerate until needed.

To make the soufflé: In a nonreactive medium saucepan combine ¼ cup of the sugar, the butter, and lemon juice, and cook over moderate heat, stirring constantly, until the sugar and butter are melted. Remove the pan from the heat and stir in the egg yolks one at a time, mixing well after each addition. Add the lemon zest and cook over moderately low heat, stirring, until slightly thickened, about 2 minutes. Do not let the mixture come to a boil or the lemon curd will curdle. The recipe can be prepared to this point up to 4 hours ahead. Press plastic wrap directly onto the surface of the lemon curd and let stand at room temperature.

Preheat the oven to 425°. Butter six 8-ounce ovenproof ramekins and freeze until set. Butter the ramekins again and coat with sugar. Rewarm the lemon curd over moderately low heat, stirring constantly, just until hot to the touch.

In the bowl of a well chilled electric mixer fitted with a balloon whip beat the egg whites until soft peaks form. Add the remaining ¼ cup of sugar and continue beating until the whites are glossy and stiff, about 1 minute. Stir one quarter of the egg whites into the lemon curd, then gently fold the mixture into the remaining whites until just combined.

Spoon the mixture into the prepared ramekins and smooth the surface with a rubber spatula. Run a thumb inside the edge of the dish in order to create a "hat." Bake the soufflés in the lower third of the oven for about 16 to 20 minutes or until risen. Dust the top with confectioners' sugar and serve immediately. Garnish with raspberries, blueberries, raspberry sauce, and fresh mint.

LEMON PARFAIT WITH FRUITS AND SAUCES

Chris Northmore

CHEROKEE TOWN & COUNTRY CLUB
ATLANTA, GEORGIA

SERVES 8

Frozen Lemon Parfait

¼	cup water
½	cup plus 2 tablespoons sugar
½	tablespoon light corn syrup
2	egg whites
	Zest of 1 lemon
¼	cup lemon juice
1⅓	cups heavy cream
¼	cup plain yogurt

Praline Batter

1	cup (2 sticks) unsalted butter
1	cup sugar
10	ounces almonds, finely ground
1	cup corn syrup

Mango Sauce

2	cups diced ripe mango, approximately
1	tablespoon fresh lemon juice
2	to 3 tablespoons confectioners' sugar or to taste
½	cup to 1 cup orange juice
½	pound bittersweet chocolate

Optional Garnishes

	Marzipan flowers
	Star fruit
6	strawberries
6	blackberries

☙ **To make the parfait:** In a medium heavy-bottomed saucepan combine the water, sugar, and corn syrup and heat until the temperature reaches 243° on a candy thermometer. In a large mixing bowl beat the egg whites until they turn foamy. Stir the syrup mixture into the egg whites and whip together until the mixture cools slightly to room temperature. Fold the lemon zest and lemon juice into the cooled egg whites.

☙ In a separate mixing bowl whip the heavy cream until soft peaks form. Whisk in the yogurt. Gently fold the egg whites into the cream and yogurt mixture. Spoon the parfait into 4-ounce molds and freeze overnight.

☙ **To make the praline batter:** Preheat the oven to 325°. Line a baking sheet with parchment paper, and have a second sheet of parchment paper the same size as the first ready. In a heavy-bottomed saucepan melt the butter over medium heat. Add the sugar, ground almonds, and corn syrup and stir until the mixture is smooth. Remove the pan from the heat and spread onto a parchment-lined pan. Allow the batter to cover all but 2 inches of the pan. To even the batter's thickness, place the second sheet of the parchment onto the batter, and gently roll with a rolling pin until a uniform thickness is achieved. Remove the parchment from the top.

🍃 Place the praline batter in the top third of the preheated oven and bake about 10 to 15 minutes until golden. Remove the baking sheet from the oven. Immediately remove the praline and begin forming into basket shapes.

🍃 Using a circle cutter, cut a 6-inch round. Next cut a rectangle 1 inch wide and 4 inches long. This will be used to form the handle. Make the baskets by folding the rounds while still warm over a rounded surface such as a can or glass with a small circular bottom. The smaller the bottom, the higher the basket. Attach the handle to the basket. If the pieces become too cool to shape, they may be rewarmed in the oven.

🍃 **To make mango sauce:** Purée the mango, lemon juice, and confectioners' sugar in a food processor. Add enough orange juice to achieve a sauce that will pour. Adjust the flavoring, adding sugar or lemon juice as needed. Force sauce through a strainer, pressing with the back of a spoon to extract all the juices from the pulp. Cover and refrigerate until serving.

🍃 **To temper the chocolate:** Have a large sheet of parchment paper ready. In the top of a double boiler set over simmering water, heat the chocolate, stirring occasionally, until it reaches 120° on an instant-read thermometer. Remove the pan from the heat and let the chocolate cool to 90°. Spread the chocolate over the parchment to about ¼-inch thickness, and smooth with a rubber spatula. When the chocolate is set, cut into rounds to fit the bottom of the praline basket, and small rectangles for the handles.

🍃 **To present:** Pour mango sauce onto individual dessert plates, and place a praline basket in the center of the plate. Place a chocolate disc on the bottom of the basket, and a rectangle on each end of the handle to adhere to the basket. If desired, place a marzipan flower over one end of the handle. Remove the parfaits from the freezer, unmold, and place in the center of basket. Decorate the plate with small pieces of fresh fruit.

BERRY COBBLER

Louis Osteen
LOUIS'S CHARLESTON GRILL
CHARLESTON, SOUTH CAROLINA

SERVES 8

This is truly great tummy food. I love mine with a big dollop of crème fraîche, but I suspect the more traditional and favorite topping is simply the best vanilla ice cream.

Cobbler Binder

3   tablespoons sugar
1   tablespoon all-purpose flour

Cobbler Filling

¼   cup Cobbler Binder
6   cups juicy ripe berries (either singularly or in combination: blueberries, black-berries, and raspberries)
1   tablespoon lemon zest, grated (be careful not to use the white layer, as it is bitter)

1   tablespoon unsalted butter, diced and kept chilled
2   tablespoons heavy whipping cream

Topping

2   cups White Lily self-rising flour
2   tablespoons sugar
½   cup (1 stick) unsalted butter, cut into ½-inch cubes and kept chilled
¾   cup heavy whipping cream
2   tablespoons heavy cream for brushing tops
2   tablespoons sugar for brushing tops

🐚 **To make the cobbler binder:** In a small mixing bowl combine the sugar and flour. Set aside.

🐚 **To make the cobbler filling:** In a large mixing bowl combine ¼ cup of the cobbler binder, the berries, and lemon zest and let the berries macerate for an hour or more at room temperature. Sprinkle the butter over the filling, then spoon the cream over the butter. When ready to cook, pour the filling into a 9-inch round baking dish or individual oven-proof bowls.

🐚 **To make the topping:** Preheat the oven to 350°. In a medium mixing bowl combine the flour and sugar and mix well. Add the cold diced butter and work into the flour with a pastry cutter, fork, or fingertips until the butter pieces are a little larger than an English pea but not larger than a lima bean. If you are using your fingers, work quickly so your body heat won't melt the butter.

🐚 Pour in all of the cream. Using a plastic spatula and light pressure, fold the mixture a few times until it becomes cohesive. Do not overmix. In order to make a light cobbler topping, it is important to work the dough as little as possible.

🏵 When the dough is mixed, turn it onto a floured surface and quickly and gently knead it 6 to 10 times or until it just begins to be nearly homogenized. There will be large pieces of butter throughout. Keep a little flour under the dough to make sure that the dough doesn't stick on the bottom and lightly dust the top of the dough so that the rolling pin doesn't stick on the top. Roll the dough to about ⅝-inch thickness.

🏵 Cut the dough into 4-inch rounds. Place the rounds on top of the cobbler filling. Use as much as needed of the cream to brush the tops. Then sprinkle the tops with the sugar. Bake the cobbler in the preheated oven for about 40 to 50 minutes or until the top is cooked through completely and the cobbler is thick and bubbly. Gently lift a part of the top and make sure that it is cooked and not still liquid and raw. Remove and serve while warm.

STRAWBERRY NAPOLEON

Stephen Austin
HEDGEROSE HEIGHTS INN
ATLANTA, GEORGIA

SERVES 6

Strawberry Coulis

1   cup strawberries
1   tablespoon sugar, or to taste
½   tablespoon fresh lemon juice

Pastry Cream

3   egg yolks
6   tablespoons sugar
1   cup milk
1   tablespoon cornstarch
½   teaspoon vanilla extract
2   tablespoons heavy cream
1   tablespoon Kirschwasser

Mousseline

1   cup heavy cream
1   cup Pastry Cream

1   package gelatin, softened in cold water
1   tablespoon Kirschwasser

Macerated Strawberries

1   pint strawberries, quartered
1   tablespoon sugar
1   tablespoon Kirschwasser

Puff Pastry

¾   pound puff pastry
¼   cup sugar
¼   cup sliced almonds

Fresh mint

☛ **To make the strawberry coulis:** Stem the fresh strawberries. In a food processor or blender combine the strawberries, sugar, and lemon juice, and purée until smooth. Refrigerate until ready to use.

☛ **To prepare the pastry cream:** In a large heatproof bowl whisk together the egg yolks and sugar (the mixture will be very stiff). Add the milk and cornstarch, whisking until the cornstarch is completely dissolved. Transfer the mixture to a large, heavy-bottomed saucepan, place over medium-low heat, and bring just to a boil. Reduce the heat and simmer, whisking constantly, about 2 minutes until very thick. Transfer the hot pastry cream to a clean heatproof bowl. Add the vanilla, cream, and Kirschwasser and cover the surface with buttered waxed paper. Chill the pastry cream at least 2 hours and up to 2 days. Whisk the pastry cream before using.

☛ **To make the mousseline:** In a clean mixing bowl whisk the heavy cream to form firm peaks. Beat in 1 cup of prepared pastry cream, 1 tablespoon of Kirschwasser, and the dissolved gelatin. Be careful not to overwhip.

🍓 ***To macerate the strawberries:*** In a clean bowl combine the strawberries, 1 tablespoon sugar, and Kirschwasser.

🍓 ***To make the strawberry Napoleon:*** Preheat the oven to 400°. Cut the puff pastry into four 5 x 1-inch rectangles. Brush the puff pastry lightly with water just to moisten, and sprinkle with the sugar and almonds. Let the pastry rest in the refrigerator for 15 minutes. Remove from the refrigerator, place on a baking sheet, and place in the upper third of the oven for approximately 15 minutes or until the pastry is fully puffed and the sugar and almonds have caramelized. Remove the pastry from the oven to a rack and let cool. When the pastry is sufficiently cooled, cut each rectangle horizontally into 2 even layers.

🍓 Spread mousseline cream evenly over four bottom layers of puff pastry, and top with top layers. Decorate the sides of each serving with the macerated strawberries and serve with strawberry coulis and sprigs of fresh mint.

CARAMELIZED BOURBON APPLES

Stephen Demeter
THE CAMBERLEY BROWN
LOUISVILLE, KENTUCKY

SERVES 4

Puff Pastry Cookies

1   16 x 10-inch sheet frozen puff pastry,
      thawed
2   cups confectioners' sugar

Pastry Cream

3   egg yolks
6   tablespoons sugar
1   tablespoon cornstarch
1   cup milk
½   teaspoon vanilla extract
1   tablespoon triple sec
2   tablespoons heavy cream
2   tablespoons bottled apple butter

Caramelized Bourbon Apples

3   Granny Smith apples
2   tablespoons butter
1   whole vanilla bean, split
½   cup firmly packed brown sugar
½   cup bourbon
1   teaspoon ground cinnamon
½   teaspoon grated nutmeg

Whipped Cream

1   cup heavy whipping cream
¼   cup confectioners' sugar

      Mint sprigs for garnish
      Candied violets, optional

✿ **To prepare the pastry:** Line a large baking sheet with parchment paper. Roll out the pastry ⅛-inch thick on a lightly floured surface. Transfer to a baking sheet and dust the top with confectioners' sugar. Cover with a sheet of parchment paper, and place a second baking sheet on top to prevent the pastry from rising. Refrigerate 2 hours.

✿ Preheat the oven to 350°. Slice the pastry into twelve ¼-inch thick squares and dredge in confectioners' sugar. (The "cookies" will resemble sweetened crackers.) On a surface that has been lightly coated with confectioners' sugar, roll each piece to ⅛-inch thickness. Return the pastry to the baking sheet and bake in the preheated oven for 15 to 20 minutes or until brown. Remove from the oven and let cool.

✿ **To prepare the pastry cream:** In a large heatproof bowl whisk together the egg yolks, sugar, and cornstarch (the mixture will be very stiff). Add the milk and whisk until the cornstarch is completely dissolved. Transfer the mixture to a large, heavy-bottomed saucepan, place over medium-low heat, and cook just until it comes to boil. Simmer, whisking constantly, about 2 minutes or until very thick. Transfer the hot pastry cream to a clean heatproof bowl and add the vanilla, cream, and triple sec. Cool. Cover the surface with buttered waxed paper to prevent a "skin" from forming. Chill the pastry cream at least 2 hours and up to 2 days. Whisk the pastry cream before using, and add 2 tablespoons of apple butter.

🍮 ***To prepare the caramelized bourbon apples:*** Peel, halve lengthwise, and core the apples. Slice them thinly crosswise. In a sauté pan brown the butter. Add the vanilla bean. Add the apples to the pan and cook until softened but still firm. Sprinkle in the brown sugar and cook until melted. With a slotted spoon remove the apples to a clean plate. Pour bourbon into the pan and cook, stirring constantly, about 1 minute until the sauce is smooth and syrupy. Remove the pan from the heat and add the cinnamon and nutmeg.

🍮 ***To make the whipped cream:*** Place the whipping cream in the well-chilled bowl of an electric mixer fitted with a well-chilled balloon whip. Whip on high until the cream is frothy. In a steady stream add the sugar and whip until the cream begins to form soft peaks.

🍮 ***To assemble:*** On individual dessert plates place one cookie, cover with 2 tablespoons of pastry cream, and ⅓ cup of sautéed apples. Place a second cookie on top and continue layering with another 2 tablespoons of pastry cream, and ¼ cup of sautéed apples. Top with a third cookie, and dust with confectioners' sugar. Garnish each plate with 4 tablespoons of the syrup left in the apple cooking pan, 3 tablespoons of whipped cream, and a sprig of mint. If desired, decorate the rim with crushed candied violets.

CHOCOLATE BANANA FOSTER CAKE
WITH ORANGE FOSTER CARAMEL SAUCE

Will Greenwood
SUNSET GRILL
NASHVILLE, TENNESSEE

SERVES 8

Chocolate Banana Cake

2	cups all-purpose flour
1	tablespoon baking powder
1/3	cup cocoa
1/3	cup (5 tablespoons) unsalted butter, at room temperature
2	cups sugar
3	large eggs

Mousse

1	teaspoon gelatin
1/3	cup banana rum
1	cup mashed bananas
1/2	cup heavy cream
1/3	cup sugar

Chocolate Ganache

1/3	cup heavy cream
2	tablespoons corn syrup
1/2	pound semisweet chocolate pieces

Orange Foster Sauce

1/2	cup sugar
1/4	cup water
1/4	cup Grand Marnier
1/2	cup orange juice
2	teaspoons lemon juice
3	tablespoons butter

Puff pastry rounds

2	whole bananas, sliced
1/4	cup sugar

Grand Marnier

3	cups vanilla ice cream
	Orange zest
	Fresh mint

✍ *To make the chocolate banana foster cake:* Preheat the oven to 350°. Butter a cookie sheet and dust lightly with flour, sprinkling out the excess. Sift together the flour, baking powder, and cocoa powder. In the bowl of an electric mixer combine the butter and sugar and mix on medium-high speed until creamy. Add the eggs one at a time, beating well after each addition. Add the dry ingredients and blend well. Spoon the batter onto the prepared pan, smooth the top with a rubber spatula, and bake in the preheated oven about 20 minutes until a toothpick inserted in the center is clean when removed. Let the cake cool in the pan, set on a wire rack, for 10 minutes. (The cake can be made up to 3 days ahead.) When the cake is cooled, cut enough rounds to cover the bottom, sides, and top of individual 6-inch round molds.

To make the banana mousse: In a small bowl sprinkle the gelatin over the banana rum, and let rest for 5 minutes. Place this mixture over hot water in the top of a double boiler, and heat until it melts. In the bowl of a food processor purée the bananas. Gradually add the puréed bananas to the gelatin. In the well-chilled bowl of an electric mixer fitted with a chilled balloon whip, beat the heavy cream on high speed about 1 minute until peaks just begin to form. With the mixer on low speed, add the sugar and whip about 2 minutes until soft peaks form. Be careful not to overwhip or the mousse will be grainy. Add the whipped cream to the bananas by gently folding in the cream ½ cup at a time.

To make the chocolate ganache: In a medium saucepan combine the cream and corn syrup and bring to a boil over medium heat. Remove the pan from the heat and add the chocolate pieces, stirring until the chocolate is melted and the mixture is smooth and shiny.

To make the orange foster sauce: In a medium saucepan bring the sugar and water to a boil over medium heat, and cook about 8 minutes or until the mixture reaches a light brown color and a caramel is formed. Remove the pan from the heat, add the Grand Marnier, orange juice, lemon juice, and the butter, and return the mixture to the stove. Bring to a slow boil over low heat, and cook about 1 minute until the mixture becomes liquid again.

To make the puff pastry: Preheat the oven to 350°. Grease a large sheet with softened butter. With a rolling pin, roll the puff pastry until thin and place on the prepared pan. Cover the pastry with a second clean cookie sheet in order to prevent the pastry from rising. Cook in the preheated oven for 5 minutes or until golden. Remove the pastry from the oven and allow to cool. Top each round with 5 banana slices, and sprinkle with 1 tablespoon of sugar. Place the pastry under the broiler for about 4 minutes or until the sugar just begins to caramelize.

To assemble: Line the bottom and sides of the molds with cake rounds. Sprinkle the cake with 1 tablespoon of Grand Marnier. Fill the molds with the banana mousse, placing it inside the cake. Place a final piece of cake on top of the mousse, sprinkling again with Grand Marnier, and refrigerate the molds about 30 minutes or until set. Unmold the individual molds by turning upside down onto a rack set over waxed paper. Pour the chocolate ganache over the "bombes" until completely covered. Refrigerate about 45 minutes to 1 hour or until set.

Cut the bombes in half, place one half on each individual dessert plate. Place a banana-topped puff pastry round on top of each serving. Pour ¼ cup of the orange foster sauce around the bombe, and finish with a 4-ounce scoop of ice cream on top. Garnish with 2 strips of orange zest and a sprig of fresh mint.

BANANAS FOSTER CHIMICHANGA

Renee Anzalone
BOUND'RY RESTAURANT
NASHVILLE, TENNESSEE

SERVES 4

Banana Filling

6	ripe bananas, chopped medium
1	cup golden raisins
½	cup firmly packed light brown sugar
	Juice and zest of 1 lemon
¼	cup dark rum
2	teaspoons ground cinnamon

Rum Walnut Sauce

2	cups firmly packed light brown sugar
¼	cup instant coffee
⅔	cup half-and-half
½	cup butter
2	tablespoons corn syrup
6	tablespoons dark rum
1	cup chopped walnuts

Cinnamon Ice Cream

2	cups heavy cream
1	cup milk
3	cinnamon sticks
6	large egg yolks
¼	cup molasses
½	cup packed brown sugar
½	teaspoon ground cinnamon

4	9-inch flour tortillas
1	egg, beaten lightly with 1 tablespoon water
2	ounces white chocolate
5	cups vegetable oil for frying
2	teaspoons ground cinnamon mixed with ¼ cup sugar
4	whole strawberries for garnish

To make the banana filling: In clean medium saucepan combine the bananas, raisins, light brown sugar, lemon juice, lemon zest, rum, and cinnamon, and cook over medium heat, stirring occasionally, about 7 minutes or until the mixture is thick and bubbling. Remove the pan from the heat, cool, and refrigerate until needed.

To make the rum walnut sauce: In a medium saucepan combine the light brown sugar, instant coffee, half-and-half, butter, and corn syrup. Bring to a boil over medium-high heat. Cook this mixture, stirring constantly, about 4 minutes or until the sauce is shiny and smooth. Remove the pan from the heat. Add the rum and walnuts and mix well to combine the ingredients.

To make the cinnamon ice cream: In a large saucepan combine the cream, milk, and cinnamon sticks, and bring just to a boil over medium-high heat. Remove the pan from the heat, cover, and let rest for 15 to 20 minutes. In the bowl of an electric mixer fitted with a balloon whisk, whisk the egg yolks with the sugar, molasses, brown sugar, and cinnamon. In a steady stream, gradually whisk about one-third of the cream into the egg mixture. Add this mixture to the saucepan, set over medium-low heat and cook, stirring constantly with a wooden spoon for about 5 minutes or until the custard thickens enough to coat the back of a spoon (180° on a candy thermometer). Do not let the custard boil. Strain the custard through a fine mesh strainer into a metal bowl and cover. Refrigerate, stirring occasionally, until cold. Pour into the canister of an ice cream maker and freeze according to the manufacturer's directions. Let the ice cream soften slightly before serving.

≈ **To assemble:** Brush the edges of four 9-inch flour tortillas with 1 tablespoon of egg wash. Place ½ cup of banana filling in the center of each tortilla, top with three ½-ounce pieces of white chocolate, and roll the tortilla like a burrito, beginning with the long ends and tucking in the short ends. Heat 5 cups of vegetable oil in a saucepan over medium-high heat until the temperature reaches 350°. Fry the tortillas 2 at a time until golden brown, or about 1½ minutes. Remove the burritos to paper towels to drain, and sprinkle with the cinnamon-sugar mixture. Slice on the bias, and then place on individual dessert plates (one burrito per serving). Place a scoop of ice cream alongside the burrito, with one strawberry. Spoon ¼ cup of the rum walnut sauce on the plate.

HAVANA BANANAS
WITH RUM, CHILIES, AND CHOCOLATE SAUCE

Norman Van Aken

NORMAN'S
CORAL GABLES, FLORIDA

SERVES 4

Chile Jelly

2	ancho chilies, stems and seeds discarded
2	chipotle chilies
1	quart water
6	tablespoons red currant jelly
6	tablespoons honey
2	tablespoons sherry wine vinegar

Chocolate Sauce

½	cup whipping cream
2	tablespoons unsalted butter
2	tablespoons firmly packed brown sugar
4	ounces bittersweet chocolate, chopped

Mango Sauce

2	cups diced ripe mango, approximately
1	tablespoon fresh lemon juice
2	to 3 tablespoons confectioners' sugar, or to taste
½	cup to 1 cup orange juice

Mango Ice Cream

2	cups peeled, seeded, diced ripe mangos
1¼	cups sugar
2	tablespoons fresh lime juice
2	cups milk
5	egg yolks
1	cup whipping cream

Bananas

4	ripe bananas
2	tablespoons butter
1	tablespoon dark brown sugar
2	tablespoons prepared Chile Jelly
3	tablespoons Myers dark rum
4	tulip cookie cups

🍌 **To make the chile jelly:** Remove the stems from chilies and toast in a dry skillet over medium-high heat until they begin to release their aromas, about 3 minutes. Place them in a saucepan with 1 quart of water and simmer on medium heat until the water is almost completely evaporated. Add the currant jelly, honey, and vinegar. Bring to a boil over high heat. Remove the pan from the heat and process the mixture in a food processor until smooth. Transfer to a clean bowl and cool.

🍌 **To make the chocolate sauce:** In a small heavy saucepan cook the cream, butter, and brown sugar over medium heat, stirring constantly, until the sugar is dissolved and the mixture is no longer grainy. Add the chocolate and stir until melted. Cover and chill until serving. If made in advance, the sauce may be reheated gently over low heat.

✍ *To make the mango sauce:* In a food processor purée the mango, lemon juice, and confectioners' sugar. Add enough orange juice to achieve a sauce that will pour. Correct the flavoring, adding sugar or lemon juice as needed. Force the sauce through a strainer, pressing with the back of a spoon to extract all the juices from the pulp. Cover and refrigerate until serving.

✍ *To make the mango ice cream:* In a nonreactive mixing bowl combine the mangos, ½ cup of sugar, and lime juice. Refrigerate for 1 hour. Scald the milk in a heavy saucepan. In a small mixing bowl whisk the egg yolks and ¾ cup sugar. In a thin stream whisk in the scalded milk. Return the yolk mixture to the pan and cook over medium heat about 3 minutes until thickened. The mixture should coat the back of a wooden spoon. Be careful not to let the mixture boil or it will curdle. Strain the custard into a bowl and let come to room temperature. Stir the mango mixture into the custard. Whisk in the cream. Taste for sweetness, adding more sugar if needed. Freeze the mixture in an ice cream maker according to the manufacturer's directions.

✍ *To prepare the bananas:* Peel the bananas and cut them into ¼-inch slices on the diagonal. Heat a skillet to moderately hot. Place the bananas in the skillet with the butter and brown sugar. When the butter is melted, add the chile jelly. Toss the bananas around the pan to coat them well. Remove the bananas to a plate. Add the rum to the pan, deglaze, and reduce the sauce until thickened.

✍ *To assemble:* Divide the bananas among dessert plates. Drizzle with chocolate sauce, then mango sauce, and the sauce remaining in the banana cooking pan. Place the mango ice cream in the tulip cookie cups and place on the plates.

MOCHA TOFFEE MERINGUE

Kathy Cary
LILLY'S
LOUISVILLE, KENTUCKY

SERVES 8

Meringue

8	egg whites
½	teaspoon cream of tartar
½	teaspoon salt
2	cups sugar
½	teaspoon vanilla extract

Mocha Filling

1	cup sugar
⅓	cup water
1	ounce semisweet chocolate
3	egg yolks
1	tablespoon instant coffee dissolved in 1 tablespoon warm water
1½	cups (3 sticks) butter, room temperature, cut into cubes

Chocolate Mousse

¼	pound semisweet chocolate
1½	cups heavy whipping cream
1	tablespoon Amaretto

Chantilly

1	cup heavy whipping cream
¼	cup confectioners' sugar
½	teaspoon vanilla extract
	Semisweet chocolate for chocolate curls
	Cocoa powder
3¾	ounces Heath bar or homemade toffee, chopped

☛ **To make the meringue:** Preheat the oven to 250°. In the bowl of an electric mixer fitted with a balloon whip, combine the egg whites, cream of tartar, and salt. Whisk on high speed until soft peaks form. In a steady stream add the sugar and continue beating over high speed about 3 minutes until stiff. Add the vanilla and beat about 2 minutes until dry peaks are formed. Spoon the meringue mixture into a pastry bag and pipe 2-inch circles onto a cookie sheet that has been lined with parchment paper. Continue to spiral each circle upward to about 2½ to 3 inches, leaving the center hollow, filling only the bottom completely. Place the meringues in the preheated oven and bake 1 hour and 30 minutes until dry. Remove from the oven and cool for 45 minutes before handling.

☛ **To make the mocha filling:** In a small saucepan combine the sugar and water and cook over medium heat until the sugar dissolves. Remove the pan from the heat and let cool slightly. In the top of a double boiler over hot water melt the chocolate. Remove the chocolate from the heat and let cool. In a large bowl beat the egg yolks with a whisk until smooth. Slowly whisk in the sugar water. Continue stirring and add the coffee, chocolate, and butter. Chill in the refrigerator at least 2 hours or overnight.

To make the chocolate mousse: In the top of a double boiler over 1 inch of hot water melt the chocolate slowly. Remove the chocolate from the heat, stir until smooth, and let cool. Place the heavy cream in the well-chilled bowl of an electric mixer fitted with a chilled balloon whip and beat on high speed about 1 minute until peaks form. With the mixer on low speed, add the chocolate and continue mixing until the chocolate is completely incorporated. Add the Amaretto and whip until stiff. Chill this mixture 2 hours or overnight.

To make the chantilly: Place the whipping cream in the well-chilled bowl of an electric mixer fitted with a well-chilled balloon whip. Whip on high until cream is frothy. In a steady stream add the sugar and whip until the cream begins to form peaks. Add the vanilla and whip until stiff.

To make chocolate curls: With a swivel-blade scraper shave the chocolate in long strands to make curls.

To assemble: Sprinkle cocoa powder over individual serving plates. Place a meringue bowl in the center of each plate. Fill each meringue with 4 tablespoons of mocha filling, add 1 tablespoon of chopped toffee, and top with 2 tablespoons of chocolate mousse. Finally, finish the meringue by topping off with 3 tablespoons of chantilly cream. Decorate the tops of the meringues with chocolate curls.

FROZEN LIME GANACHE PARFAIT WITH CHOCOLATE TUILES

Christopher Malta

1848 HOUSE
ATLANTA GEORGIA

SERVES 6

Silky-smooth ganache centers put a touch of surprise in smooth, frozen lime parfaits. Fruit sauces add color and bright flavor notes. Begin a day ahead to allow time for freezing.

Ganache

1	cup heavy (whipping) cream
2	tablespoons unsalted butter
2	tablespoons sugar
12	ounces bittersweet chocolate, chopped

Lime Parfait

1	envelope unflavored gelatin
2	tablespoons cold water
3	egg yolks
2	tablespoons cornstarch
1/3	cup heavy (whipping) cream
1/3	cup sugar
	Juice of 4 large fresh limes (about 2/3 cup)
3	egg whites
1/4	cup sugar

Chocolate Tuiles (makes 24 to 30 medium cookies)

3/4	cup (1 1/2 sticks) unsalted butter
2	cups sugar
6	egg whites
1/4	teaspoon vanilla extract
2	cups all-purpose flour
1	cup cocoa powder

Garnish

1	cup Peach Sauce (see page 216)
1	cup Strawberry Sauce (see page 216)
1	cup Kiwi Sauce (see page 216)
1	cup Crème Anglaise (see page 215)
6	pansies
2	sprigs fresh mint
	Chocolate Tuiles

☙ **To make the ganache:** In a deep, heavy pan stir together the cream, butter, and sugar and bring to a boil over medium-high heat. Remove the pan from the heat and add the chocolate. Let sit for 5 minutes, then stir to blend. Cover and refrigerate until chilled. Reserving 1 cup for garnish, roll the ganache between your hands to form six walnut-size balls. Refrigerate.

☙ **To make the parfait:** Soften the gelatin in the water. In the top of a double boiler or a medium metal bowl whisk together the egg yolks and cornstarch until the cornstarch is absorbed. In a deep, heavy pan over low heat stir the cream and sugar together until the sugar is dissolved. Whisking constantly, slowly pour the cream mixture into the eggs and cornstarch. Place over a double boiler with simmering water and whisk gently for 3 to 4 minutes until thickened. Whisk in the lime juice and the softened gelatin, whisking until the gelatin is completely melted and dissolved in the custard. Remove the pan from the heat and place the pan or bowl in a large bowl of ice water to cool. In a deep bowl beat the egg whites and sugar until soft peaks form. Add the egg whites all at once to the cooled lime custard and fold until blended; the egg whites will lose about half their volume. Fill six 3 x 2-inch round molds three-quarters full with the lime parfait mixture, and press a ganache ball into the center of each. Finish filling the molds with the parfait mixture, and smooth with the back of a spoon to seal. Freeze for at least 3 hours or overnight.

To make the chocolate tuiles: Preheat the oven to 350°. Using an Xacto-type blade or razor, cut a pleasing design in a thin plastic lid of the type that covers tubs of butter. Line a baking pan with parchment paper. In the large bowl of a mixer or a food processor cream the butter and sugar. Slowly beat in the egg whites. Add the vanilla. Stir in the flour until blended. Add the cocoa powder and stir until the color is uniform.

Place the stencil on the parchment paper and spread the batter over the stencil. Lift and repeat to use all of the batter. Bake 10 minutes or until the tuiles are semi-firm. Remove from the oven and immediately lift the tuiles with a spatula, placing them over a rolling pin or bottles to mold them.

To serve: Prepare the dessert plates. Warm the reserved ganache until liquefied and place it in a squeeze bottle. Draw a multi-petaled flower or other pleasing design on each plate with the ganache. Place each fruit sauce and the crème Anglaise in a separate squeeze bottle. Fill in the "petals" of the design with a mosaic of different colored fruit sauces, ending with a center of crème Anglaise.

Dip each mold up to the rim in warm water for 5 to 7 seconds to loosen, then unmold onto a large plate or platter. Cut through about one quarter of one parfait. Place both pieces on one of the serving plates, separating the pieces to reveal the ganache center. Garnish with a pansy and mint leaves. Repeat with the remaining molds.

STACKED KEY LIME PIE

Kenneth Hunsberger

OYSTERCATCHERS

TAMPA, FLORIDA

SERVES 8

Pastry Wafers

1   cup confectioners' sugar
1/2   cup all-purpose flour
3   egg whites
1/4   cup (1/2 stick) butter, melted
1/4   teaspoon vanilla extract

Key Lime Custard

    Zest of 3 key limes
1   cup sweetened condensed milk
1/2   cup key lime juice
3   egg yolks

Whipped Cream

1¾   cups heavy cream
1/4   cup sugar
1   teaspoon vanilla extract

Pastry Cream

2   egg yolks
2   tablespoons plus 2 teaspoons sugar
4   teaspoons cake flour
4   teaspoons cornstarch
2/3   cup milk
1/2   vanilla bean, split and scraped
2   teaspoons unsalted butter

Key Lime Sauce

1/4   cup key lime juice
1/4   cup Pastry Cream
1   drop green food coloring

    Fresh raspberries
    Mint sprigs
    Key lime slices

☙ **To make the pastry wafers:** Preheat the oven to 350°. Lightly film a baking pan with vegetable spray. Draw sixteen 2-inch circles (leaving 1 inch between circles) onto the baking pan, using either a round biscuit cutter or a glass. In a large mixing bowl sift together the confectioners' sugar and flour. Whisk in the egg whites, working them into the flour and sugar until smooth and well incorporated. Whisk in the melted butter and vanilla. Spoon the mixture onto the drawn circles, using a circular motion to fill the space completely. Bake for 8 to 10 minutes or until golden brown. Remove the cookies from the oven and cool on a rack. Use a cake spatula to carefully lift the baked cookies off the pan.

☙ **To make the key lime custard:** Preheat the oven to 325°. Lightly grease a small baking dish with butter. In a large mixing bowl combine the zest from the key limes, sweetened condensed milk, and key lime juice and whisk together. Add the 3 egg yolks and whisk together until well blended (the mixture will turn bright yellow). Pour the mixture into the prepared baking pan, and place in upper third of the oven. Bake for 20 minutes or until set. The center of the custard will feel firm to the touch. Remove to a rack and let cool overnight.

To make the whipped cream: Place the heavy cream in the well-chilled bowl of an electric mixer fitted with a well-chilled balloon whip. Whip on low speed until the cream is frothy. In a steady stream add the sugar and whip, gradually increasing the mixer's speed until the cream begins to form peaks. Add the vanilla and whip until soft peaks form. Or you may make by hand in a large mixing bowl, with a large balloon whisk.

To make the pastry cream: In the clean bowl of an electric mixer fitted with a whisk, beat the egg yolks with sugar on high speed until the mixture is thick and pale yellow. Sift the flour and cornstarch together and whisk into the egg yolk mixture. In a noncorrosive saucepan scald the milk with the vanilla bean. Pour about one-fourth of the hot milk into the egg yolk mixture, whisking constantly. Return this mixture to the saucepan, whisking constantly until the mixture thickens, reaching a pudding-like consistency. Remove the pan from the heat and blend in the butter. Strain into a bowl and cover with film wrap, pressing down on the surface of the cream so that a skin will not form. Cool. Refrigerate until needed.

To make the key lime sauce: In a medium mixing bowl whisk together the key lime juice, pastry cream, and green food coloring.

To assemble: In the center of a dessert plate place one pastry wafer. On one side of the wafer place a 2-ounce scoop of key lime custard. Place a second wafer on top of the custard, and top with another 2-ounce scoop of custard. Repeat for one more layer, finishing with a fourth wafer. Dust the top with confectioners' sugar, and garnish the plate with key lime sauce, whipped cream, raspberries, mint, and slices of lime.

LEMON CHEESECAKE

Jose Gutierrez
CHEZ PHILIPPE
MEMPHIS, TENNESSEE

SERVES 8

This makes a wonderful light-as-air cheesecake that would be an ideal ending for a summer meal.

Crust

12	ounces hazelnuts, ground
12	ounces almonds, ground
9	tablespoons butter, melted
½	cup sugar

Filling

2½	pounds cream cheese, softened
1¼	cups sugar
7	whole eggs
5	egg yolks
¼	cup freshly squeezed lemon juice
	Zest of 2 lemons
2	tablespoons vanilla extract
6	tablespoons heavy cream, whipped to soft peaks

Lemon Sauce

½	cup lemon juice
½	cup orange juice
1½	tablespoons cornstarch
2	tablespoons unsalted butter
¼	cup sugar
1	tablespoon grated lemon zest

Sweet Potato Garnish

1	sweet potato, peeled
5	cups vegetable oil for frying
½	cup confectioners' sugar

Light brown sugar for dusting cake

☛ **To make the crust:** Position the rack in center of the oven and preheat to 350°. Finely grind the nuts in a food processor. Add the butter and sugar, and blend using on/off turns just until moist. Press the nut mixture firmly onto the bottom of a 10 x 13-inch sheet pan. Bake about 10 minutes or until the crust is set. Cool. Lower the oven temperature to 250°.

☛ **To make the filling:** In the bowl of an electric mixer, beat the cream cheese and sugar together. Add the eggs and egg yolks, one at a time, beating just until combined. Add the lemon juice, lemon zest, and vanilla and beat until smooth. Fold in the whipped cream. Pour the filling into the crust, spreading evenly. Bake about 18 minutes until the center moves only slightly when the pan is shaken and the top is lightly colored. (The cake will continue to firm up in the refrigerator.) Transfer the cake to a rack and cool for 5 minutes.

✍ To make the lemon sauce: In a medium bowl whisk the juices and cornstarch until the cornstarch dissolves. In a small heavy saucepan melt the butter over medium-high heat. Whisk in the sugar, lemon zest, and orange juice mixture, and cook about 4 minutes or until the sauce boils and thickens slightly. Remove the pan from the heat and cool. (Can be made 2 days ahead, covered, and chilled. Bring to room temperature before serving.)

✍ To make the sweet potato garnish: Using a mandolin, cut the sweet potato into strings. In a saucepan heat the vegetable oil over medium-high heat until the temperature reaches 350°. Dredge the sweet potato strings in confectioners' sugar and fry (if necessary, lower the heat to prevent the strings from burning) until crisp. Remove to paper towels to drain.

✍ To finish and present: Set the broiler rack so the cheesecake will be 2 to 3 inches from heat and preheat the broiler. Sift light brown sugar evenly over the cheesecake and broil about 2 minutes until the sugar is melted and caramelized. (Alternately, raw sugar may be sprinkled over cake and caramelized with a blowtorch.) With a cookie cutter, cut the cheesecake into 3-inch rounds. Drizzle ¼ cup of lemon sauce on individual dessert plates. Center a cheesecake round on the dessert plate, top with sweet potato strings, and repeat, adding 2 more layers of cake and sweet potato strings and finishing with a layer of strings.

WHITE CHOCOLATE BLACK JACK ICE CREAM SANDWICHES

Allen Rubin White

HERMITAGE HOTEL
NASHVILLE, TENNESSEE

SERVES 4

White Chocolate Black Jack Ice Cream

½	cup heavy cream
1	cup cold whole milk
½	vanilla bean, split lengthwise and scraped
5	egg yolks
½	cup sugar
5	ounces white chocolate
2	tablespoons Jack Daniel's whiskey

Pecan Meringues

5	egg whites
1	cup sugar
½	cup finely chopped pecans
	Pinch of salt

Sauce

1	cup white wine
2	cups water
6	peaches
¼	cup honey
2	tablespoons fresh lemon juice
2	vanilla beans

Fresh blackberries for garnish

❧ **To make the white chocolate black jack ice cream:** In a large saucepan combine the cream, milk, and vanilla bean, and bring just to a boil over medium-high heat. Remove the pan from the heat, cover, and let rest for 15 to 20 minutes. In the bowl of an electric mixer fitted with a balloon whisk, whisk the egg yolks with the sugar.

❧ Remove the vanilla bean from the saucepan. In a steady stream gradually whisk about one-third of the cream into the egg mixture. Add this mixture to the remaining cream-milk mixture in the saucepan and cook over medium-low heat, stirring constantly with a wooden spoon for about 5 minutes or until the custard thickens enough to coat the back of a spoon (180° on a candy thermometer). Do not let the custard boil. Strain the custard through a fine mesh strainer into a metal bowl set in an ice bath. Stir occasionally, until cold.

❧ In the top of a double boiler set over simmering water melt the white chocolate. Stir the chocolate into the cooled custard and strain once more. Stir in the whiskey, cover, and refrigerate until chilled. When well chilled, pour into the canister of an ice cream maker and freeze according to the manufacturer's directions. Remove the ice cream from the ice cream maker and spread in a shallow 10 x 12-inch pan to a thickness of about ½ inch. Freeze until firm. While the ice cream is freezing, prepare the meringues that will be used to make the sandwiches.

✍ **To make the pecan meringues:** Preheat the oven to 250°. Line a baking pan with parchment paper. Trace 4-inch circles onto the parchment paper. In the bowl of an electric mixer beat the egg whites and salt together until they just hold soft peaks. Add the sugar in a stream and beat until the meringue holds stiff, glossy peaks. Gently fold in the chopped pecans. Spoon the meringue mixture into pastry bag and pipe spirals onto the drawn circles. Fill in the circles completely. Completed circles should be about ¼-inch thick. Smooth the tops with a rubber spatula or table knife. Place the meringues in the preheated oven and bake 1 hour and 30 minutes or until dry. Remove the paper with the meringues and cool on a wire rack. When cooled, lift the meringues from the paper. Set aside until ready to use.

✍ **To make the ice cream sandwiches:** Remove the ice cream from the freezer, and using a cookie cutter, cut the ice cream into circles the same diameter as the meringues. Carefully lift the ice cream circles from the pan with a rubber spatula, and place on the smooth side of one of the meringue shells. Top with another shell. The sandwiches may be assembled and stored in the freezer while the sauce is prepared.

✍ **To make the sauce:** In a heavy-bottomed saucepan bring the wine and water to a simmer. Split and scrape the vanilla beans into the simmering mixture. Add the peaches to the liquid and poach until the skin begins to pull away. With a slotted spoon remove the peaches from the pan, and place them in a bowl of ice water just long enough to stop the cooking process. Meanwhile, reduce the peach cooking liquid over high heat to 1 cup or until a syrupy consistency is achieved. Strain the liquid into a container to remove the vanilla seeds, and add the honey and lemon juice.

✍ Remove the peaches from the ice water. Peel, slice in half, and remove the pit. Slice the peach halves into 4 sections and remove any remaining pit material with a small melon baller. Add the peaches to the bowl with the syrup, and let steep until the syrup has cooled.

✍ **To serve:** Preheat the broiler. Dust an assembled ice cream sandwich with confectioners' sugar and lightly caramelize the top by placing under the broiler for 10 seconds. Place the sandwiches in the center of individual dessert plates and surround with the peach sauce. Garnish with fresh blackberries and finely chopped pecans.

STRAWBERRY APPLE CHEESE STRUDEL

Shane Gorringe

ZOE'S BAKERY
COVINGTON, LOUISIANA

SERVES 8

This luscious dessert is not without effort, but the results are well worth it. Be advised, however, when you begin making the strudel dough, you must be prepared to complete the recipe, as once the dough is stretched it will quickly dry and become brittle.

Apple Crisps

2   Granny Smith apples
2   tablespoons sugar

Apple Filling

2   pounds Granny Smith apples

Strawberry Sauce

2   cups hulled and sliced fresh strawberries
1/4   cup sugar
1   tablespoon lemon juice
1   cup fresh strawberries, hulled and left
     whole

Cheese Filling

8   ounces cream cheese, softened
1/4   cup sugar
2   teaspoons lemon juice
1   teaspoon freshly grated lemon zest
1   large egg yolk

Cinnamon Sugar

1   tablespoon sugar combined with
     1/4 teaspoon cinnamon

Strudel

3   cups unbleached all-purpose flour
1   large egg, beaten
3/4   cup warm water
1/2   teaspoon lemon juice
1/4   cup vegetable oil
     Pinch of salt
1/2   cup (1 stick) butter, melted
1/2   cup dry breadcrumbs

Confectioners' sugar for dusting
Vanilla ice cream
Fresh mint

🍃 **To make the apple crisps:** Preheat the oven to 125°. Line a sheet pan with parchment paper. Peel, core, and slice the apples crosswise into 1/4-inch thick slices. Arrange the apple slices in a fan shape on the prepared pan, cover with sugar, and bake in the oven for 3 hours or until dried.

🍃 **To prepare the apple filling:** Peel and core apples, and slice crosswise in 1/4-inch slices.

🙟 **To make the strawberry sauce:** In a medium heavy-bottomed saucepan combine the sliced strawberries, sugar, and lemon juice, and heat just to a boil, stirring occasionally to prevent scorching. As soon as the sauce comes to a boil, remove the pan from the heat, strain, and add the whole strawberries. Let the whole strawberries remain in the sauce until soft. Remove the whole berries and reserve the sauce.

🙟 **To make the cheese filling:** In the bowl of an electric mixer cream together the cream cheese and sugar. Add the lemon juice and zest, and finally add the yolk. Beat until smooth. Cover the filling and chill for at least 1 hour and up to 24 hours.

🙟 **To make the strudel:** Sift the flour onto a pastry board and make a well in the center. Add the egg, water, lemon juice, oil, and salt to the well and thoroughly mix. Work the flour in with your fingertips to form coarse crumbs. If the crumbs seem dry, add water. Press the dough into a ball, wrap in plastic, and let rest in the refrigerator for 2 hours.

🙟 Flour the work surface and knead the dough for 5 to 7 minutes. Or you may knead the dough in a mixer fitted with a dough hook. Remove the dough to a clean mixing bowl, cover with a towel, and let rest 30 minutes.

🙟 **To finish and assemble the strudel:** Preheat the oven to 400°. After the dough has rested, cover the worktable with a lightly floured cloth, and roll the dough as thin as possible. If necessary, cut the dough so that you have a very thin 9 x 18-inch rectangle. Cover the dough with a damp towel and let rest for 15 minutes. Brush the dough with melted butter and proceed immediately with filling. Place a layer of breadcrumbs at one end of the dough, then add the sliced apples. Next add the sliced strawberries. Spoon the cream cheese mixture on top, and sprinkle with cinnamon sugar. If necessary, trim the thick outer edges of the dough.

🙟 Fold the short ends of the dough over the filling. Fold the long side over the filling and then roll up to enclose. Arrange the strudel on an unbuttered baking sheet, seam side down, and paint with melted butter. Bake the strudel for 15 minutes. Reduce the temperature to 375° and bake about 25 minutes longer until deep golden brown. Immediately slide a long spatula under the strudel to loosen it from the baking sheet. Transfer the strudel to a platter and let stand 10 minutes. Cut away 1 inch from each end. Slice diagonally, sprinkle with confectioners' sugar, and place on a serving tray. Arrange the apple crisps alongside. Place a scoop of vanilla ice cream on the crisps, top with more crisps, and place some of the macerated strawberries on the plate. Drizzle with the strawberry sauce and add a sprig of mint.

CARDAMOM CAKE WITH SAFFRON ICE CREAM

Anoosh Shariat

SHARIAT'S
LOUISVILLE, KENTUCKY

SERVES 8

Cardamom Cake

4	large eggs
1	cup sugar
1	cup (2 sticks) butter
1	teaspoon ground cardamom
3	teaspoons rose water
1	cup plain yogurt
2	cups all-purpose flour
1	teaspoon baking powder

Saffron Ice Cream

2	cups cream
1	gram saffron, ground
8	egg yolks
1	cup sugar
½	cup toasted and chopped pistachio nuts

Caramel Sauce

2	cups sugar
½	cup hot water
½	gram saffron

✒ *To make the cardamom cake:* Position the rack in the center of the oven and preheat to 325 °. Butter two 8-inch round cake pans with 2-inch-high sides. Line the bottom of the pans with waxed paper and butter the paper. In a metal bowl set over a pan of barely simmering water, beat the egg yolks and sugar with a whisk about 5 minutes until creamy. Remove the pan from the heat and transfer to the large bowl of an electric mixer. Beat on high speed until cool. In a separate pan melt the butter over low heat. Remove the butter from the heat and let cool. To the egg mixture add the ground cardamom, rose water, yogurt, and melted butter, and mix on low speed. In a medium bowl sift together the flour and baking powder. Slowly add the dry ingredients to the egg mixture. (To prevent the flour from flying out of the mixer, make sure the mixer is set on low speed.) Divide the batter equally between the prepared pans. Bake about 25 minutes until golden brown and a tester inserted into the center of the cakes comes out clean. Transfer pans to racks. Cool 10 minutes. Using small sharp knife, cut around sides of pan to loosen cakes. Turn out cakes onto racks and cool completely. Peel off the waxed paper. (Can be prepared 1 day ahead. Wrap tightly in plastic and store at room temperature.)

✒ *To make the saffron ice cream:* In a large saucepan combine the cream and saffron and bring just to a boil over medium-high heat. Remove the pan from the heat, cover, and let rest 15 to 20 minutes. In the bowl of an electric mixer fitted with a balloon whisk, whisk the egg yolks with the sugar. In a steady stream, gradually whisk about ⅓ of the cream into the egg mixture. Add this mixture to the saucepan and cook over medium-low heat, stirring constantly with a wooden spoon for about 5 minutes or until the custard thickens enough to coat the back of a spoon (180° on a candy thermometer). Do not let the custard boil. Strain the custard through a fine mesh strainer into a metal bowl. Cover and refrigerate, stirring occasionally, until cold. Pour into the canister of an ice cream maker and freeze according to the manufacturer's directions. Let the ice cream soften slightly before serving. Garnish with pistachio nuts.

To make the caramel sauce: In a large, deep, heavy skillet cook the sugar over moderately high heat, stirring constantly with a fork, until it is melted and turns a deep golden caramel. Remove the skillet from the heat, and carefully pour the water into the side of it a little at a time. Cook the mixture over moderate heat, stirring constantly, until the caramel is dissolved. Simmer it for 2 minutes. Remove the skillet from the heat, add the saffron, and stir the mixture. Pour the sauce into a heatproof pitcher or glass measure, and let it cool slightly. (The sauce will thicken as it cools. To return the sauce to a liquid state, set the pitcher in a saucepan of barely simmering water and stir the sauce until it reaches the desired consistency.) Serve the sauce warm over ice cream.

To present: After the cake has cooled, run a sharp knife around the edges of the cake pans, and invert onto a cake rack. Peel off the waxed paper and invert the cakes onto a clean plate. Cut each cake into quarters and place on individual dessert plates. Drizzle with saffron caramel sauce and place 2 scoops of ice cream on the cake.

RICH DENSE CHOCOLATE PECAN TORTE

Elizabeth Terry
ELIZABETH'S ON 37TH
SAVANNAH, GEORGIA

SERVES 8

Caramel Pecan Crust

1	cup (3½ ounces) pecan pieces
⅓	cup firmly packed light brown sugar
¼	teaspoon grated nutmeg
2	tablespoons all-purpose flour
2	tablespoons butter, chilled and cut into pieces

Filling

6	ounces sweet chocolate
2	ounces bitter chocolate
2	egg yolks
1	scant cup heavy cream

Chocolate Whipped Cream

1¾	cups heavy cream
¼	cup sugar
3	tablespoons cocoa
1	teaspoon vanilla extract

Berry Purée

2	cups strawberries and raspberries
1	to 1½ tablespoons sugar
1	teaspoon triple sec
1	tablespoon lemon juice

English Cream

3	egg yolks
6	tablespoons sugar
1	tablespoon cornstarch
1	cup milk
½	teaspoon vanilla extract
2	tablespoons heavy cream
1	tablespoon triple sec

Fresh strawberries
Fresh mint leaves

To make the pecan crust: Preheat the oven to 325°. Line an 8-inch springform pan with parchment paper. In the bowl of a food processor combine the nuts, brown sugar, nutmeg, flour, and butter. Process until the nuts are crushed and the butter is entirely incorporated. Spread the crumbs on top of the paper in the springform pan, press gently, and bake 8 minutes. Remove the crust from the oven and let cool.

To make the filling: Place the chocolates in the top of a double boiler over hot water. Stir the chocolates until melted. Whisk in the egg yolks. Remove the pan from the heat. In a small saucepan heat the cream over medium heat until hot but not boiling. Immediately whisk the cream into the melted chocolate. When thoroughly combined, the mixture will be smooth, with a rich dark brown color. Pour the filling into the prepared crust. Chill in the refrigerator at least 1 hour. Run a knife around the edge of the pan, and remove the sides. The torte should remain at room temperature for 15 minutes before serving.

To make the chocolate whipped cream: Place the whipping cream in the well-chilled bowl of an electric mixer fitted with a well-chilled balloon whip. Whip on low speed until the cream is frothy. In a steady stream add the sugar and cocoa and whip, gradually increasing the mixer's speed until the cream begins to form peaks. Add the vanilla and whip until soft peaks form. Spoon the whipped cream into a pastry bag fitted with a metal tube.

To make the berry purée: In the bowl of a food processor combine the strawberries and raspberries, sugar, triple sec, and lemon juice. Blend until liquid, and refrigerate until needed.

To make the English cream: In a large heatproof bowl whisk together the yolks and sugar (the mixture will be very stiff). Add the milk and cornstarch, whisking until cornstarch is completely dissolved. Transfer the mixture to a large, heavy-bottomed saucepan, place over medium-low heat, and bring just to a boil. Simmer, whisking constantly, about 2 minutes until very thick. Transfer the hot pastry cream to a clean heatproof bowl and add the vanilla, cream, and triple sec. Cover the surface with buttered waxed paper. Chill the pastry cream at least 2 hours and up to 2 days. Whisk the pastry cream before using.

To assemble: Pipe the whipped cream over the torte, completely covering the torte. Cut into individual slices and place on dessert plates. Spoon ⅓ cup of berry purée and ¼ cup of English cream onto each plate. Garnish with sliced fresh strawberries and fresh mint.

WARM CENTER CHOCOLATE PYRAMID CAKE

Gene Bjorkand

AUBERGINE
MEMPHIS, TENNESSEE

SERVES 6

Because the chocolate cakes need to freeze 24 hours before they can be baked, this dessert takes some advance planning.

Nuggets

5	ounces semisweet chocolate
1	cup heavy cream
1/4	cup (1/2 stick) butter
1/2	cup plus 2 tablespoons water

Chocolate Cake

2	eggs, separated
1/4	teaspoon cream of tartar
1/4	teaspoon salt
1/2	cup sugar
4	ounces semisweet chocolate

3	tablespoons cake flour, sifted
3	tablespoons butter, at room temperature
3	tablespoons almond powder
6	tablespoons sugar

Chocolate Sauce

5	tablespoons sugar
7	tablespoons water
2	tablespoons cocoa powder
1/4	cup heavy cream

Confectioners' sugar for dusting cakes

☞ *To make the nuggets:* In a heavy-bottomed saucepan melt the chocolate, cream, butter, and water over low heat. Mix gently until well combined and pour into a small ice cube tray. Freeze for 24 hours. While the nuggets are freezing, proceed with the cake recipe and let the cake remain in the refrigerator until you are ready to complete the dessert.

☞ *To make the chocolate cake:* Lightly butter and dust with flour six 4-ounce cupcake molds or cups in a muffin tin. Separate the eggs. Place the egg whites, cream of tartar, and salt in the bowl of an electric mixer fitted with a balloon whip. On high speed whisk until soft peaks form. In a steady stream add the sugar and continue beating on high speed until stiff. Melt the chocolate in the top of a double boiler over simmering water. While maintaining a very low heat, gradually add the cake flour, mixing until a paste is formed. Add the softened butter, mixing until it is well incorporated. Mix in the almond powder and sugar. Remove the pan from the heat and add the egg yolks. Gently fold in the egg whites, and set aside. The cake batter will be somewhat grainy. Fill the prepared molds with the cake batter. Place the frozen nuggets in the center of each mold (not the bottom) and let the molds rest in the freezer 24 hours before baking.

✑ **To make the chocolate sauce:** In a medium saucepan combine the sugar, water, cocoa powder, and cream, and simmer over low heat for 30 minutes. Remove the pan from the heat and transfer to a clean container. Cover and chill for 24 hours.

✑ **To assemble:** Preheat the oven to 350°. Place the cake molds in the upper third of the oven and bake for 15 minutes or until firm. While the molds are baking, decorate individual dessert plates with the chocolate sauce. The chef likes to serve the sauce cold to contrast with the warm cakes but, if you prefer, the sauce may be warmed slowly over a low heat. Remove the cakes from the oven and let cool on a rack. To remove the cakes from the molds, carefully run a sharp knife around the inner edge of the mold and invert onto dessert plates. Sprinkle with confectioners' sugar.

CHOCOLATE GENOISE TRUFFLE TORTE WITH FRESH BERRIES

Libby Stritch

SLIGHTLY NORTH OF BROAD
CHARLESTON, SOUTH CAROLINA

SERVES 8

Although the ingredient list and number of techniques may seem formidable, this elegant dessert is actually quite easy to execute.

Chocolate Genoise

5	eggs
3/4	cup sugar
1/3	cup all-purpose flour
1/3	cup cocoa powder
1	tablespoon butter
1	tablespoon brandy

Simple Syrup

1	cup sugar
1	cup water

Chocolate Truffle Cream

17	ounces dark chocolate, chopped
1½	cups heavy cream
3	egg yolks
6	tablespoons Chambord

White Chocolate Truffle Cream

17	ounces white chocolate, chopped
1½	cups heavy cream
3	egg yolks
6	tablespoons Chambord

Macerated Raspberries

½	cup sugar
	Zest and juice from 2 oranges
	Zest and juice from 2 lemons
6	tablespoons Chambord
3	pints fresh raspberries

Garnish

	Fresh raspberries
	White chocolate shavings
	Fresh mint

✒ **To make the genoise:** Preheat the oven to 350°. Line the bottom of a greased 10½-inch springform pan with waxed paper, grease the paper, and dust the pan with flour, knocking out the excess. In the large bowl of an electric mixer beat the eggs with the sugar on high speed for 5 minutes or until the mixture is pale yellow and forms a ribbon when the beaters are lifted. In a separate bowl sift the flour and cocoa together. Fold the dry ingredients into the egg mixture until the batter is just combined. In a small saucepan over low heat melt the butter with the brandy. Fold the butter mixture into the batter gently but thoroughly. Pour the batter into the pan, smoothing the top. Bake the cake in the middle of the oven for 20 minutes or until a tester comes out clean. Transfer the cake to a rack and let cool.

🥄 ***To make the simple syrup:*** In a small heavy-bottomed saucepan combine the sugar and water and let this mixture come to a slow simmer over medium heat. Cook, stirring occasionally, until a syrup is formed. Remove the pan from the heat.

🥄 ***To make the chocolate truffle cream:*** In a metal bowl set over a pan of barely simmering water, melt the dark chocolate with 1¼ cups of heavy cream, stirring until the mixture is smooth. Remove the bowl from the heat and let the mixture cool. In the large bowl of an electric mixer combine the egg yolks, Chambord, and ¼ cup of cream and beat on high speed until the mixture is tripled in volume. Fold in the dark chocolate mixture gently but thoroughly.

🥄 Brush the genoise with 2 tablespoons of simple syrup. While still in the springform pan, spoon the chocolate truffle cream onto the cake, spreading to cover, until cream is about 1 inch thick. Refrigerate while making the white chocolate truffle cream.

🥄 ***To make the white chocolate truffle cream:*** In a metal bowl set over a pan of barely simmering water melt the white chocolate with 1¼ cups of heavy cream, stirring until the mixture is smooth. Remove the bowl from the heat and let the mixture cool. In the large bowl of an electric mixer combine the egg yolks, Chambord, and ¼ cup of cream and beat on high speed until the mixture is tripled in volume. Fold in the white chocolate mixture gently but thoroughly.

🥄 ***To make the macerated raspberries:*** In a clean mixing bowl combine the sugar, orange juice, orange zest, lemon juice, lemon zest, Chambord, and raspberries. Stir until smooth and refrigerate, covered.

🥄 ***To assemble:*** Remove the cake from the refrigerator and spread the white chocolate truffle cream onto the chocolate truffle cream and smooth with a rubber spatula. The cream should be level with the top of the pan. Refrigerate for at least 30 minutes. Run a sharp knife around the edge and remove the side of the pan. Decorate the finished cake with fresh raspberries and white chocolate shavings.

🥄 ***To present:*** Place slices of cake on individual serving plates and spoon macerated raspberries on the plates. Garnish with sprigs of fresh mint.

STUFFED STRAWBERRIES WITH A TOMATO-CINNAMON CONFITURE, BALSAMIC VINEGAR, AND TOMATO LIQUEUR

Robert Waggoner
WILD BOAR RESTAURANT
NASHVILLE, TENNESSEE

SERVES 4

Stuffing

1	pound Roma tomatoes, peeled and seeded
1¼	cups sugar
2	sticks cinnamon
¼	cup water

Strawberries

12	strawberries
12	sprigs fresh mint
½	pint fresh raspberries
¼	cup balsamic vinegar

✍ **To make the stuffing:** Coarsely chop the tomatoes and place them in a heavy-bottomed medium saucepan. Add the sugar, cinnamon, and water. Cook about 15 minutes until thickened and the mixture is the consistency of jam. As the mixture cooks, brush the sides of the saucepan with a damp pastry brush to keep the sugar from caramelizing. Remove the tomato jam to a clean bowl. Let cool, cover, and store in the refrigerator.

✍ **To make the strawberries:** Wash the strawberries and remove the stems. Carve the tops and trim the bottom of the strawberries so that they will stand. Spoon 1 teaspoon of tomato jam into each strawberry. Place 3 strawberries on each of 4 individual dessert plates. Garnish the top of each strawberry with a sprig of fresh mint, and arrange fresh raspberries decoratively around the plate. Drizzle each strawberry with 1 teaspoon of balsamic vinegar.

THE CHEFS

JAMIE ADAMS

Veni, Vidi, Vici
Atlanta, Georgia

Veni, Vidi, Vici's executive chef, Jamie Adams, was born and raised in Atlanta. Following studies in English at Georgia State University, he worked his way through the restaurants, hotels, and resorts of Italy while indulging his passion for Italian food and learning the nuances and techniques of the cuisine. He was the sous chef at the Locanda Del Sant Uffizzio near Asti, and the sous chef in Restaurant Ceresole in Cremona. He even taught a five-day cooking course in Venice's grand hotel, the Hotel Cipriani.

With skills in Italian preparation learned, Adams returned to the US to work for the Buckhead Life Group of restaurants. During his tenure he has served in several positions – working at the original Fish Market, and as sous chef at the group's highly regarded Pricci restaurant. In 1993 he was promoted to executive chef at Veni, Vidi, Vici, an ambition he had long aspired to. As chef, Adams practices the fine art of Italian cookery, employing his familiarity with Italy's bounty and concepts to develop original and delectable dishes. One of the kitchen's highlights is a wide selection of antipasti picoli (small appetizers) that includes grilled eggplant rolls stuffed with

goat cheese on panzanella salad and speck (smoked prosciutto with a tomato and mozzarella salad).

Jamie Adams's recipe for Gnocchi Stuffed with Fonduta in Parmesan Cheese-Cream Sauce is on page 11.

PAUL ALBRECHT

Pano's and Paul's
Atlanta, Georgia

Since the day he opened Pano's and Paul's, Paul Albrecht has been revolutionizing dining in Atlanta, Georgia. Today, nearly two decades later, he and his partner, Pano Karatassos, head their Buckhead Life Restaurant Group, which includes nine of the city's most flourishing restaurants and food operations.

Albrecht began his career learning the restaurant business at the Hotel and Restaurant School in Munich, Germany. After graduation, he cooked at the Beaurivage and Restaurant Grand Chene in Lausanne, Switzerland, before proceeding to the Hotel Sonesta in Washington, D.C. During a stint at the Lodge of the Four Seasons in Missouri, he met and formed a partnership with Pano Karatassos, and in 1979 the team opened their first restaurant—Pano's and Paul's.

Together they have been credited with single handedly raising the culinary standards of Atlanta. As Anne Bryn reported in the *Atlanta Journal-Constitution*, "Turning Atlantans on to fine food was about as easy as getting Scarlett to give up Ashley. If any credit is due, it goes first to the team of Pano Karatassos and Paul Albrecht, who pooled their savings, left Lake of the Ozarks, Missouri, and opened Pano's & Paul's in January of 1979. The duo's commitment to Atlanta's fine dining has given us excellent restaurants . . . worthy of their stars."

The American/Continental menu is replete with enticing dishes, such as crisp potato- wrapped Florida grouper fillet with sesame spinach; batter-fried lobster tails; and sautéed almond-crusted veal steak with osietta pasta, mushrooms, and a Marsala sauce. Albrecht is no less concerned with the quality of the ingredients than he is with the innovation on the menu. Fish is purchased whole from a select list of suppliers, veal saddles are used exclusively, and all food on the menu is prepared fresh. Mâche and arugula are flown in from Belgium, wild mushrooms and miniature vegetables arrive from California.

Over the years awards and prizes have been heaped on Albrecht and his team. There is scarcely a toque, a fork, a platter, or a prize in the industry that they have not received. For example, *Esquire* magazine named Pano's and Paul's the "Second Best Restaurant in the Country for Service"; they were selected by the *Zagat Guide* as "Atlanta's Favorite Fine Dining Restaurant," by *Connoisseur* magazine as "One of the World's Top 40 Restaurants," and *Atlanta* magazine's "Best Overall Restaurant." The restaurant is a consistent Mobil four-star and AAA four-diamond winner.

Paul Albrecht's recipe for Maine Lobster with Celery Root and Apple Salad is on page 48, and Guinea Hen "Souva Roff" Modern with Foie Gras, Truffles, and Morels is on page 99.

SCOTT ALDERSON
Criolla's Restaurant
Grayton Beach, Florida

Scott Alderson, chef at Criolla's, likes to think of his cooking as a kind of new Florida fare, the result of years of study at some of the South's finest restaurants. A graduate of the Asheville-Buncombe Community College in Asheville, North Carolina, Alderson received an A.A.S. degree in culinary technology in 1988. While in school, he landed his first job with Mark Rosenstein at the Marketplace in Asheville. During a three-year tenure he rose to sous chef. His next stops were on the Cashiers, North Carolina country club circuit—first at the Wade Hampton Golf Club, then at Chatooga Club. From there it was back to his native Florida and Café Maxx in Pompano Beach.

In 1990 he was able to realize a dream to work with Jeremiah Tower at his famous Stars restaurant in San Francisco. From there, inspired by the high energy, sophisticated cuisine, he traveled across the countryto take on the sous chef's position at the Harbourwatch in Harwichport, Cape Cod, Massachusetts. But it wasn't long before Alderson was eager to return to his homeland, and in 1992 he went to work as the sous chef at Casa Vecchia in Ft. Lauderdale. A year later, he left Ft. Lauderdale for Bud & Alley's in Seaside, Florida, and then in April 1995 Johnny Earles hired him to take on the chef's position at Criolla's.

Alderson is delighted to be in the chef's chair at what many consider to be the "dining gem" of the Florida Gulf Coast. He is experimenting with the Florida products that he loves, adding new original recipes to the menu. He is proud to work with owner Johnny Earles in the creation of the New Orleans/Caribbean dishes that have made the restaurant famous. *Florida Trend* magazine called the menu a "masterpiece," declaring the recipes a blend of "the Cajun spices of the back-bayou with the finesse of French flavor." Alderson truly believes in Earles's philosophy "I just do it right, and people get off on it." It works for Alderson as well, who was recently invited to consult on the menu at a neighboring restaurant, Bayside Grill in Orange Beach, Alabama.

Scott Alderson's recipe for Scallop Escabeche is on page 4.

RENÉE ANZALONE

Bound'ry Restaurant
Nashville, Tennessee

Renee Anzalone learned to cook at her mother's knee, that is, her mother's knee in the kitchen of the restaurant she owned. Anzalone recalls hours of enjoyment at the stoves and in the dining room of the family's Hook n' Ladder restaurant in western New York State. But making pastries was always her favorite activity, so when she moved to Los Angeles she sought a job in a pastry kitchen. Ultimately, she landed a position making desserts and confections for some of the country's best-known celebrities at Schatzi's on Main. A favorite recollection is the night she cooked for Arnold Schwarzenegger.

Now at Nashville's Bound'ry, Anzalone has found her southern home in the restaurant's sweet-smelling pastry and bread kitchen. Here she works her indulgent magic on guests who are captivated by her delicate dessert creations and crusty breads. And it is certainly her end-of-meal triumphs that have contributed to restaurant accolades that include *Nashville* magazine's "Best New Restaurant," of 1996.

Renee Anzalone's recipe for Bananas Foster Chimichanga is on page 148.

NICK APOSTLE

Nick's
Jackson, Mississippi

Nick Apostle grew up in the restaurant business, working in his father's restaurant during his high school and college years. After graduating with a business degree from the University of Mississippi, Apostle went to work full-time at his father's place, Paul's Restaurant. He remained there until 1983 when he opened his present Nick's in Jackson. He has been busily building restaurants ever since.

In 1986 Apostle helped cofound the Crescent City Seafood Grill, Mahogany Bar, and the Purple Parrot Café in Hattiesburg, Mississippi, and in 1989 he assisted in the establishment of Capitol Seafood in Jackson. In 1992 Apostle cooperated in the construction of Rodeo's and Stockyard Steaks, two restaurants in which he now shares ownership.

Despite running a myriad of restaurants, Apostle finds time to work in community activities. For the last four years he has cochaired the menu selection and served as a judge for the March of Dimes Gala. He was responsible for coordinating the food service for the Southern Governor's Conference in 1989 and has been involved in coordinating the last two Governor's Inaugural Balls.

A leader in the restaurant community as well, Nick is past president and current chairman of the board of the Mississippi Restaurant Association as well as president of the Jackson chapter of the association. He is one of the founders and presently serves as chairman of the board of trustees for the Mississippi Service Industry Self Funded Workmen's Compensation Fund, and he is president of the board of directors for Metro Jackson's Convention and Visitors Bureau. He is a past guest chef at the Salute to Southern Chefs, which benefits Share Our Strength.

Nick Apostle's recipe for Spicy Scallops

with Chili Sauce is on page 21, and Paneéd Catfish with Crayfish Stuffing in Herb Butter Sauce is on page 80.

STEPHEN AUSTIN

Hedgerose Heights Inn
Atlanta, Georgia

Stephen Austin celebrates his love of food in every dish he prepares for the Hedgerose Heights Inn. Atlantans adore the romance of Austin's beautiful food with its deep roots in some of France's most glorious restaurants.

Indeed, Austin's biography reads like a "Who's Who" of the world of great restaurants. He trained under Michelin three-star chef Joel Robuchon at Jamin and Guy Savoy at his namesake restaurant. He studied and worked in the renowned kitchens of Gilles Epie at Miraville, Jacque Martines at Tour D'Argent, and George Blanc at La Mere Blanc. In New York, Austin was educated by David Burke at the River Café and with the preeminent chef Gilbert Le Coze at the four-star Le Bernadin. In 1994 Austin moved to Atlanta as opening executive chef at Brasserie Le Coze.

Rewards and enthusiastic patrons have followed him to Hedgerose Heights Inn. Atlanta food critic Terrell Vermont named Austin "1994's Best Chef in Atlanta." Writing for *Conde Naste Traveler*, Mimi Sheraton listed Hedgerose Heights as one of "America's Fifty Best Restaurants."

Austin's strength is to create dishes that are visually beautiful as well as exciting to the palate. He specializes in seafood dishes that are flavored with herb-infused oil; and the restaurant has been made famous by some of his signature dishes—created from his favorite game: quail, pheasant, and venison.

Austin's recipe for Salad Niçoise is on page 49, and Strawberry Napoleon is on page 142.

JEAN BANCHET

Riveria Restaurant
Atlanta, Georgia

In 1973, When Jean Banchet opened Le Francais, his Wheeling, Illinois restaurant, foodies from all over the Continent traveled to this Chicago suburb to worship at what was often referred to as a culinary temple. For two and a half decades since that seismic opening, Banchet has led the culinary field, acquiring along the way legions of admirers.

Born the first of triplets in Roanne, France, Banchet knew very early in life that he was destined to be a chef. He was only thirteen when he took his first culinary job as kitchen boy in the Troigros restaurant. Owners Jean and Pierre Troigros immediately recognized his extraordinary talent, and they encouraged him to transfer to what was then the most famous restaurant in the world, La Pyramid, in Vienne, France. At La Pyramid Banchet worked fourteen-hour days cooking for owner Madam Point. At the end of two years, he had been promoted three times and held the first comis position. Banchet now felt it was time to pursue a culinary internship—defined in France as working in a series of high quality restaurants in order to gain world-class experience. He transferred to the Hotel de Paris in Monte Carlo, followed by stints in three additional well-known restaurants before leaving for two years of service in the army.

Banchet returned home to the Hotel de Paris as chef poissonier (fish chef). After several months Banchet moved on to the Pavilion Eden Roc on the French Riviera, where he rose to sous chef. As his reputation grew, he was offered a chef's position in a London casino. In England, Banchet made a gastronomic reputation for himself and his employer. By 1986, Banchet's reputation had spread across the Atlantic, and noted restaurateur Arnold Morton enticed him to the Midwest. After five years in Chicago, Banchet opened Le Francais with French chef Henry Coudrier. Within a year ill health forced Coudrier to leave the restaurant and Chef Banchet and his wife became sole owners. In 1989 Banchet decided to take a hiatus from the restaurant business and he leased Le Francais. In 1992 he founded Ciboullette restaurant in Atlanta, and in 1995 he opened Riviera Restaurant. At the Riveria, Banchet is able to indulge his passion for the cooking of the south of France in his Mediterranean menu.

Over the years a multitude of honors have been heaped upon Banchet. His Wheeling restaurant has received the Mobil five-star rating every year since 1979, was *Playboy* magazine's Critic's Choice Award winner in each of three polls, and has been a frequent award winner in the *Zagat* poll of favorite U.S. restaurants. He has been featured on national television—including appearances on *Lifestyles of the Rich and Famous* and *Great Chefs of Chicago*.

Jean Banchet's recipe for Nage of Dover Sole Riviera is on page 78, and Grilled Vegetable Terrine with Lobster and Red Pepper Coulis is on page 2.

DONALD BARICKMAN

Magnolia's
Charleston, South Carolina

Donald Barickman has loved food from his early childhood days in Charleston, West Virginia—days that were spent in his grandparents' kitchen and at his family's dining table.

After studying forestry for a year at West Virginia University, Barickman realized that his true passion was food and he started cooking at a local restaurant. When he moved on to help a friend open a small deli, he was certain that he wanted to spend a lifetime working in restaurants. In 1983 he enrolled at the Culinary Institute of America. He graduated

in 1985, and immediately moved to the "other" Charleston, in South Carolina.

He began as a roundsman at Wild Dunes Resort and within a year he was hired as sous chef at The Wine Cellar. In March of 1987 he was offered the executive chef's position at what was to become Charleston's hottest restaurant—Carolina's. Quick to recognize and appreciate Barickman's creative use of southern ingredients, Charleston residents swarmed the restaurant. Two years later Barickman's talents were so appreciated that the owners of Carolina's asked him to open their next new venture, Columbia's.

In 1989 Barickman returned to Charleston to become a stockholder and vice president of Hospitality Management Group, Inc., the corporation that owns Magnolia's. Within thirty days of the restaurant's opening in July, 1990, Magnolia's was listed by the local newspaper as "the place to dine" in Charleston.

Barickman describes the food at Magnolia's as "uptown American cuisine with down South flavor." The eclectic menu includes accents of the Southwest, Pacific Rim, Cajun country, France, Italy, the South Carolina Upstate, and Charleston. "But no froufrou," Barickman insists. Skillet-seared grit cakes with tasso gravy and yellow corn relish are typical of Barickman's reinvented southern dishes. "Our theory at Magnolia's was local ingredients with a twist, food that no one—or hardly any one—had done before in Charleston," he says.

In May of 1993 Barickman opened a second restaurant for the Hospitality Management Group, Blossom Café. And in 1994, busy Barickman authored his first book, *Magnolia's Uptown/Down South Southern Cuisine*, published by Wyrick & Company. The cookbook has been as successful as Barickman's restaurants.

Donald Barickman's recipe for Spicy Shrimp, Sausage, and Tasso Gravy over White Grits is on page 59.

BEN BARKER

Magnolia Grill
Durham, North Carolina

The impetus behind Magnolia Grill's rise to national prominence is certainly the Barkers' inspired and unwavering dedication to the improvement of their craft. A native of Chapel Hill, North Carolina, Ben Barker met his wife and pastry/chef/partner, Karen, on their first day at New York's prestigious Culinary Institute of America. To date, they have amassed a combined thirty years of experience in top quality restaurants, including such fine dining establishments as Bill Neal's La Residence and The Fearrington House, where Barker initiated the "Cuisine of the New South" as the restaurant's mission statement.

In 1986 the Barkers converted a neighborhood grocery store into the Magnolia Grill, where their motto, "not afraid of flavor," is evident in every item served. As Judith Olney said, "Barker is a man obsessed with freshness," and his dedication to using the freshest local produce in a creative, densely flavored fashion continues to surprise and delight diners.

The Barkers' engaging personalities and bold flavors gained the Magnolia Grill instant popularity and national press attention. That recognition has been ongoing and includes the following honors: nominated in 1992, 1995, 1996 & 1997 as James Beard Best Chef, Southeast; selected by Delta Air Lines to create a southern regional menu, with original recipes to be served to passengers on Delta's international flights; chosen as 1995 "National Pork Restaurant of the Year"; selected as one of four chefs in the nation to cook at the 1994 James Beard Foundation Journalism Awards Dinner; served as guest chef instructor at La Varenne at the Greenbrier; listed as one of 1993's "Ten Best New Chefs in America," by *Food & Wine;* named *Esquire* magazine's 1992 "Rising Star Chef."

Opening another restaurant was the obvious next step in the Barkers' passion for providing superior cuisine to as many Triangle area people as possible. Pop's, a high-energy Italian trattoria-style restaurant, opened in January 1995 to rapturous acclaim.

Barker is the founding organizer of Share Our Strength's Taste of the Nation event in Durham as well as a charter member of the Piedmont America Institute of Wine and Food. In 1994 he initiated an annual fund-raising effort to start The Magnolia Fund, which provides grant assistance. The fund is targeted at promoting collaborative efforts among various Triangle-based AIDS service agencies. One hundred percent of proceeds, a total of $147,000 in three years, has gone directly to grant funding.

Barker's recipe for Wild and Exotic Mushroom Salad with Marinated Tomatoes and Warm Sherry-Bacon Vinaigrette is on page 46, and Panfried Rainbow Trout with Green Tomato and Lime Brown Butter Salsa on Sweet Potato, Artichoke, and Crayfish Hash is on page 83.

GENE BJORKLUND

Aubergine
Memphis, Tennessee

Memphis has some claims to food fame. Barbecue would have to top any list, followed by fried catfish. But a European chef coming to the banks of the Mississippi from cooking stints in France, Monte Carlo, Key West, Copper Mountain, and Morrocco might seem like fish out of water.

Not so, insists Gene Bjorklund, who received his primary training at the Lycée Technique d'Hotelière in Nice and cooked under more than one Michelin three-star chef before setting his sights on Memphis. With Bjorklund in the kitchen at Aubergine, the city famous for Graceland now cooks with grace as well.

At Aubergine, Bjorklund'd province is Provence, that herb-kissed and sun-drenched blending of France and Italy, with memories of Greece strewn about in between. Bjorklund has been chef/owner here since June 1993, having earned his Memphis stripes as places as diverse as Bosco's Pizza Kitchen and Brew Pub, Anthony's, La Tourelle, and Chez Phillipe at The Peabody Hotel.

This chef's encounters with France, primarily it's southern exposure, go back as far as his 1980 apprenticeship at Chez Antoine in Aix-en-Provence. Other formative experiences included work with Alain Ducasse at the three-star restaurant Le Louis XV in Monte Carlo, with Marc Meneau at the three-star L'Espérance in St.-Père-sous-Vézelay and, early on, at Club Med in Tetuåan, Morocco, and Arc 2000 in the French Alps.

Today, however, Bjorklund seems mighty pleased to find himself in Memphis. Though the city may still be better known for music on Beale Street, Bjorklund can be proud to have created a famed bit of Provence in the heart of Tennessee.

Bjorklund's recipe for Tempura-battered Frog Legs with Arugula Creamy Tartar Sauce is on page 36, and Warm Center Chocolate Pyramid Cake is on page 168.

MARTY BLITZ

Mise en Place
Tampa, Florida

New York-born and Detroit-raised Marty Blitz has always loved to eat. By the age of twelve his love of food was propelling him (on bicycle) to the local deli for his favorite sandwich. His formal initiation into the culinary world was at an apprenticeship with European-trained master chef Milos Ghelka. Three years of intense training and discipline taught Blitz the classic precepts that readied him for a future position as head chef of RG's North. Four and a half years later, Blitz was ready to work hard in his own kitchen.

He is today, as he has been for more than a decade, the hands-on chef at his urban bistro, Mise en Place. The restaurant gained instant popularity when it opened in the mid 1980s as a small catering and take-out establishment. When he opened for dinner, he garnered raves for eclectic specialties and "killer" desserts. Andre Gayot, writing in Gault Millau's *Best of Florida* raved, "If they'd just open for breakfast, we'd be tempted to move in and pay rent." In 1992 Mise en Place moved to larger quarters. The new and better than ever restaurant attracted enthusiastic observation by Kurt Loft in the *Tampa Tribune:* "the menu simmering with Ambrosian imagination, the presentation of each entrée a minor study in edible elegance." Blitz's reputation continues to soar. *The Zagat Guide to Central Florida/Gulf Coast Restaurants* rated the restaurant at the top of the list, with a score of 28 out of 30 for food. The trendsetting restaurant also holds four consecutive Golden Spoon awards from *Florida Trend* magazine.

During his tenure Blitz has been chosen a "Rising Star" at the James Beard House and invited to participate in their First Annual New World Cuisine Festival on Amelia Island. He was a participant in the NFL Taste of the Nation and his recipe for Cuban Spiced Shrimp with Manchego Cheese Grits was the cover photo of the league's cookbook.

Still, after many years, Blitz's culinary philosophy remains simple and straightforward. "My aim is to serve good food at a good price and to have fun doing it." That probably sums it up!

Marty Blitz's recipe for Smoked Scotch Bonnet Jerk Spice Mahimahi Stuffed with Christophene, Carrot, and Pepper with Mofongo Broth is on page 66.

JAMES BURNS
J. Bistro
Charleston, South Carolina

James Burns's culinary roots are in the scores of Sunday dinners enjoyed at his Irish grandmother's table in New York. In the honest flavors of the hearty roasts and superbly fresh vegetables of her kitchen, Burns discovered the virtues of real food, and a passion for food and cooking.

He began his career at Iona College in New Rochelle, New York, working weekends at the Bronx steakhouse Doubledays. He left there in 1983 with a B.A. in marketing to go to work in a nouvelle Mexican restaurant in Hunter Mountain, New York. He was learning the grill while waiting for an opening at the Culinary Institute of America. He spent two hard years at CIA, learning cooking processes and restaurant business practices while supporting himself by cleaning the bar under his residence.

After graduation from the CIA in 1986, Burns was hired as the chef at the American Express corporate dining room. At the age of twenty-five, he prepared meals and designed menus for some of the nation's most powerful men: James Robinson, Lou Gerstner, Malcolm Forbes, and Donald Trump. Even Gerald Ford popped into the kitchen to greet Burns and his staff.

Tavern on the Green followed. The Tavern on the Green of the late 1980s was the maelstrom of the social set, and Burns was part of a crew preparing dazzling plates for guests as glamorous as the food—Pavarotti and Gotti. A year after his arrival, Burns had risen to banquet sous chef.

In 1989, three months before Hurricane Hugo hit, Burns, his wife, and daughter moved to South Carolina. In Charleston, James Burns, who was raised in New York, adapted his training and artistry to the culinary products of the Low Country. He enjoyed continuous success; for two years commanding the stoves at Carolina's restaurant, then at Anson's.

In November 1994, Burns took on his most ambitious project to date—the creation of J. Bistro, his own restaurant in the Charleston, South Carolina suburb of Mt. Pleasant. Here he remains loyal to a basic formula of good ingredients cooked to order and rendered marvelous with the addition of sophisticated or innovative twists.

James Burns's recipe for Chocolate Soufflé is on page 126.

FRANK CAPUTO
The Kiawah Island Club
Charleston, South Carolina

Chef Frank Caputo says, "I was raised in the food industry dating back to the 1940s. Both parents were born in a small town in southern Italy where hard work, eating, and drinking are a way of life. Traditions, culture, and the love for food followed our arrival to America." Out of this background and a desire to "express my love for food, because without that pleasure my life is unfulfilled," came the decision to spend a career cooking.

In 1989, after graduation from the Culinary Institute of America, Caputo took his first job as sous chef at the Gina Rosa restaurant in Voorhees, New Jersey. There he was responsible for supervising the preparation of the popular restaurant's upscale northern Italian recipes. Caputo learned the intricacies of banquet operations next—at the Mansion at Main Street in Vorhees. In 1991 he headed south to accept the position of executive sous chef at The Bay Colony Club in Naples, Florida. As part of the club's opening team, Caputo was able to impact all aspects of a multifaceted food operation—from special events and meetings to restaurants. A stint at the Club at Nevillwood in Pittsburgh,

Pennsyvlania, followed, where he developed innovative menus for the members and hosted special events that included such celebrities as golf professional Jack Nicklaus.

In 1992 Caputo headed south to Bonita Springs, Florida where he was executive working chef at the Miramar Beach and Tennis Club. Caputo's generous regional Italian and French cooking were made to measure for the food-loving clientele at Miramar. With his reputation spreading, it was not surprising that word of his gifts reached South Carolina, and in 1993 The Kiawah Island Club lured Caputo to their shores. Here he maintains total responsibility of the culinary department, which includes a staff of fourteen and features the Italian and French foods he loves, brightened up with more than a little imagination.

Frank Caputo's recipe for Galliano Crêpes with Seasonal Berries is on page 120.

Kathy Cary

Lilly's
Louisville, Kentucky

One reviewer, thrilled with the flavors presented at Lilly's, called Kathy Cary "an Einstein in a toque." Cary, who also has two gourmet-to-go shops and the Louisville catering operation La Pêche, was named one of the "Ten Trendsetter Chefs" by *Food Arts* magazine, and won rave reviews for her debut with the James Beard House "discovery" dinner. Cary has made three addional appearances as a guest chef at the James Beard House in New York in tribute to her skill in regional cuisine. She founded a cooking and gardening educational program, "From Seed to Table," benefiting the Cabbage Patch Settlement House. Cary grew up in Kentucky and credits her knowledge and love of local foods to her Kentucky roots. She apprenticed to a Cordon Bleu-trained chef in Washington, D.C., and

later set up her own catering firm there, serving the likes of Senator Edward Kennedy, Henry Kissinger, and the movie cast of *All the President's Men*. Returning to Kentucky, she opened her first gourmet-to-go shop in 1979 and has been "on the go" ever since. She considers her menu to be a French-inspired use of traditional Kentucky ingredients, with some unusual twists.

Kathy Cary's recipe for Sea Scallops with Mango and Jalapeños is on page 58, and Mocha Toffee Meringue is on page 152.

Joe Castro

The English Grill
Louisville, Kentucky

"Mother knows best," according to Louisville's best chef, the award-winning Joe Castro. Having a father who was a doctor did not hurt, either, for the thirty-four-year-old hometown boy made good. "I tell my cooks, don't ever put anything on the table you wouldn't serve your mother," says Castro. "I know how I feel about my mom, so the food I serve is the best I can make." Indeed, food is everything to this young chef—his career, his hobby, his passion, and his family. His wife is a pastry chef, and his brother and brother-in-law are chefs.

Castro's beloved mother is from an old Kentucky family who were used to baking country hams. His Filipino father loved to fix fish heads, which he often fed his son at midnight. The diversity gave Castro an interesting balance and an unusual perspective. Although never formally trained, Castro learned at every job and from every chef he worked with—from an internship in Taiwan where he learned about simplicity and integrity in cooking, to five years at the stoves of the Embassy Row Hotel in Washington D.C.

Now back at home, Castro's food has a strong regional accent blended with the understatement that is the backbone of classical techniques. He likes to feature local ingredients and produce and makes many of his own vinegars and oil. He is excited about the excellence of the local produce, which he attributes to the limestone layer that the Louisville groundwater passes through.

His passion and his skills have been richly rewarded. *Louisville* magazine rated The Brown as having the best hotel restaurant in town and the *Louisville Courier-Journal* called The English Grill the best restaurant in town.

Joe Castro's recipe for Roulade of Salmon with Egg and Capers is on page 34.

THOMAS CATHERALL

Tom Tom
Atlanta, Georgia

Tom Tom is the pet name for Thomas Catherall, the restaurant's talented, flamboyant chef/proprietor. The chef's international fusion cuisine is the outgrowth of his growing up in Newcastle, England, and an apprenticeship at the Royal Turks Head Hotel in Newcastle. At the Culinary Institute of America, Catherall received his Certified Master Chef certificate. Following his formal education, he traveled and trained in London, Bermuda, Barbados, and the U.S., acquiring the skills and tastes that have catapulted him into fame as one of the South's top chefs. He was inspired by mentors Jeremiah Tower of San Francisco Stars' fame, and Atlantan Paul Albrecht, co-owner of the Buckhead Life group of restaurants.

Atlantans first discovered Catherall's talents when he was the chef at the Cherokee Town & Country Club. He left to start up his first Atlanta restaurant, Azalea, which received raves for its dazzling, contemporary American cuisine. Now, as chef and owner at Tom Tom, his cutting-edge cuisine continues to draw throngs. Fans have followed him to Tom Tom for signature dishes like Hot Chili

Squid, Whole Sizzling Catfish, Sesame Almond Lace Basket, and a "fun for everyone" menu. Catherall defines his style as "food for the 90s with an emphasis on healthy ingredients and cooking preparations." It is also equal parts bistro and world amalgamation, or as he says, "East meets West."

Catherall's skills have been recognized in an impressive list of competitions. In 1988 he was awarded a gold medal with a perfect score at the Culinary Olympics in Frankfurt, Germany, as a member of the U.S.A. Culinary Team. In 1990 Catherall received the "Best Seafood Chef in the U.S.A." in a competition in New Orleans, and in 1993 he won the "Taste of Elegance" pork competition.

Thomas Catherall's recipe for Whole Sizzling Catfish with Sizzling Black Bean Sauce is on page 82.

JOHN CURRENCE

City Grocery
Oxford, Mississippi

City Grocery was born out of the frustration of its co-owners, John Currence and Palmer Adams. When a search of Oxford, Mississippi yielded no restaurant offering the fine flavors and subtle sophistication they yearned for, they decided to open one themselves. So, these two young, urban New Orleanians opened City Grocery to satisfy their own need, and in the process fulfilled the wants of many, many more.

John Currence is a New Orleans native, but his cooking was born in Chapel, North Carolina. There, under the tutelage of one of the founders of regional American cooking, Bill Neal of Cook's Corner, he learned classic French techniques and traditional deep southern American cuisines. In 1985 Currence left Neal's employ to assume the pasta chef's job at Chapel Hill's upscale Aurora restaurant. There he expanded his repertoire, and studied the basics of traditional Italian preparations.

In 1989, at the request of his future partner, Palmer Adams, then general manager at Gautreau's in New Orleans, and Larkin Selman, Gautreau's chef and co-owner, John returned to New Orleans as sous chef at Gautreau's. Eighteen months later, Currence took the executive sous chef job at the Brennan family's soon-to-be-opened Italian restaurant, Bacco's. In preparation for his position at Bacco's, Currence spent eight months training at Mr. B's Bistro and Commander's Palace, learning management skills and the art of running a high-volume and highly skilled kitchen. Although the decision to leave the Brennans, one of the country's premier hospitality families, was troublesome, the lure of private ownership pulled. In the spring of 1992, Currence and Adams opened the City Grocery and are today enjoying the popularity of their restaurant and the fine praises of their customers.

John Currence's recipe for Pecan Flour-dusted Softshell Crab with Roasted Garlic Tomato Butter is on page 61.

Peter de Jong

The Beaufort Inn
Beaufort, South Carolina

Born and raised in Amsterdam, Holland, Peter received an "old-fashioned" European training. De Jong worked in the most recognized European kitchens as a chef and professional baker. He graduated from the University of Amsterdam and became a Master pastry chef. The success of his traditional training was established with his winning several gold medals at national competitions. Peter received a masters in food arts before migrating to the United States and New York.

In New York, de Jong and chef Albert Kumin opened their own restaurant and taught classes at the International Pastry Art Center in Elmsfore. Together they received

the grand prize of the Culinary Salon in New York City.

In 1994 de Jong migrated to Beaufort, South Carolina to open the Beaufort Inn. Local produce and regional products provide inspiration for the constantly evolving menu that de Jong defines as modern southern cuisine with a personal twist. Oysters, shrimp, blue crab, and grits regularly appear on his menus. True to his master pastry chef heritage, each plate is thoughtfully and artistically presented. And, as the flavors of the region marry on the plate, the taste buds quiver with delight.

De Jong's recipe for Chocolate Crème Brûlée with Sweet Basil Vanilla Sauce is on page 122.

Stephen Demeter

The Camberley Brown
Louisville, Kentucky

As a child in Cleveland, Ohio, Stephen Demeter often found dinner to be the very best part of the day. It was then that he got to help his mother cook the wonderful evening meals she prepared for the family; and it was at that table that he began what was to become a lifetime enchantment with food. It helped also that on Sunday visits to his grandparents, Demeter played sous chef in his grandfather's kitchen, assisting in the preparation of "the world's best stuffed cabbage."

So it seemed natural that when Demeter enrolled at the Villa Angela St. Joseph Parochial School in Cleveland, he would discover himself working with the priest/chef. Every Christmas Stephen assisted the priest in the preparation of the holiday meals served to the local children. Stephen loved baking the bread and assisting with the savories in the priest's kitchen. He knew then that when he graduated he would enroll in a culinary school.

Chef Demeter spent two years at the Sullivan College, National Center for Hospitality Studies in Louisville, Kentucky, and graduated in 1995 with an associate degree in culinary baking and pastry arts. He spent part of his beginning year there working his first professional job in the pastry kitchen of the Big Springs Country Club.

Since graduation from Sullivan, Demeter has been at The Camberley Brown, where he has traveled up the kitchen ladder from roundsman at the hotel's four-star restaurant, the English Grill, to banquet chef, to his current position as executive sous chef. In his current role at the hotel, Demeter supervises the sous chefs for the hotel's two restaurants, supervises a busy banquet kitchen, and acts as roundsman for the entire hotel's food operations.

As a young chef, Demeter was "often overwhelmed by the hundreds of new ingredients constantly being introduced." But even in his short time at the professional stoves he has been able to determine that the best ingredients are the often the simplest and always the freshest.

Stephen Demeter's recipe for Caramelized Bourbon Apples is on page 144.

JOHNNY EARLES

Criolla's Restaurant
Grayton Beach, Florida

With his innovative equatorial cuisine, Johnny Earles is one of the country's cutting-edge chefs, combining ingredients from around the globe for today's sophisticated American palate. Restaurant reviewers and food critics from publications such as *Southern Living*, *Nation's Restaurant News*, the *Atlanta Journal-Constitution*, *Cook's*, and *Self* have praised the cuisine served at Criolla's for its inspired pairings and lively presentation.

"*Criolla* is the name of a European born in the West Indies after Columbus's arrival," Earles explains. "The French took this Spanish word and changed it to Creole. It embodies a type of people and a type of cuisine. It's expanded into the Caribbean, South America, France, Spain, Africa, India, and the lower Caribbean. I call it equatorial cuisine."

Earles's first formal food experience came as a teen, when his family moved from their home in Bogalusa, Louisiana, to Baton Rouge. Earles developed an interest in jazz and blues and landed a job as the pizza cook at a cowboy bar and pizza restaurant. Some years later, he returned to Baton Rouge to attend Louisiana State University, initially planning to study medicine. He paid his way through school while living at home and running crawfish traps with his father.

Self-taught, Earles's early culinary mentors were his mother, grandmother, aunt Erma, and the guides of Paul Prudhomme, including the *River Roads Cookbook* and *Paul Prudhomme's Louisiana Kitchen*.

In 1983 Earles moved to Grayton Beach, Florida to open the Paradise Café. His first kitchen consisted of a screened back porch with a hot plate and backyard barbecue grill. Writing in *Cook's* magazine, Mark Bittman described the Paradise Café as "so popular that people frequently drove in from as far as Tallahassee. There were nights when Earles ran out of food." The only problem was the restaurant had no stove. Wearing swimming goggles to avoid the smoke, Earles cooked fresh fish and beef on a homemade grill on the back porch. Other items were cooked in the "kitchen" in a variety of devices—an electric wok, an electric slow cooker, or an electric skillet.

Today, Criolla's is a much different place. Earles cooks in a state-of-the-art kitchen and mentors a highly trained staff. Each year the restaurant has been open, *Florida Trend* magazine has named Criolla's one of the state's top twenty restaurants. *Southern Living* executive travel editor, Michael Carlto, has called Criolla's "by far the best dining experience on the Gulf Coast."

Johnny Earles's recipe for Grouper Pibil is on page 75.

JONATHAN EISMANN
Pacific Time
Miami, Florida

"I cook Asian-influenced American food with a French sensibility," says chef/proprietor Jonathan Eismann. So defines the food that has been luring people to Pacific Time on Miami's trendy Lincoln Road. Indeed, Eismann has been drawing raves for his clever, exciting dishes with their Asian flair. *Esquire* magazine named the restaurant in its list of "Best New Restaurants," and for three consecutive years it has been voted "Best Restaurant in South Florida by both *South Florida* magazine and the *Miami New Times*. Pacific Time is the first South Florida restaurant to receive Mobil's sought-after four stars. Eismann was awarded the "Robert Mondavi Award for Culinary Excellence," and he has appeared on the accompanying PBS series.

Eismann typically spends three mornings a week in Asian markets and with local fishmongers buying new ingredients to test in his kitchen. He says that he develops recipes through a process of experimentation, and that "nine times out of ten, I don't have any idea how the dish is going to taste in the end." The end is, as his patrons will tell you, always terrific. This inventive, sensual approach to his ingredients gives his cuisine a seductive charm that is simply irresistible.

Eismann attributes his success to his training at the Culinary Institute of America, followed by a lifetime of just plain old hard work in restaurants After graduating the Culinary Institute, he led the stoves at New York's

Acute Café, then went on to head the kitchens of some of the hottest restaurants of the 1980s—including Baton's Fadango, Mondial, China Grill, and Busby's. He has consulted for restaurants in Miami Beach and New York City. He conceived and opened the wildly successful Googies Italian Diner in New York City and worked with the staffs of The Strand, 720 Ocean, and A Fish Called Avalon. It was there that he met his partners in Pacific Time.

Eismann comments that it was the sum of these experiences that taught him that "being a talented cook was not enough to make a restaurant prosper. To thrive, one must constantly refine the menu and service. It means working with other people who understand the nuances of the business." Indeed, Eismann has found a formula that works, "a balance of distinctive food and warm service that supplement each other. It is the synergy of just these components that has made Pacific Time a triumph."

Eismann's recipe for Barbecued Breast of Duck with Crushed Pepper, Plums, and Plum Wine is on page 103.

JOHN FLEER
The Inn at Blackberry Farm
Walland, Tennessee

North Carolina-born chef John Fleer says, "It is southern food that lies at the heart of my cooking." Fleer has many memories of summers spent at his grandparents' home in Tidewater, Virginia, and of their large garden and the couple's "mad rush from the crab pot to the boiling pot." There were also trips to Europe during his childhood and young adulthood, and even two six-month stays in England and Italy. Fleer is convinced that the early exposure to European culture broadened his culinary horizons and profoundly affected his love of food.

Yet Fleer did not begin his education with the study of food. His first degree was a B.A. in religion from Duke University. Next he enrolled in the master's program in religion and culture at the University of North Carolina, Chapel Hill. It was while pursuing his graduate degree there that Fleer worked as the head baker at Aurora restaurant in Carrboro, North Carolina. This led to work on a master's thesis on the community of the dining table as a model for aesthetic, ethical, and political judgments.

Fleer's formal training was at the Culinary Institute of America, where he earned his degree, graduating with honors in 1991. He completed a fellowship at the school's St. Andrew's Café under chef Jonathan Zearfoss, who taught him how to appreciate freshness and seasonality in ingredients, and to think about the nutritional value of food. He had the opportunity to expand his experience with healthy cooking techniques while working as the private chef of Mary Tyler Moore and her husband in their New York home.

Since arriving at Blackberry Farm, Fleer has developed a cooking style that he likes to refer to as "Foothills Cuisine"—a style that "wanders the line between the refined and the rugged, classical and traditional." Although his dishes are native to the region, they are peppered with influences from the regions of Gascony, Alsace, and the Basque. He feels that it is these regions, because of their small farms and lack of urban concentration, that share a way of life with America's South. He hopes that his food at Blackberry Farm "strikes a chord of the familiar in our guests," but will also "bring flashes of the original."

Fleer's cooking style and recipes have been featured in publications and broadcasts including *Veranda, Southern Living, Country Home, Food & Wine*, and *Inn Country Chefs*.

John Fleer's recipe for Bacon-wrapped Trout Stuffed with Crawfish is on page 86, and Blackberry-glazed Quail is on page 41.

WILHELM GAHABKA
The Registry Resort
Naples, Florida

Wilhelm Gahabka, the son of a brewmaster and a cook, was destined to become a great chef. A native of Erlangen, Germany, Gahabka's enthusiasm for food was born in his mother's kitchen and learned at the Culinary Institute in Nuremberg. After three years at the Institute, Gahabka moved on to learn and explore the cuisines of St. Moritz, Munich Gamisch-Partenkirchen, Milan, and Monte Carlo. But his aspirations were to live in a place where he could spend Christmas on the beach.

So Gahabka found his way to Southwest Florida, where he took the executive chef job at the Landings Yacht and Gold Club. It was not long before he was lured to the Lafite Restaurant at The Registry Resort. As the executive chef he is at the helm of a kitchen that is putting out some of the most exciting and original cuisine found in the Southeast. Dishes like his Sugar Cane-speared Gulf Shrimp with Tamarind-Orange Honey Glaze have earned him an enthusiastic following. As has initiating new dining ideas, like his monthly Chef's Table, five gourmet courses with accompanying wines.

Chef Gahabka is frequently seen participating in industry events. As a member of the American Culinary Federation, he is a frequent entrant in their competition and in the past several years has won three gold medals, four silver medals, and one Best of Show. In November 1995 Gahabka was invited to cook at the James Beard Foundation's Best Hotel Chefs of America Series. He has cooked at the Culinary Institute of America in Hyde Park, New York and at Martinique's Club Med. Still his favorite kitchen is at The Registry Resort, where Florida's pristine fish and beautiful local produce continue to inspire him.

Wilhelm Gahabka's recipe for Sugar Cane-speared Gulf Shrimp with Tamarind-Orange Honey Glaze is on page 17.

GREGORY GAMMAGE

Bones
Atlanta, Georgia

As the name suggests, the stylish, clubby restaurant Bones is acclaimed for its beef. Yet chef Gammage, whose motto is "Don't be afraid to experiment," is known no less for his flawless meals with a southern emphasis.

Gammage says that he "likes to initiate trends, not follow them. I strive to be on the cutting edge with something different and be ahead of the crowd." And Bones's patrons seem to thrive on Gammage's experimentation, as they come back time and time again to savor dishes such as grit fritters, salmon on a bed of sautéed collards topped with crawfish, grilled salmon with frilled Vidalia onions and a red pepper sauce, Georgia pecan pie and crème brûlée with a light cookie-crust shell, and black-eyed pea soup with a sweet relish.

Gammage's cooking style, which he describes as "new southern cuisin," was developed during more than fifteen years at Bones, building from his southern heritage and the traditions of southern foods. His history in the restaurant business is certainly the story of a humble beginning. Starting out as a busboy at Atlanta's Tango restaurant, he "got talked into doing a few days in the kitchen as a line cook, and I've been cooking ever since." Along the culinary circuit, Gammage stopped at more Atlanta kitchens—Scarborough's, Zasu, and Joseph's. In 1979 he took a part time position at Bones, but within six months was elevated to chef. In 1990 he was named executive chef.

In his tenure at Bones, Gammage and the restaurant have earned repeated praise from the local and restaurant community, including: election to "Who's Who Among Chefs in Atlanta" by the *Atlanta Business Chronicle*, named one of the top ten restaurants in Atlanta two consecutive years by the *Atlanta Journal-Constitution*, and recipient of the Best Steakhouse award from *Atlanta* magazine for eight consecutive years.

Gregory Gammage's recipe for Roasted Chicken with Collards, Red Onion, and Sweet Potato Chips is on page 92.

LARRY GOBER

Criolla's Restaurant
Grayton Beach, Florida

Criolla's pastry chef, Larry Gober, has worked with the restaurant's chef, Johnny Earles, since 1986. But while Earles's creations may satisfy the diners' yen for the adventurous, Gober tends toward the classical. A man who gently discusses the philosophies of Escoffier and conceptual art as he describes his desserts, Gober offers a studied contrast to Earles's "Indiana Jones" approach to the food. "Johnny is the Ying, and I'm the Yang," Gober says. "We're at odds, but it works."

While Gober relishes using the ingredient building blocks of equatorial cuisine—tropical fruits, sweet potatoes, and spice—he finds the ultimate satisfaction in serving desserts with gentle layers of flavor, such as Cardamom Ice Cream with a Homemade Chocolate "Krunch" Bar and Praline Cream Sauce. "If you want powerful flavors, eat chocolate," the pastry expert counsels. "But I've often found that the subtle surprises are what people remember."

Gober grew up in Milton, Florida, and planned to be a high school teacher until the culinary world lured him to San Francisco. He worked at the London Wine Bar, the first wine bar in the U.S., and watched from a ringside seat as the then fledgling California wine industry fought into a class of its own. Portland was his next stop, and he sharpened his skills on classical French cookery as sous chef under Leif Bensen at the Timberline Lodge.

Seven years later, armed with his new-found sensibilities and a love for old-guard favorites, Gober returned to his native Florida. His skills sustained him as he cooked for several well known restaurants, including the Sandestin Resort, Anthony's in Pensacola, the Paradise Café in Grayton Beach, Café Maxx in Pompano Beach, and the Ocean Reef Club in Key Largo.

At Criolla's he continues to insist on flavor and presentations that complement the elements of his desserts. "Dessert is not a prerequisite course," the chef says simply. "It's one place diners can sin a little."

Larry Gober's recipe for Aunt Irma's Banana-Pecan Beignets is on page 119.

SHANE GORRINGE

Zöe's
New Orleans, Louisiana

A native of Surrey, England, pastry chef Shane Gorringe ("rhymes with orange," he says) apprenticed at Sweet Vienna Pâtisserie, a renowned Austrian pastry shop south of London. Thereafter, he was assistant pastry chef at luxury hotels in England, Germany, Holland, Venezuela, and the Middle East. Coming to New Orleans, he took over as pastry chef of the frequently honored Windsor Court Hotel.

Gorringe has been about the business of making pastries since he was sixteen years old. "After twenty years in this field, you learn that when you come to a new city, you don't assume that just because the desserts you did at the previous location worked there they're going to work here." Because the Windsor Court in New Orleans catered to an international clientele, his desserts shied away from strictly regional favorites like bread pudding, but he quickly found New Orleanians, no matter how sophisticated, still have affinities

for chocolate, desserts with apples, sorbets, exotic fruits, and crème brûlée. Having established himself in New Orleans, Gorringe followed his heart's desire and opened Zöe's on the rapidly developing north shore of Lake Pontchartrain, across from the city. The bakery, named for his daughter, gives him free rein to develop his talents. His advice to the nonprofessional cook is not to be put off by the presentation of elaborate desserts. Simplifying the garnishes does not change the essential flavor of the dish, but does sometimes make it more accessible to at-home cooks.

Shane Gorringe's recipe for Coffee Cup Sabayon is on page 129 and Strawberry Apple Cheese Strudel is on page 162.

WILL GREENWOOD

Sunset Grill
Nashville, Tennessee

American cooking in the hands of Will Greenwood has been delighting food aficionados throughout the region. Known for his devotion to the history of American food, Greenwood paired international techniques with regional ingredients to create his signature dishes.

A native of Oklahoma, Greenwood is a graduate of the Culinary Institute of America and studied with Madeleine Kamman at the Beringer Vineyards School for American Chefs. He was executive chef at the Maryland Inn in Annapolis and cooked in other acclaimed hotel restaurants, including La Brasserie in the Peabody Court Hotel in Baltimore. In 1989 Greenwood joined the Jefferson Hotel in Washington, D.C., as executive chef. In the five years spent there, he revitalized the dining room with his new Virginian cuisine, creating dishes in the spirit of culinary experimentation epitomized by Thomas Jefferson.

Hearing of Greenwood's culinary prowess,

the Clintons invited him to apply for the chef's position at the White House. As one of three finalists for the job, Greenwood was featured in a *Washington Post* "Style" section cover story, and on CNN. That same year—1994—members of the Restaurant Association of metropolitan Washington named Greenwood "Chef of the Year."

At Sunset Grill, Greenwood managed to revamp a menu responsible for serving 1,200 meals, while receiving *Nashville Scene* magazine's "Best Restaurant in Nashville" and the American Academy of Restaurants' "Best Chef in America" award. Greenwood and his recipes have been featured on ABC's *Good Morning America*, CNN *News*, and in *Gourmet*, *Bon Appetit*, *Conde Nast Traveler*, and *People* magazines, and *USA Today*.

Will Greenwood's recipe for Chocolate Banana Foster Cake with Orange Foster Caramel Sauce is on page 146.

Richard Grenamyer

The Governor's Club
Tallahassee, Florida

Richard Grenamyer's cooking philosophy is as straightforward as he is. It's "not about 'fou-fou cuisine,' it's about the freshest ingredients, no matter the cost, and simple, logical, intelligent preparation." But as one reviewer put it, to be Grenamyer's kind of chef one also needs "the spirit of an artist to see the vision, the daring of an explorer in order to take risks, and the instincts of a chemist to achieve flavor and textural balance."

Grenamyer's achievement of all these attributes is the result of growing up in his family's restaurant, the Kismet Inn, on Fire Island, New York. He started at the restaurant at the age of twelve, washing dishes. By age fifteen, he was at the stoves. His mentor was his father, and at twenty-four he was already running the restaurant. In his career he has

owned and operated a total of six restaurants. His Jacksonville restaurant, Sterling's Flamingo Café, was chosen as one of very few in Florida to receive the prestigious Florida Gault-Millau Award.

Now, as executive chef at The Governor's Club, Grenamyer is at the height of his powers. His talent for bringing out the best in his remarkable ingredients is exemplified in dishes like his classic Italian carpaccio served with a rich horseradish pesto sauce, or an entrée of duck breasts accented with a red wine cream sauce. It's no wonder the word about Grenamyer has traveled through the gourmet pipeline. But Grenamyer remains an unassuming chef who is not at all comfortable with admiration. He'd much rather cook; the delight of creating, it seems, is far more important to him than applause. One might guess that he cites his hobbies as "family, friends, and food."

Richard Grenamyer's recipe for Roasted Portabello Caps is on page 8.

Jose Gutierrez

Chez Phillipe
The Peabody Hotel
Memphis, Tennessee

Convincing diners that some of America's finest French cuisine is served in the city of Elvis's Graceland and barbecue has never been an easy task. But in a grande dame southern hotel most famous for its daily parade of ducks, anything is possible.

Cooking at Chez Phillipe, the small and elegant dining room of the Peabody, Gutierrez has made a happy alliance between his French heritage and the South's traditional tastes. Guests at The Peabody love the pairing, and so do the people of Memphis.

In recent years, the cross-cultural borrowing has become more complex. Now more and more dishes are showing the Pacific Rim influence that fascinates so many chefs these days.

At the same time, this fine French restaurant has been updated for the nineties. The dress code has been relaxed and prices have been lowered. As a result, this cuisine has become more accessible to more people.

"We can do very nice things with produce grown locally and people are more familiar with them," observes Gutierrez. "It helps bring the cost of food down." Such considerations are basic to traditional French cuisine, which seeks to use regional foods at their best. And Gutierrez learned his art from some of the finest masters of this tradition.

Starting his career at the Professional Culinary School in Manosque, France, he followed up with two years at the Hôtel de France at Jura under the direction of chef Roger Petit, who in turn had studied unter the legendary Fernand Point. Gutierrez then put in an instructive year with chef Francis Trocelier, followed by another year at La Réserve de Beaulieu on the French Riviera.

After working in several other restaurants, Gutierrez spent a year cooking with the celebrated Paul Bocuse at his namesake restaurant near Lyons, then headed for the Restaurant de France at the Meridien Hotel in Houston. From there, Chez Phillipe at The Peabody seemed a logical step.

Gutierrez's recipe for Shrimp with Sugar Cane and Papaya Ketchup is on page 22, and Lemon Cheesecake is on page 158.

CLIFFORD HARRISON

Bacchanalia
Atlanta, Georgia

Hawaiian-born Clifford Harrison had already graduated from the University of Hawaii before deciding to enroll at San Francisco's California Culinary Academy. When he gradu-

ated from culinary school in 1987, he did a stint with Judy Rogers at the Zuni Café in San Francisco, and then traveled to Nantucket Island, Massachusetts, to work with Bob Kinkead at 21 Federal. He spent a few years in New York perfecting his cuisine in the kitchens of Bimini Twist, La Petite Ferme, and the Grolier. It was during this time that the James Beard Foundation elected Harrison to their roster as a "Rising Star Chef."

In 1990 Harrison and his wife and partner, Anne Quatrano, moved to Atlanta to take over her family's farm in Cartersville, Georgia. They restored it to an organic herb and vegetable garden with an orchard, and the inspiration followed to open a small restaurant. The energetic couple took over and lovingly restored a sixty-year-old Tudor-style house in Atlanta's Buckhead neighborhood. Their romantic, charming restaurant is now the setting for the elegant cuisine that evolved through the years of Harrison's experience. It is a cuisine based on the organic and pesticide-free ingredients grown either on his North Georgia farm or acquired from small farmers. And it is a cuisine based on the philosophy that "good food is simple food. I am not trying to be clever." Sometimes Harrison labels his food "fresh flavors with subtle complexities." In sum, the food at Bacchanalia is simply contemporary American at its finest. Harrison and his partner have made an impression on Atlanta residents, who voted it a "welcome addition" in the *Zagat Guide to Atlanta*. As Christine Laueterbach said in *Atlanta* magazine, "Bacchanalia seems bound to become what Quatrano and Harrison have always wanted: 'a nice, long-lasting place.'"

Clifford Harrison's recipe for Horseradish-crusted Sea Bass with Shiitake Mushroom and Miso is on page 77.

ROBERT P. HOLLEY
Brasserie Le Coze
Atlanta, Georgia

Native New Yorker Robert Holley graduated from the Culinary Institute of America, and in 1987 went to work for the brother-and-sister team of Maguy and Gilbert Le Coze at New York's extraordinary Le Bernadin Restaurant. Under the tutelage of *New York Times* four-star chef Gilbert Le Coze, Holley learned the special skills of fish preparation. In his four years at Le Bernadin, Holley worked hard learning the techniques of a fine French kitchen. In 1991 the Le Cozes opened Brasserie Le Coze in Miami, and Holley joined them as executive chef.

Holley gave Miami residents something to celebrate in the more casual, but still elegant and disciplined, Brasserie Le Coze. The immediate praise and accolades encouraged the brother-and-sister team to open a second Brasserie Le Coze in Atlanta in 1994. One year later, Holley moved to Atlanta to become executive chef. His reception there has been as warm and enthusiastic as it was in Miami.

Atlantans embraced and celebrated the young and talented Holley, while being amazed and delighted by such dishes as skate with brown butter scattered with capers and salmon over French lentils splashed with vinegar. Food writers have alternately described Holley's dishes as "downright mesmerizing," "magical in its essence," and "miraculous." Writer Terrell Vermont said, "I'm grateful for this new restaurant, and applaud its every effort."

Holley was chosen to represent the United States in the Culinary Olympics in Germany in 1987. He was the team captain for the hot food competition, where his team bested culinary teams from around the world to capture a silver medal.

Robert Holley's recipe for Coq au Vin is on page 94.

SCOTT HOWELL
Nana's
Durham, North Carolina

North Carolina native Scott Howell can proudly say that his culinary career has been an expedition through some of the country's and the world's greatest restaurants. En route Howell has worked with some of America's brightest talents and innovators.

During his tenure at the Culinary Institute of America, Howell interned with America's premier movers of the American cooking movement on both coasts, New York's Jonathan Waxman and California star Paul Bartalotta. Following graduation he appeased a passion for Italian cuisine, and traveled to Imola, Italy, to work at San Domenico. Howell is certain that working in Italy, learning the basics of the cuisine, was an integral step in his development as a chef. From Italy he returned to the States to work with David Bouley, the chef/owner of the restaurant that bears his name and that is one of only a few restaurants to receive four stars from the *New York Times*. Although he felt honored to participate in a kitchen that had emerged as one of the country's finest, Howell was ready by 1991 to return to his home state.

Back in Durham, Howell went to work for talented chefs Karen and Ben Barker at Magnolia Grill, who were already creating a national stir with their refined southern cooking. In 1992 he took the executive chef's job at Café Atlantique in Wilmington, North Carolina, where he was responsible for serving some of the region's finest French cuisine.

By 1993 Howell felt he was ready to venture out on his own and opened Nana's Restaurant. At Nana's, Howell's study of Mediterranean and European techniques hass been the inspiration for a menu that features "new American" food with French and Italian accents. The well-thought-out combinations and delicate flavors created an immediate stir in the press and were a hit in the dining room. *Esquire* magazine recognized Nana's as one of the best new restaurants in the country, and Howell and his recipes were featured in *Food & Wine* magazine.

In 1995 Howell formed a partnership with his former boss and mentors, the Barkers, to open Pop's Trattoria in Durham. Immediately, *Bon Appetit* magazine named Pop's to their "Best of the Year's Hot-Spot" list.

Scott Howell's recipe for Risotto with Bacon, Silver Queen Corn, and Catfish is on page 9.

KENNETH HUNSBERGER

Oystercatchers
Tampa, Florida

Kenneth Hunsberger's cooking career started at the Saddlebrook Resort in Wesley Chapel, Florida. In three years there he worked as the first cook in the resort's fine dining restaurant, the Cypress Room, and as kitchen manager at "the little club."

In 1985 Hunsberger joined the Hyatt Regency in Tampa, Florida, as first cook at the Westwinds restaurants. A stint at the Hyatt's Armani's, Tampa's highest rated restaurant, followed. There Hunsberger learned to create the rich concoctions and traditional northern Italian dishes that consistently win the restaurant praise. His accomplishments did not go unnoticed and Hyatt soon elevated the young cook to garde manger sous chef and then garde manger chef. He spent a year as chef at Petey Brown's, serving three meals a day and fulfilling the expectations of a demanding, busy restaurant.

Hunsberger assumed the chef's position at Oystercatchers in 1994. Since his arrival he has been wowing the patrons at this all-Florida seafood restaurant. Hunsberger's seafood dishes and desserts, featuring regional ingredients ingeniously prepared, have

encouraged accolades that include *Tampa* magazine's "Best Weekend Brunch" and "The Best Place to Take Visitors." The *Weekly Planet* gave Oystercatchers the vote for the "Best Business Lunch" for two consecutive years, and "Best Waterfront Restaurant."

Kenneth Hunsberger's recipe for Stacked Key Lime Pie is on page 156.

ROGER KAPLAN

City Grill
Atlanta, Georgia

In February 1993, Roger Kaplan brought his culinary expertise and fresh American styled regional cuisine to The Peasant Restaurants' City Grill in Atlanta, Georgia.

A native of Morristown, New Jersey, Kaplan learned the basics at the Culinary Institute of America. His first job was at Washington, D.C.'s Jockey Club in the Ritz-Carlton Hotel. During his three years there he worked his way up to sous chef. In 1983 he was one of the founding kitchen talents at what was to become D.C.'s next hot spot—the Ebbit Grill. In 1990 Kaplan joined the Rosewood Group as executive sous chef, working at the Dallas Crescent Court and assisting in the opening of the Resort La Samanna in St. Martin.

Tireless and determined, Kaplan created for City Grill a menu full of original southern and southwestern dishes. The foods from his menu are bold and courageous in both flavor and concept. There are southern classics and dishes that are intensely whimsical. Important to Kaplan is his belief in cooking healthy foods. "I don't want people to go home after eating dinner here and say, 'I've eaten too much fat,'" says Kaplan. That philosophy, combined with his use of only the freshest meat and poultry products and organic produce, earned him *Fitness* magazine's recognition as one of the nation's healthiest chefs in their July/August 1994 issue. He relies on marinades and cures rather than fats to boost flavors in his preparation. Although, he says, he "likes to stay centered in the South, " Kaplan realizes that "conventioneers come to Atlanta from every part of the country, so I'm going to cook things they can all relate to." His latest experiment is dishes of the Northwest—including mushrooms, earthy sauces, wild rices, and Asian ingredients.

In addition to his duties at City Grill, Kaplan oversees menu development for The Peasant Restaurants' casual dining concept, Mick's, and the company's other white linen establishments.

Roger Kaplan's recipe for Barbecued Duck with Wilted Greens is on page 101.

FRANK LEE
Slightly North of Broad
Charleston, South Carolina

Chef Frank Lee's food is as southern as he is. As a native South Carolinian he grew up surrounded by the flavors and bounty that characterize the region. The rich resources of the state's farms and waters provided Lee's inspiration and created his passion for cooking. Lee has always has loved to cook, and says he has no interest in doing anything else. Excited daily by the smells and textures of the gardens and farms that he has helped inspire, he is continually inventing new dishes, creating new recipes, and inventing new combinations. But his dishes are never the inept manifestations of the novice. They are the result of more than two decades of working with food and training with some of America's most talented professionals.

Lee began his career working in small restaurants in Columbia, South Carolina. With some of the basics behind him, Lee felt he was ready for the big city. The two years of training under chef Jovan Trboyevic at Le Per-

roquet in Chicago refined his talents and his approach and provided the classical training that is still the core of Lee's food. He learned finesse, subtlety, and the fine art of great sauces from chef Yannic Cam at Le Pavilion in Washington, D.C. But Lee wanted to return to his homeland. He came back to South Carolina as sous chef at Charleston's Relais et Chateau Restaurant Million. In 1991 Charleston Restaurateur Richard Elliott asked Lee to take on the chef's position at Charleston's oldest restaurant, The Colony House. When Elliott sold The Colony House and opened Slightly North of Broad in December, 1992, Lee moved with him as executive chef. Today he oversees not only Slightly North of Broad, but also Elliott's new restaurant, Slightly Up the Creek.

Calling his food "maverick southern cuisine," Lee has distinguished his food with his use of multicultural flavoring that employs a variety of herbs and spices. It is, he says, "southern food with a twist, or, perhaps, international with a Low-country interpretation." The innovation and diligence have paid off. He has earned much praise and legions of loyal followers. *GQ's* Alan Richman was so overwhelmed by Lee's Shrimp and Grits that the magazine awarded Lee with their coveted Golden Dish Award, which recognizes the ten best dishes of the year, a list that includes national and international entries. He has appeared on television, his recipes have been published in cookbooks, and travel writers always list Lee as one of Charleston's very best. Although appreciative of the acknowledgments, Lee says his best reward is "in the satisfied smiles of his diners."

Frank Lee's recipe for Grilled Barbecued Tuna is on page 74.

CHRISTOPHER MALTA
1848 House
Atlanta, Georgia

Raised in Rochester, New York, Christopher Malta got his first kitchen job in high school at the Perkins' family restaurant. When his high school's culinary team won second place in a chocolate competition, Malta knew he had found his true vocation. He enrolled at the State University of Cobleskill in New York, and graduated with an associate degree in occupational studies with a culinary major.

Malta's first job after college was first line cook at the Hyatt Regency in St. John in the U.S. Virgin Islands. From there he moved to southern California to take a job in the pastry shop at the Hyatt Grand Champions Resort. Anxious to return to the East Coast, Malta then did a stint in Atlanta at the Atlanta Hilton and Towers, beginning as a pastry cook and moving up to supervisor before leaving in 1994. His next position was at Atlanta's Mobil four-star Nikolai's Roof, where he learned the art of the restaurant's elegant Continental Russian-accented pastries.

In 1994, at just twenty-three years of age, Malta was offered the pastry chef's position at Atlanta's 1848 House. William B. Dunaway, who sold a chain of drugstores and lovingly and painstakingly restored the Marietta property in order to create a fine southern experience, had purchased the restaurant in 1992. The kitchen keeps the award-winning menu current with a rotation of fine southern ingredients. Malta shares the same culinary philosophy and says that "with the changing of the seasons, comes the changing of the menu." And with a new menu every three months, Malta is free to unleash his considerable imagination on his confections. It is his aspiration that every meal conclude with a crescendo of delectable flavors at dessert.

Christopher Malta's recipe for Frozen Lime Ganache Parfait with Chocolate Tuiles is on page 154.

CORY MATTSON

The Fearrington House
Pittsboro, North Carolina

For more than a decade, chef Cory Mattson has been heading up Fearrington House's kitchen, creating the classic southern specialties that have earned the inn its membership in the prestigious Relais & Chateaux, AAA's five-diamond award, and Mobil's four-star award.

When Mattson graduated from the Culinary Institute of American in 1986 and arrived at The Fearrington House shortly thereafter, he probably did not realize that his work would continue there for over a decade. But the appeal of managing the elegant dining room, working closely with his staff, and overseeing the daily preparation of the four-course menu has kept him there.

The Fearrington House has thrived under Mattson, gaining strength from his growing reputation as one of the region's great culinarians. Articles featuring Mattson's talents have appeared in *Travel & Leisure*, *Food & Wine*, *Southern Living*, *Mid-Atlantic*, *Country Journal*, *Country Inns Magazine*, *Family Circle*, and the *New York Times*. The Fearrington House was the subject of a one-hour episode of "Great Country Inns" on The Learning Channel, and was also featured on the series *Great Country Inn Chefs*.

Fetzer Vineyards chose Mattson to represent "The New Cuisine of the Old South" in a national wine and cuisine promotion in 1990. He was a consultant to the North Carolina Department of Agriculture in Caracas, Venezuela, in 1994 for the American Harvest Festival, a three-week menu promotion sponsored by the Southern U.S. Trade Association featuring North Carolina food products.

Cory Mattson's recipe for Potato Crisp Pizza is on page 10, and Rice Paper-wrapped Tuna Loin with Ginger Sauce is on page 84.

Michael McSweeny

Dux
The Peabody Orlando
Orlando, Florida

Michael McSweeny has been in love with food and cooking since he was twelve. Born to a U.S. Navy family based in Ankara, Turkey, he spent his youth traveling the world and experiencing its cuisines. McSweeny reminisces about going to school with a lunch box packed with his mother's favorite exotic dishes—like Turkish kofta, ground lamb with rice and herbs. Today, with over twenty years of culinary credentials, McSweeny has combined his experiences to create an American cuisine for the twenty-first century.

A devotee of healthy food, McSweeny's grand passion is daily apparent on the menus that he creates at Dux. Menus that take diners on a Jules Verne-like culinary world tour— from Hawaii to Thailand, from Europe and back to the U.S. McSweeny is not limited by traditional pairings, but instead uses his imagination and skills to produce a unique profusion of tastes.

Perhaps it's the Irish in McSweeny that brings out the metaphysical poet, the lyricist in him. "Food is such a sensuous thing," he says. "At my table, I want to provide people with a new sensation, a new taste treat." He is likely, as well, to burst into song as he visits his happy guests in the dining room. But his feet are firmly planted on the ground, and his recipes are always harmonious. Contrasts, too, are frequently the hallmark of his dishes, hot and cold, robust and delicate, crunchy and smooth.

Under McSweeny's leadership, Dux has become the most celebrated restaurant in Orlando and is the only restaurant in town with a Mobil four-star rating. The restaurant has won the AAA four-diamond award, *Epicurean Rendezvous's* "Top 100 Restaurants in Florida" list, *Florida Trend's* "Golden Spoon"

award, and *Orlando* magazine's "Top 10 Restaurants in Central Florida" list.

Before joining The Peabody Orlando, McSweeny held positions ranging from souschef to executive chef at the Poipu Bay Resort and the Hyatt Regency on Kauai. Prior to that he worked under the direction of chef Ernest Herzog at the famous Couch Street Fish House in Portland, Oregon, and at the Veranda restaurant in Wild Dunes Beach and the Racquet Club, Isle of Palms, South Carolina. Stints in Florida kitchens included the Fountainbleau Hotel Resort & Spa, Miami, and Mark's Place in North Miami Beach.

Michael McSweeny's recipe for Stone Crab Cakes with Curried Potatoes and Thai Butter is on page 25.

Matthew Medure

The Dining Room, The Ritz-Carlton
Amelia Island, Florida

At the young age of twenty-six, Matthew Medure, chef of The Grill at The Ritz-Carlton, Amelia Island, was one of only two AAA five-diamond chefs in Florida, and one of only four in the Southeast. The Grill, under his leadership, is a winner of *Florida Trend* magazine's 1996 Golden Spoon awards, making it one of the top twenty restaurants in the state. *The Zagat Guide to U.S. Hotels, Resorts, and Spas* said "don't miss a meal in The Grill."

With a passionate desire to create beautiful food with simplicity, Medure creates new menus daily, combining his imagination with the freshest available ingredients.

The youngest chef ever to hold The Grill's top job, Medure began his career at twelve working in his family's catering business. Under his father's tutorship, Medure acquired a taste for cooking and a talent for making the ordinary extraordinary. He attended the Pennsylvania Institute for Culinary Arts while working full-time as a line cook at Maggie

Mae's Italian Restaurant in Pittsburgh. In 1990 he completed an externship at The Ritz-Carlton, Buckhead. By graduation, he had been promoted to first cook at The Café. In 1991 he was invited to be a member of the opening team for The Ritz-Carlton, Amelia Island. Shortly thereafter he was promoted to his current position.

Inspired by the world's great chefs, Medure continues to master and perfect his craft. Although he may consider himself still an apprentice, winemakers attending his dinners agree that the young chef is certainly one of tomorrow's rising stars. "Chef Medure's flair for marrying the right food to a winemaker's product reveals the creative genius within him," said executive chef Steven Schaefer.

In 1996 Medure completed a stage with Alain Ducasse, the Michelin five-star chef who owns and operates a Michelin three-star restaurant in Paris and Michelin 2 star restaurant in Monte Carlo. Medure was a 1996 nominee for the James Beard Perrier-Jouet "Rising Star Chef of the Year."

Matthew Medure's recipe for Poached Vidalia Onions with Foie Gras and Marmalade is on page 44.

DANIEL MELLMAN

Greenhouse Grill
Sanibel, Florida

Daniel Mellman's food is very much like him—well balanced, unpretentious, and extremely likable. At the heart of Mellman's personal and culinary successes are his creative energies fueled by a boundless enthusiasm for learning and exploration. It is these qualities that have built the success of the Greenhouse Grill.

The history of Mellman's career is a story of achievements. Pennsylvania native Mellman attended Muhlenberg College before he

began traveling and studying in France and Italy, learning classic techniques and regional cuisines. In France he studied with Michelin three-star chef Roger Verge. Returning to the U.S., Mellman presided over some of the most prestigious kitchens on the East Coast. While he was executive chef at Cape May's Mad Hatter, the restaurant was named to John Mariani's list of "America's Best Dining." His talents were touted and his story told in the *Washington Post*, the *Los Angeles Times*, and the *New York Times*.

In 1988 Mellman was ready to venture out on his own and he opened his original Greenhouse Restaurant on Captiva Island, Florida. From the start the restaurant was hailed by the press as one of Florida's best. In 1993 he and Ariel, his wife and partner, moved their restaurant to the Casa Ybel resort on Sanibel Island. Critics and reviewers continue to flock to the new location. *Florida Trend* named the Greenhouse to their list of Florida's "top restaurants," and the restaurant's wine list won an Award of Excellence from the *Wine Spectator*.

Mellman's pursuit of absolute freshness in ingredients and clear, pure flavors continues. He accomplishes this by maintaining his own herb garden and nurturing relationships with local growers. The quality of the ingredients is the key to the successes of dishes like this Greenhouse Grill Rack of Lamb; Wild Mushroom and Spinach Stuffed Risotto with Rosemary Glace; and Pan-seared Florida Quail on Frisee and Lentil Salad.

Daniel Mellman's recipe for Greenhouse Grill Rack of Lamb is on page 112.

HEATHER MENDENHALL

The Fearrington House
Pittsboro, North Carolina

Fearrington House is certainly North Carolina's most prestigious inn, and Heather

Mendenhall, the property's extraordinarily talented executive pastry chef, has helped to make it so. Yet Mendenhall did not immediately decide to become part of the world of pastry and butter. She began her studies in French at Northern Illinois University in Dekalb, Illinois. It wasn't long, however, before she discovered the restaurant kitchen and in 1992 she completed her A.A.S. degree in culinary arts at Kendall College in Evanston, Illinois. Determining to concentrate on pastries, Mendenhall continued her training at the Ewaldland Susan Notter International School of Confectionery Arts in Gaithersburg, Maryland.

Mendenhall's first professional job was at Il Palio Ristorante in Chapel Hill, North Carolina, where she tested new products and new recipes. She left North Carolina in 1992 to spend two years in Jean Banchet's chic French bistro in Atlanta, Ciboulette. It was there that she learned the intricacies and finesse of French pastries. At Fearrington House since 1994, Mendenhall works closely with her staff, overseeing the baking of pastry and the dessert production that keep the inn's patrons swooning.

At Fearrington House, Mendenhall is responsible as well for pastry production for all the weddings, receptions, and special occasion banquets held both in the restaurant and in the Fearrington Village meeting facilities.

Heather Mendenhall's recipe for Fearrington House Chocolate Refreshmint is on page 124.

DEAN MITCHELL

Morel's Restaurant
Banner Elk, North Carolina

Dean Mitchell's inspired classic cuisine has been attracting gourmets to his charming North Carolina mountain restaurant for nearly a decade. At Morel's Restaurant,

Mitchell turns out perfectly tuned dishes with imagination. Guests are frequently seduced by preparations that include local trout, game, and vegetables. Enchanting, too, are dishes like tortellini filled with quail and sun-dried apples that simply melts in your mouth, or the fennel and walnut couscous that accompanies the perfectly cooked seared salmon. It is the chef's pride that every item on the menu is carefully prepared and presented with flair.

Mitchell's special knack for updating classic dishes is the result of more than two and a half decades in the restaurant business. He began as a young man working for his father in country clubs and hotels in South Florida. He broadened his experiences and his food knowledge while traveling through Europe and North America, ceaselessly working all the while to improve his skills.

Before starting Morel's, Mitchell opened several top-rated restaurants in South Florida, including Café La Europe and the Epicurean Palm Beach, and was the evening sous chef at the Breaker Resort. *Food & Wine* magazine recognized his accomplishments in their 1983 "Honor Roll of American Chefs."

Dean Mitchell's recipe for Duck and Sweet Potato Hash with Quail Eggs, Sunny Side Up is on page 38, and Morel-crusted Trout Salad with Apple and Walnut Vinaigrette is on page 51.

FREDERICK MONTI

Brasserie Le Coze
Atlanta, Georgia

"Brasserie Le Coze is absolutely perfect" screamed Atlanta's insider guide *Knife and Fork*. And, absolutely perfect is the way to describe Frederick Monti's pastries that have helped earned the restaurant such grand accolades.

Monti's exquisite pastries and desserts are

the results of long years of study at the Pastry School in the south of France in Avignon and training at the famous Lenotre Restaurant and Bakery in Paris. As sous chef at Bechart Touget Bakery in Aix-en-Provence, Montl refined his skills and studied his craft—always seeking the perfection, taste, and innovation that would ultimately win him such praise.

The study also earned Monti the chance to travel across the Atlantic to New York and land the chef's position at Frederic's Bakery. There Monti trained with well-known pastry chef Herve Poussot of New York's Le Bernadin. When in 1994 he was asked to assume the executive pastry chef's position at the new Brasserie Le Coze in Atlanta, he knew that his lifelong work had been recognized and rewarded.

Frederick Monti's recipe for Praline Mousse with Chocolate Meringue is on page 133.

Norma Naparlo

Magnolia's
Charleston, South Carolina

Norma Naparlo was born in the small community of Black River Falls, Wisconsin, the youngest of eight children. Later the family moved to a 240-acre dairy farm in the northern part of the state, which they farmed for the next twelve years. Because vegetable gardens, pigs, and fruit orchards were also part of the property, cooking, baking, and canning were a part of everyday life. It was the lifestyle that stimulated Naparlo's passion for food and cooking.

Shortly after high school graduation, Naparlo moved to the East Coast and spent time in Washington, D.C. and Virginia Beach. She moved to Charleston, South Carolina in 1985. Her first job was with a small caterer and local resort, Wild Dunes. When Hurricane Hugo blew through town in 1989, Wild

Dunes was shuttered, and Naparlo moved on to be pastry chef for well-known caterer Stephen Duvall. When a short time later the business was sold, Naparlo accepted the pastry chef position at Charleston's new restaurant, Anson's.

By 1993 word of Naparlo's skills in the pastry kitchen had spread, and Donald Barickman offered her the executive pastry chef job at his Hospitality Management Group, which operates two of Charleston's most popular restaurants, Magnolia's and Blossom Café. Since her ascent to the head of Magnolia's pastry kitchen, the restaurant has become Charleston's most sought-after destination for dessert. A connoisseur of the region's traditional dishes, the chef uses the best local produce to prepare her fresh baked confections, and the homemade breads and pastries are arguably the best in town.

Norma Naparlo's recipe for Baked Creams with Orange Custard Sauce is on page 127.

Chris Northmore

Cherokee Town & Country Club
Atlanta, Georgia

Chris Northmore, executive pastry chef at Atlanta's Cherokee Town & Country Club since 1986, inherited his creative eye from his commercial photographer father. Years of training taught Northmore the art of working with his hands. The aggregate of his talents— his artistic eye, agile hands, and imagination— has won him a Master Pastry Chef certification from the Culinary Institute of America in Hyde Park—one of only three certified in the United States through the American Culinary Federation. It was high praise, indeed, from his alma mater, the result of years of dedication and hard work.

Northmore studied business administration at Eastern Michigan University, but found his niche studying pastry at the Culinary Institute of America. When he graduated in 1979, he decided to try a stint in a pastry shop and landed a job at Atlanta's Omni Hotel with Gunther Heiland, master pastry chef and an Olympic team veteran. More than two years later, Northmore followed Heiland to Philadelphia's Fairmont Hotel (now the Bellevue Stratford), as assistant pastry chef. After two and a half years there, Northmore moved to Boston as executive chef at the Parker House.

Northmore considers Heiland his "father in the pastry business. He gave me direction and got me involved in culinary competitions." Among the competitions Northmore refers to is the 1988 U.S. Culinary Olympics in Frankfurt, Germany. As a member of the team, Northmore was responsible for the dessert platters and plates that the national team presented. It was Northmore that dreamed up the Big Apple Dessert served during the hotel food competition that helped win the team the first-place prize.

Order and discipline define Northmore's work. As he says, they come with the territory. "You have to be constantly aware of proper temperatures and consistencies." Although he feels his strength is chocolate work, he is not content to confine his talents to one area of the pastry kitchen. Working with sugar and yeast fascinate him as well, and he has studied sugar pulling and sugar blowing, and taken bread dough courses. Yet despite the seeming complexities of his desserts, his philosophy remains that of "simplistic elegance." He is aware that "it's too easy to produce very complex desserts." His goal is simple, straightforward presentations coupled with a light touch and intense flavors.

Chris Northmore's recipe for Lemon Parfait with Fruits and Sauces is on page 138

DANIEL O'LEARY
Buckhead Diner
Atlanta, Georgia

When chef Daniel O'Leary arrived at the Buckhead Diner in Atlanta, he brought with him over fifteen years of culinary experience from some of the country's most prestigious restaurants. This Massachusetts native graduated from the Culinary Institute of America, before beginning his career as a grill cook at La Bagatelle in Washington, D.C.. From there he became sous chef at Maison Blanche, and then chef tourant at Le Lion D'Or, two of the District's most popular restaurants. O'Leary's next stint was at two of Dallas's famous spots—the Hotel Crescent Court and the Mansion on Turtle Creek. While executive sous chef at the Mansion, he was credited with revamping the menu from French to California cuisine. O'Leary remarks that his refined skills are due to mentors Dean Fearing at the Mansion on Turtle Creek and Pierre Chambrin, executive chef at the White House.

Under his guidance, the Buckhead Diner's menu combines the appeal of southern comfort foods with tinges of southwestern and Asian flair. Free-range chicken and game birds play a big part in his menu. He believes that the preparations at the Buckhead Diner counter the misconception of fat-laden southern food. He aims to bring out the natural flavors in the foods, "without just masking or adding to it."

O'Leary has been the recipient of many awards and honors. While executive chef at the Hotel Crescent Court in Dallas, the restaurant was selected by *Esquire* as "Best New Restaurant" for 1990. At the same time, he was honored by the magazine as "Top Chef of Texas." In 1992 O'Leary was featured in the *Lifestyles of the Rich & Famous Cookbook*. During his tenure the Buckhead Diner has been the recipient of numerous national and international culinary honors.

Daniel O'Leary's recipe for Barbecued Spiced Oysters on Creamy Succotash is on page 31.

LOUIS OSTEEN

Louis's Charleston Grill
Charleston, South Carolina

Louis Osteen, chef/creator of Louis's Charleston Grill was born in Anderson, South Carolina, the son and grandson of theater owners. In 1975 he left the traditional livelihood of his ancestors to pursue his passion for cooking and the regional foods of the South and began an apprenticeship with Atlanta's then most acknowledged chef, Francoise Delcrosse.

In 1980 he and his wife, Marlene, moved to Pawleys Island, South Carolina, to open the Pawleys Island Inn. Immediately, Osteen became a leader in the exploding movement for indigenous American cuisine, developing recipes and participating with other young chefs to create an American consumer audience for their uniquely American product. The originality of his recipes, the honesty of his food preparation methods, and his overwhelming enthusiasm for his locale stirred the attention of the regional and national press. *Nation's Restaurant News* said "Southern-born Osteen is celebrated as one of the chief proponents of Low-Country cuisine."

In 1989 Louis's desire to reach a larger audience combined with the interest of the owners of the Omni Hotel at Charleston Place to reformat their existing restaurant. In October 1989, Louis's Charleston Grill opened to immediate praise, receiving national media attention when it was selected by *Esquire* magazine as one of the country's "Top 25 New Restaurants." He has been called by one admiring food writer "the pride of Charleston," and recognized by Bryan Miller

of the *New York Times* as "the spiritual general of . . . the new Charleston chefs." Osteen and his recipes have been featured in *Gourmet, Bon Appetit, Southern Living, GQ, Esquire, Saveur, Food & Wine*, and *Town & Country*.

His numerous awards include: 1996 James Beard nominee, Great American Chef, southeast; *Restaurants & Institutions* magazine's Ivy Award; 1994 recipient of *Nation's Restaurant News* "Fine Dining Hall of Fame." GQ magazine's food and wine writer, Alan Richman, awarded Osteen the Golden Dish Award for having created one of the ten best dishes of 1994. Osteen serves on the board of directors of DiRoNa, is a former member of the food board of the New England Culinary Institute, and is a founding co-organizer of Charleston's Share Our Strength Taste of the Nation event.

Osteen's recipe for Lamb Ribs with Shallot-Pepper Butter Sauce is on page 42, and Berry Cobbler is on page 140.

PASCAL OUDIN

The Grand Bay Hotel
Miami, Florida

Selected by *Food & Wine* magazine as one of America's "Best New Chefs" in 1995, and by *Esquire* magazine's restaurant critic, John Mariani, as one of "America's New Chefs to Watch" in 1995, Pascal Oudin has set new standards on the South Florida regional American culinary map.

Born in Moulin, France, Oudin received his chef's training in the great kitchens of France, under the guidance of three-star Michelin luminaries Roger Verge, Alain Ducasse, Gaston Lenotre, and Joseph Rostang.

Oudin has modified the way Florida and new world cuisine are perceived by combining his French cooking techniques with the tropical ingredients and ethnic influences of the region. Accolades have followed. The *Wine Spectator* said of Oudin's cooking that it "has achieved a delicate balance of tastes and textures, one that many other Florida chefs might well copy." The Grand Café was honored by *South Florida* magazine as one of the best restaurants in the region and best in Dade County. The *Zagat* survey lists The Grand Café in Miami's "Top 20 Food Rankings," calling it " a treat in all respects," and saying that "the serious regional American restaurant offers some of Miami's finest dining . . . with impeccable food."

In 1989 Oudin won the prestigious Florida Chef of the Year Award from Chefs of America while opening the Colonnade Hotel in Coral Gables. Prior to assuming his position at the Grand Bay Hotel, Oudin was part of the opening team of "Festival Disney" at Euro-Disney in Paris.

Pascal Oudin's recipe for Tropical Tiramisu is on page 135.

DEBRA PAQUETTE

Bound'ry Restaurant
Nashville, Tennessee

A native of Ft. Lauderdale, Florida, Debra Paquette describes her cuisine as Fusion-Mediterranean-Asian-Southern. Or, as she says, " I could be buried in capers." *Atlanta Journal-Constitution* restaurant reviewer Ann Bryn described Paquette's ingenious inventions at the Bound'ry as reading "like some multicultural crossword puzzle—sushi with poblano peppers or southern porkchops seasoned with Japanese wasabi." She also adores vegetables, especially the wild mushrooms and morels she and her family forage on their farm in Kingston, Tennessee. Braised venison with morels and raisins is one of her favorite dishes to cook and eat.

Raised in a family of great male cooks—her first mentors were her father and grandfather—she learned early on to appreciate the pure essence of flavors and to respect the

integrity and individuality of her ingredients. A culinary career was the natural outgrowth of her upbringing, and in 1978 Paquette graduated from the Culinary Institute of America. From there she continued her education at Florida International University and in 1989 received a bachelor in hospitality service. She spent seven years as executive chef at Nashville's Cakewalk restaurant before taking the executive chef position at the Bound'ry.

Culinary specialties like Curried Lobster Flapjacks; Southwestern Sushi (salmon, rice, and vegetables in a flour tortilla served with poblano dipping sauce); Double Porkchop Grilled over Hickory and Glazed with Sorghum and Wasabi have earned her culinary fame. *Nashville Life* magazine named Paquette "Chef of the Year" two consecutive years, and the restaurant was voted Best New Restaurant in 1996. Recognized as well for her accomplishments by her peers in the local restaurant community, she is vice president of the Middle Tennessee Culinary Association of the American Culinary Federation. Paquette was the first woman in the state to become a certified executive chef. She is currently busily at work planning menus for the two new Bound'ry restaurants scheduled to open in 1998.

Paquette devotes her spare time to her favorite charity—she is cochair of Nashville's Taste of the Nation—boxing classes, her husband, and two children.

Debra Paquette's recipe for Salmon South-by-Southwest is on page 88.

REIMUND PITZ

Disney-MGM Studios
Lake Buena Vista, Florida

German-born Reimund Pitz immigrated to the United States through a European apprenticeship program to attend the Disney School of Culinary Arts. His employment began with The Walt Disney World Co. in

1978 as a culinary assistant at the Disney Village Restaurant. He quickly advanced through the culinary ranks and was promoted to area chef in 1979. By 1984 Pitz had progressed to sous chef at the Walt Disney World's Polynesian Resort and in 1986 was again promoted to chef de cuisine for Epcot Center. In 1988 at just thirty years of age, he was promoted to executive chef at Disney-MGM Studios.

At the Disney-MGM Studios restaurants he oversees—the Hollywood Brown Derby and 50's Prime Time Café—Pitz is known for his innovative culinary contributions. A polished pro, his ingenious and delightful dishes have won him accolades that include the American Culinary Federation's top honor, "1992 National Chef of the Year." In culinary competitions, he has acceded to the highest honors, winning a perfect score at the 1988 Culinary Olympics. In June 1992 he was the youngest chef to be inducted into "The Honorable Order of the Golden Toque"—an organization that recognizes only one hundred culinary professional in the U.S. He has won also the "Chef's Professionalism Award," twenty-six gold medals (including six international), several silver and bronze medals including Best of Show, the Florida Governor's Cup Seafood Challenge two years in a row, and the 1995 ACF President's Medallion. In 1992 Pitz served as adviser to the Culinary Olympic Team U.S.A.

Active as well in his community, Pitz devotes time to a host of children related programs. He has chaired the National Children's Foundation, Inc., the function of which is to provide funds for medical treatment, his work on children's daily nutritional needs was featured on a CNN *Nutri News TV* broadcast, he frequently prepares monthly breakfasts and dinners at the Orlando Boy's Ranch, and he is a volunteer at the career day programs at the Seminole County School.

Reimund Pitz's recipe for Fruited Cobb Salad is on page 54.

STEVEN SCHAEFER
The Ritz-Carlton
Amelia Island, Florida

Steven Schaefer wears two toques at The Ritz-Carlton, Amelia Island. As executive chef he leads a culinary team that serves award-winning cuisine for the resort's restaurants. As director of food and beverages, he positions the hotel as a leader in the industry with The Festival of Wine and New World Cuisine; The Smoker—A Cigar Connoisseur's Dinner; monthly cooking schools, winemakers' dinners, and children's Storybook Teddy Bear Teas.

At fourteen, Chicago native Schaefer was looking for a part-time job after school and landed a dishwashers position in a small restaurant. Most teenagers would have considered this a pretty thankless job, but Schaefer became fascinated by what was going on in the kitchen. As he got older he increasingly found jobs in kitchens. "You could say that I was always in the right place at the right time," said Steve, "because as soon as I would take a lower-level kitchen job in a small place, someone above me would leave, and I'd get promoted immediately." At the age of nineteen, Schaefer was already the head chef of the Richmond Mill Inn in Ann Arbor, Michigan. He eventually got a job as one of the chefs at Chicago's acclaimed Ritz-Carlton. It was then and there that he decided his future was as a hotel executive chef. Other stints followed, including the Century Country Club in Westchester, New York. Then Schaefer got a call from the Executive Hotel in San Diego. He left California for a stint at the Fairmont in Dallas, vowing to return. There was an interval stop at Washington, D.C.'s Four Seasons Hotel before his eventual return to the West Coast—initially at The Doubletree Hotel in Marina del Ray, and in 1991 joining the opening team at The Ritz-Carlton, Amelia Island, as executive chef.

Schaefer's cooking secret is to pay attention to the little details. "It's very important how you display the food on the dish," says Steve, "since eye appeal is one of the most important factors in enjoying your meal." But as beautiful as Schaefer's cuisine is, even more important, it tastes sublime. He is passionate about his trade, continually creating ingenious and imaginative new sensations for the palate while fostering the personal development of his staff.

Steven Schaefer's recipe for Roasted Game Hen with Goat Cheese and Spinach is on page 96.

GUENTER SEEGER

The Dining Room
The Ritz-Carlton Buckhead
Atlanta, Georgia

Chef Seeger acquired his love for the fruits and vegetables of the land from his family's produce business in Baden-Baden, Germany. He acquired his passion for cooking at the age of thirteen when he began his apprenticeship at the Hotel School Montana in Lucerne, Switzerland. There he learned all the fine arts of the restaurateur: food, wine, bartending, the genteel skills of the maître d'. By the age of twenty-eight Seeger was ready to open his own fifty-seat restaurant near Germany's Black Forest. In 1980 after operating his restaurant just three years, Seeger received the prestigious Michelin Guide star.

In 1985 a fellow German and then general manager of the Ritz-Carlton Hotel persuaded Seeger to bring his talents and prestige to their growing hotel chain. In his capacity as executive chef of the hotel's Dining Room, Seeger blends his traditional European haute cuisine with regional American cuisine, a synergy that has won him praises and accolades since his arrival. The Dining Room can count among its prizes the AAA five-diamond,

Mobil four-star, and the *Zagat America's* "Top Restaurant," and "Triple Crown" awards. The Dining Room was recognized as one of the top twenty-four restaurants in the U.S. by *Food and Wine* magazine, and was ranked sixth of the nation's top fifty in *Conde Naste Traveler's* January 1995 readers poll.

Seeger is not one to rest on his laurels. He works tirelessly for the restaurant community, and has lent his talents to various charity events including Meals on Wheels–A Meal to Remember, and Share Our Strength Taste of the Nation. He has achieved much, but still works to increase his skills, always testing new methods—and, of course, searching for new produce suppliers.

Guenter Seeger's recipe for Asparagus Charlotte is on page 1.

DAWN SEIBER

Cheeca Lodge
Islamorada, Florida

Dawn Seiber probably did not know when she enrolled at the University of Miami to pursue a degree in psychology that she would someday be analyzing the impact of food combinations on taste rather than the combination of personality traits on behavior. But somewhere along the path to a degree in psychology, Seiber's own analysis took her to the Baltimore International Culinary Arts Institute, where she graduated first in her class with a dual degree.

Not long after graduation, Seiber opened and operated The Red Star, a successful forty-seat bistro in historic Baltimore. A short time later, in 1988, Cheeca Lodge reopened following a $30 million renovation, and lured Seiber to Florida as their executive sous chef. It was not long before Seiber was promoted to executive chef, where she has stamped her signature style and "new American" cuisine on the menu.

President Bush dined twice at chef Seiber's table, and *Esquire, Food & Wine, Travel & Leisure,* and the *Miami Herald* have all lauded her talents. She has cooked at the prestigious Masters of Food and Wine at the Highlands Inn in Carmel, California, on the CBS *Morning Show,* and at Julia Child's gala birthday dinner, which was hosted and filmed for television by Boston's Channel 2.

Not complacent to restrict her talents to the stoves, Seiber recently hosted the American Institute of Wine and Food weekend of fishing, food, and fun and the Celebrity Chefs Eco-Challenge. As part of the Eco-Challenge, which pitted celebrity chefs against participating foodies, the agenda included a discussion of environmental responsibility in the kitchen. The forum opened a discussion of the pros and cons of using farm-raised food products versus the exhaustion of natural resources. Concerned about the delicate ecological balance, Seiber's goal is "to bring more public awareness to our fragile reef ecosystem and depletion of our natural resources by focusing our event on earth-friendly methods in our industry."

Seiber's dedication to her craft and her pledge to the environment symbolize the strong sense of responsibility and community that chefs across America are displaying.

Dawn Seiber's recipe for Yellowtail Snapper Encrusted in Yuca with Roasted Pepper-Orange Salsa and Sizzling Black Beans is on page 68, and Stone Crab Cakes with Red Pepper Remoulade is on page 24.

JAMIE SHANNON

Commander's Palace
New Orleans, Louisiana

Jamie Shannon says that 70 percent of the ingredients he uses come from within one hundred miles of New Orleans. Commander's Palace, honored as the best in the U.S. by the James Beard Foundation, is the destination of choice for locals and visitors alike in New Orleans. Its kitchen has seen chefs such as Paul Prudhomme, Emeril Lagasse, and Frank Brigtsen; now Shannon upholds the tradition. As guests walk through his kitchen on their way to other parts of the mansion housing the restaurant, he creates a menu that is at once contemporary and traditional New Orleans.

Shannon's first job was in a cafeteria, where he worked his way from busboy to cook. Enticed to make the culinary arts his career, he studied at the Culinary Institute of America under the tutelage of chef Tim Ryan. After working at Trump Tower in Atlantic City, he moved to New Orleans at Ryan's suggestion, became saucier at Commander's Palace, and progressed to executive chef. Under Shannon, Commander's culinary staff makes its own Worcestershire sauce, sausages, and cheeses. Shannon has steadfastly supported local suppliers and farmers, and is commited to fresh, seasonal products. "For American cuisine to grow, we're going to have to support local producers. And be flexible as chefs and consumers—and not demand what's not available. The best cuisine is to cook and eat what's in our own backyard," he says.

Jamie Shannon's recipe for Pressed Duck is on page 105.

ANOOSH SHARIAT

Shariat's
Louisville, Kentucky

Like many of today's chefs, Persian-born Anoosh Shariat began his culinary career at a young age. He was only fourteen when he left Iran in 1972 to attend high school in West Germany. Jobs in a European restaurant kitchen helped cover his expenses and expand his cooking horizons. Although he left Europe for the U.S. to further his education in electronics, Shariat was by this time an accomplished cook and decided that he would really rather spend time in a kitchen than a college library.

Shariat has a truly multicultural background. From his Iranian birthplace and schooling in West Germany, Shariat moved to Texas to learn the fine points of southwestern and Mexican food. There, during the late 1970s and early 1980s, Shariat was honing his culinary talents as executive chef at Remington's. His reputation soon spread to Louisville.

When he opened Shariat's in 1993 with wife and partner, Sharron, he combined elements from all the diverse cuisines he had been exposed to. The end result, which he describes as "global cuisine," has received accolades from the beginning. *Nation's Restaurant News* and *Restaurant Business* have both raved about Shariat's accomplishments. On the local scene, the restaurant received a near perfect rating and was deemed "a flawless delight" by the *Courier Journal*. The same year it was voted "Best New Restaurant" by *Louisville* magazine. Shariat's continues to remain at the top of the critics' "A" list for fine dining.

A vegetarian for more than thirty years, Shariat has received praise for his innovative vegetarian preparations. His wild mushroom stew and vegetarian sushi were featured in *Restaurant Business* magazine, and his portabello mushroom and quinoa and shiitake timbale with sesame-cactus pear fusion were the subject of an article for *Restaurant Hospitality*

Chef Shariat and his wife, Sharron, are busy as well with a range of community activities that include Dare to Care Kid's Café, the Louisville Orchestra, Share Our Strength, the Healing Place, Earth Save, and the March of Dimes.

Anoosh Shariat's recipe for Herb-crusted Red Snapper with Pine Nut-Herb Sauce is on page 000, and Cardamom Cake with Saffron Ice Cream is on page 70.

SUSAN SPICER

Bayona
New Orleans, Louisiana

"I use an eclectic mixture of ingredients and styles, but it all makes sense. My taste is the filter. And I have a good grasp of what's agreeable to my customers," says Susan Spicer, chef-proprietor of Bayona, discussing her menu that ranges from Boudin Noir with Apples and Onions to Crawfish Curry with Lime Pickle.

Spicer served a three-year apprenticeship in New Orleans at the Louis XVI restaurant and, in the summer of 1982, apprenticed under chef Roland Durand at Hotel Sofitel in Paris. "That was a turning point in my career. It gave me a real solid sense of where I was and a chance to compare myself to other professionals."

Spicer returned from France to become the executive chef at Savoir Faire restaurant in New Orleans where she cooked for celebrities such as Clint Eastwood. In 1985, after three years at Savoir Faire, she took a Wanderjahr and traveled extensively through Europe and California.

In 1986, as chef, Spicer opened the Bistro at Maison de Ville, and in 1990, as owner, she opened Bayona.

Spicer started receiving media acclaim in 1989—and the good reviews keep coming in. In 1989, she was featured in *Time* and *Esquire* magazines, and *Food & Wine* named her one of its "Ten Best New Chefs." Gault-Millau named Bayona among its "Top 40 Places to dine in the U.S.," and she was honored at the James Beard Foundation "Rising Star" Dinner in 1991, and again as the "Best Southeast Chef" in 1993.

She believes that in American cuisine, "trends develop through products as they become available." Some of her favorite flavors include citrus zest, soy sauce, Indonesian sweet soy sauce ("I lived in Holland as a kid"), curry pastes, lemon verbena, and chives. And she finds birds—quail, pheasant, duck, chicken, turkey—among the most versatile products to work with.

Spicer's recipe for Bayona Crispy Smoked Quail Salad is on page 52, and Beef Tenderloin Stuffed with Herb Cream Cheese with Sauce Bordelaise is on page 108.

FRANK STITT
Highlands Bar & Grill
Birmingham, Alabama

For a boy from Cullman, Alabama, Frank Stitt has certainly developed an international palate. He studied philosophy at the University of California at Berkely, where he met Alice Waters of the renowned Chez Panisse, and Frank Olney. Stitt worked in France with Olney, Simca Beck, and wine authority Stephen Spurrier. Returning to Alabama, he blended his culinary heritage with Mediterranean influence to launch two of Birmingham's most inventive restaurants, Highlands Bar & Grill and Bottega Restaurant. Both have been lauded for Stitt's wonderful food and originality. Stitt was named one of *Food & Wine's* "Top 25 Hot New American Chefs," and was named a "Rising Star" by the James Beard Foundation. Highlands was named "Best Regional Restaurant" by *Esquire*, and placed in the 1992 Fine Dining Hall of Fame by DiRoNa. The locals say it best: Highlands has been voted Birmingham's best restaurant every year since 1991.

Frank Stitt's recipe for Grilled and Braised Rabbit with Molasses, Bourbon, Slab Bacon, and Stone Ground Grits is on page 106, and Pork Tenderloin "au Poivre" is on page 110.

ELIZABETH A. STRITCH
Slightly North of Broad
Charleston, South Carolina

Elizabeth Stritch, or Libby, as she is known to friends and family, learned to bake by baking. The Baltimore, Maryland, native apprenticed at the whisks and mixers of Randall Peck, pastry chef at Baltimore's Donna's in Mt. Vernon, and at Donna's at the Baltimore Museum of Art. It was there that she acquired the skills to assume the demanding job of preparing the desserts, daily specials, cakes, sauces and mousses for Slightly North of Broad.

Peck taught his rising star how to maintain and service the garde manger station, a lesson that includes baking as well as management skills. She learned there, too, how to work the pasta and sauté station and use the restaurant's brick oven to maximum efficiency. She was such an impressive student that in 1994 she landed the kitchen manager's job at Donna's Café in Baltimore. There she organized the kitchen and its staff, did the daily ordering, and created the daily pasta specials.

She was so good at her job that Slightly North of Broad's chef, Frank Lee, took notice. In 1995 Lee persuaded Stritch to join him as pastry chef at his growing restaurant. Her desserts have been wowing Charleston residents and visitors since her arrival, and have helped secure the restaurant's status as one of the city's best and most sought-after dining destinations. Still learning and growing, Stritch says that she loves being at a place where "I have the opportunity to challenge my skills and broaden my experience." She values her association with chef Frank Lee, whom she considers a second and valuable mentor and tutor.

Elizabeth Stritch's recipe for Chocolate Genoise Truffle Torte with Fresh Berries is on page 170.

ALLEN SUSSER

Chef Allen's
North Miami, Florida

Allen Susser remembers the Brooklyn of his childhood as a place that loved the celebration and warmth of food. Recognizing his destiny, Susser embraced a culinary career early on and has never wavered.

By 1976 he had cooked his way through the New York City Technical College Restaurant Management School at the top of his class, receiving the Ward Arbury Award. The years immediately after were spent absorbing classic French cooking and discipline, both at the Bristol Hotel in Paris and at Le Cirque in New York. This, he says, gave him "balance and respect for foods."

Despite the culinary wonders of New York, Susser was drawn to the warmth of Miami and what was then undiscovered culinary territory. As a chef at the elegant Turnberrry Isle Resort, he began to explore the native foods of South Florida, combining fresh local fish with tropical fruits.

In 1986 Susser opened his own place, Chef Allen's. "Crisp," "satisfying," and "refreshing" are some of the adjectives Susser uses to describe what he is about in a kitchen that he defines as "new world cuisine." The Caribbean, Latin America, and the United States are all resources for Susser's pantry, which includes mango and star fruits, cobia, wahoo and pompano fish, Scotch bonnet chilies, and exotic spices and flavorings.

In his spare time Susser picked up another degree, with honors, at the Florida International University School of Hospitality Management, and stayed on to teach classes.

As first Miami and then the rest of the world began to recognize and appreciate this new cuisine, Susser began to achieve national recognition. His press book is a litany to what can be achieved. Beginning in 1981 with a silver medal from the American Culinary Federation, to *Travel & Leisure's* 1989 "Top 20 Chefs in the U.S.A.," and on to *Food & Wine* magazine's 1991 "Best New Chef," and culminating with the industry's highest award, the James Beard Perrier-Jouet Great American Chef, Southeast. He is justifiably proud of such high praise, and gladdened particularly that the South Florida cuisine he helped to engineer has attained such high regard.

Joining chefs around the country, Susser takes time to help feed the homeless and the homebound elderly. He chairs both Share Our Strength's Taste of the Nation and the Miami branch of Meals on Wheels. As he puts it, "I love to cook; I make food my hobby, my profession, and my charity." For Allen Susser, all three began at home.

Allen Susser's recipe for Brioche Pain Perdu with Orange Balsamic Syrup is on page 116, Roast Bahamian Lobster with Chilis, Saffron, Vanilla and Rum is on page 63, and Stone Crab Cobbler with Coconut Milk, Chilis, Key Lime, and Coriander is on page 26.

CASEY TAYLOR

The Rhett House Inn
Beaufort, South Carolina

Growing up in Memphis, Tennessee, Casey Taylor spent weekends fishing with his dad in the freshwater rivers of Mississippi and Arkansas, and afternoons with a local farmer's wife learning to cook greens, succotashes, and chicken and dumplings. There were also holidays spent in his grandmother's kitchen observing preparations of large family feasts. Then in the summer of his sixteenth year, Casey helped a friend build a house in Asheville, North Carolina, and found himself immersed in a budding ecological movement, surrounded by enthusiastic gardeners who were experimenting with exotic fruits and vegetables. From these experiences, fused with a love of the earth and a fundamental culinary education, the son of an accountant and industrial engineer developed a passion for food and cooking.

In 1984, Casey began biomedical engineering studies at Christian Brothers College in Memphis, Tennessee, and simultaneously launched his culinary career at a barbecue pit owned by the famed impresario of Memphis's international barbecue contest, John Wills. It hadn't been his intention to become a chef, but after stints at more restaurants, including The Peabody Hotel, Taylor realized that his future was at the stoves.

In 1988 he enrolled at Johnson and Wales in Charleston, South Carolina. When he was not studying, Casey worked at Charleston's busiest restaurant, Carolina's, under chef Donald Barickman. It was at Carolina's that Casey cut his culinary teeth and learned the techniques and discipline required to run a kitchen and develop recipes.

When, in 1989, Barickman left Carolina's to assume stewardship of Magnolia's restaurant, Casey joined him as his sous chef.

Now, at The Rhett House Inn, Taylor is hard at work developing a southern pantry and creating memorable and creative dishes that focus on the best ingredients of the Low Country and products from his own garden in Wadmalaw Island, South Carolina.

Taylor's recipe for Stuffed Collard Greens with Roasted Chicken, Carolina Goat Cheese, and Blackeyed Pea Salad is on page 6.

ELIZABETH TERRY

Elizabeth's on 37th
Savannah, Georgia

Elizabeth's on 37th in Savannah, Georgia, opened in May of 1981 as the creation of chef Elizabeth Terry and her husband and wine steward, Michael. The simple elegance of their turn-of-the-century Southern mansion sets the perfect tone for her subtle and stunning new regional cooking based on wonderful old southern recipes. Chef Terry's devotion to classic southern cooking is such that she has extensively researched Savannah cooking of the eighteenth and nineteenth centuries. She found that inhabitants of this cosmopolitan port town have always eaten well, and her creations ensure that this will continue.

Terry's philosophy is that southern cooking is both country, back-of-the-stove cooking and her favorite, elegant and entertaining front-of-the-stove cooking. The food should be contemporary but must maintain recognizable old-fashioned flavors. Her goal is to "refine the experience" by making the most out of the wonderful bounty that is found along the southern coast, using the most beautiful basic ingredients and working to combine and enhance the flavors, textures, and preparation.

The South is known for its hospitality and award-winning Terry is known for her ability to create magic in the kitchen. With her cookbook, *Savannah Seasons: Food and Stories from Elizabeth's on 37th*, chef Terry, working with daughter Alexis, brings all the warmth of the South and the secrets of her culinary wizardry into the kitchens of home cooks everywhere.

Terry's reputation as an innovator and leader in the cuisine of the "New South" has brought her thousands of inches of print and a long list of industry prizes. She has been profiled in national magazines including *Town & Country, Time,* and *Harper's Bazaar,* and honored with the industry's top awards. In 1995 the James Beard Foundation named chef Terry the Perrier-Jouet America's Best Chef, Southeast. Elizabeth's on 37th received a four-star award from the *Mobil Travel Guide* in 1997 for being one of the best restaurants in America. *Restaurants & Institutions* distinguished Terry with their 1995 Ivy Award. Elizabeth's on 37th was named one of *Food & Wine* magazine's "Top 25 Restaurants in America," and to the *Nation's Restaurant News's* 1993 "Fine Dining Hall of Fame."

Terry is a 1966 graduate of Lake Erie College for Women with a degree in psychology. She currently serves on the board of Savannah's Small Business Assistance Corporation and the Savannah Area Chamber of Commerce-Tourist Board. She is the mother of two teenage daughters, Alexis and Celestine, who participate in the activities of the thriving Elizabeth's on 37th.

Elizabeth Terry's recipe for Shad Stuffed with Shad Roe is on page 87, and Chocolate Pecan Torte is on page 166.

GUILLERMO THOMAS
The Hermitage Hotel
Nashville, Tennessee

Chef Guillermo Thomas admits that before he arrived in Nashville he didn't know what a grit was. But that has not stopped him from incorporating some southern dialect into his menus at The Hermitage Hotel's Capital Grille.

In fact, the chef says, "We're heading toward using more local products and presenting them with a little bit of flair. Our cuisine here is based on classic French training and we're trying to add a southern flavor to it, and at the same time lighten it up." Thomas mentions a special cornmeal-seared redfish with crawfish and country ham dumplings in a black-eyed pea vinaigrette with fried green onions as an example of a recent southern-styled entrée. Other signature dishes include sautéed red snapper with garlic mashed potatoes, fresh spinach, and crispy onion rings in a red wine butter sauce, and soft shell crawfish panfried and served on a medallion of eggplant with honey roasted nuts, and finished in a lemon butter sauce.

Thomas was born in Gijón, Spain, but grew up in Pittsburgh. After getting his culinary degree from Johnson & Wales University in Rhode Island, Thomas spent two years

cruising the Virgin Islands, working as a chef on a private yacht. Though he loved the nomadic lifestyle, the experience left him craving a restaurant kitchen. He disembarked in the U.S., and spent the next five years moving seasonally—summers at the esteemed Chillingsworth Restaurant on Cape Cod, and winters at the Chills East Vail Bistro in Vail, Colorado. In 1993 he landed at The Hermitage Hotel.

Thomas's innovative, creative fare earned the restaurant the distinction of being one of *Esquire* magazine's "Top New Restaurants" of 1995, and one of the "Best Hotel Restaurants" in *American Way* magazine. *Diversions* magazine mentioned Thomas's bread pudding as one of the best in the country, and Nashville food critics have raved about the food at the Grille, describing it as "nirvana . . . and desserts that were orgasmic."

Guillermo Thomas's recipe for Pan-seared Scallops with Zucchini and Summer Squash, Cheddar Grits Soufflé, and Salmon Roe Butter Sauce is on page 56.

JEFFREY TUTTLE
Pawleys Plantation
Pawleys Island, South Carolina

Native New Yorker Jeffrey Tuttle learned the basics of cooking in his mother's kitchen. The self-taught chef's culinary education is really a melding of that foundation with tips learned in restaurant kitchens in New York and Maine.

As a chef of "regional American cuisine," Tuttle is free to draw upon the innumerable helpful hints he picked up in discussions with chefs during his travels to Atlanta, Houston, San Francisco, Philadelphia, New York City, and Williamsburg. One exceptionally informative opportunity, was the chance, in 1992, to study with Madeleine Kamman at the School for American Chefs at Beringer Vineyards in St. Helena, California, one of the most prestigious culinary schools in America. He was thrilled when, later, Kamman invited him to assist her at the James Beard House in New York City for her 1993 dinner saluting "Great American Chefs."

Since assuming the executive chef's position in 1990, Tuttle has earned a reputation for his creativity and plate presentation skills. His regional specialties have been featured in *Southern Living* magazine and *The State* newspaper. The innovative crawfish dishes that he prepared at the South Carolina Aquaculture and Crawfish Festival have three times won him the first-place prize. He has participated in the Georgetown, South Carolina County's Taste of the Tidelands and won awards in several categories at that competition. In December 1995, Tuttle was again invited to the James Beard House to prepare a Low Country Christmas dinner in collaboration with two other South Carolina chefs.

Tuttle stays busy at Pawleys Plantation managing the kitchen, dining room, grill, snack bar, banquet, and catering facilities. And he couldn't be happier doing so much. "Being a chef, especially at a place like Pawleys Plantation, is the best job I could have. I really enjoy coming to work every day, because for me it's not work to be able to do something that you love and to get paid for it."

Jeffrey Tuttle's recipe for Spicy Crawfish and Black Bean Phyllo Burritos with Cilantro Cream and Fresh Salsa is on page 29.

NORMAN VAN AKEN

Norman's
Coral Gables, Florida

He has been called a "Picasso in the kitchen," "a living legend among Epicureans everywhere," and "an artist of succulent talents." He is, in fact, Norman Van Aken, the chef credited with inventing the stylish south Florida nouvelle-tropical melting pot genre over a decade ago, first at his original Louie's Backyard in Key West, and then at a Mano in Miami Beach.

In 1995, following a two-year hiatus from the restaurant business to write a cookbook, Van Aken returned with his newest venture, Norman's and his followers have been exuberant. At the new "pistol hot" Norman's, Van Aken mans the stoves, astonishing his patrons with new taste delights and new applications for his native South Florida products. The dishes that come to the table at Norman's are a beguiling combination of exotic elements and colors.

Van Aken was nineteen in 1971 when he and friends in Champaign-Urbana, Illinois decided to drive a day and a half straight to Key West, Florida. "It was just like Candy Land," Van Aken reminisced years later. It wasn't long before his wonder of the place impelled him to relocate there. He began learning about South Florida's tropical fruit in small Cuban restaurants and was immediately mesmerized by the array of drinks made from the region's exotic fruits. Not impressed with the structured, as he called it, "French-toque guy" approach to cooking, he began forging his own style. "I began to consciously tear myself away from the French and the Italian and drive myself to find out more about Spanish, Caribbean, Central and South American cuisines—influences that I felt would give my cuisine a much more regionalized stamp and flavor and appeal."

In the late 1980s he brought this signature cuisine to the rest of the nation with his first cookbook, *Feast of Sunlight. The Great Exotic Fruit Book* followed in 1995. A third book, *Norman Van Aken's New World Cuisine*, was recently released.

Van Aken has been featured live on *Good Morning America*, TVFN, CNBC, and appeared on the pages of *Bon Appetit*, *USA Today*, *Food Arts*, *Food & Wine*, *The Wine News*, and *Art Culinaire*. In 1997 he received the industry's highest award, the James Beard

Perrier-Jouet Great American Chef Award, Southeast.

Norman Van Aken's recipe for Havana Bananas with Rum, Chilies, and Chocolate Sauce is on page 150, and Yuca-stuffed Shrimp with a Sour Orange Mayonnaise and Scotch Bonnet Tartar Sauce is on page 19.

GUILLERMO VELOSO

Yuca Restaurant
Miami Beach, Florida

Yuca, the acronym that stands for Young Urban Cuban American, is also the tuber that is one of the central ingredients in Cuban cooking. Yuca was the first Miami restaurant to combine the traditional flavors of the Cuban and Caribbean cuisines, and Veloso, the restaurant's new executive chef, has continued the menu and the concept in this vein. Using yuca and other exotic ingredients like plantains, bonitos, tamarinds, and fiery Scotch bonnet peppers, Veloso is reworking old-fashioned traditions and concepts.

Early in his professional career, Veloso made a dramatic change, switching from archaeology and anthropology studies at Rutgers University to culinary courses at Johnson & Wales. After graduation he honed his skills in the kitchens of several New Jersey restaurants before coming to Coral Gables to work at Restaurant San Michel. In 1991 Yuca's owners, Elaine Levy and Efrain Vega, lured him to Yuca, where he is now happily ensconced, creating the bold, bright dishes that have made the restaurant famous.

In 1996 a second Yuca opened on Miami Beach's rejuvenated Lincoln Road. Veloso's new menu at the second location is again drawing crowds, amassing a loyal clientele infatuated with Veloso's contemporary Cuban cuisine. As one writer so aptly put it, "Some chefs were born to replicate, some to innovate. Chef Veloso is clearly the latter. His imagination and keen sense of taste provide each individual diner with the ultimate blend of style, texture, and of course, Flavor!!!"

Guillermo Veloso's recipe for Shrimp and Plantain Torte is on page 13, and Cuban French Toast is on page 117.

ROBERT WAGGONER

Wild Boar Restaurant
Nashville, Tennessee

When Robert Waggoner arrived at the Wild Boar Restaurant, it was a Gaelic touching down. He had spent more than a decade in French kitchens learning the classic techniques and exquisite preparations that are the hallmark of French haute cuisine.

The California native received his first on-the-job training at Trumps in Los Angeles, from Michael Roberts. A series of stints working with Michelin starred chefs in France followed including Jacques Lameloise, Charles Barrier, Pierre Gagnaire, Gerard Boyer, and Marc Meneau. Briefly leaving France for a year to work in Caracas, Venezuela, as chef at Jean-Paul Coupal's Members, Waggoner was able to expand his culinary repertoire. In 1986 he returned to France as chef at the Hotel de la Poste in Avallon. After two years he was ready to try out his entrepreneurial hand, and he opened Le Monte Cristo in Moneteau. In 1991 Waggoner closed the restaurant to join Jean-Pierre Silva at Le Vieux Moulin. Then in 1994 he returned to the U.S. to work briefly at Turnberry Isle in Florida, before Nashville restaurateur Tom Allen lured him to the Wild Boar.

Waggoner is enthusiastic about Nashville and enjoys the challenge of showing the world that this mid-south city can produce some highly sophisticated cooking prepared with fresh ingredients imported from throughout the world. Diners at the Wild Boar often feel that they are on a culinary safari as Waggoner takes particular delight in creating a few unusual and unexpected, but always elegant, dishes.

Although still a relative newcomer in the U.S. culinary arena, Waggoner has been quietly capturing attention with his menus of unusual ingredients combined with time-honored methodologies. Food critic John Mariani commented in a recent *Wine Spectator* story that "Waggoner's cooking is classically precise, based on the finest ingredients money can buy, with a touch of modernism that makes this an exciting as well as a very refined place to dine. The Wild Boar under Waggoner has. . . emerged as one of the finest restaurants in the South."

Robert Waggoner's recipe for Crepinette of Turbot and Foie Gras on Salsify Mousseline with White Asparagus and Morel Jus is on page 32, and Stuffed Strawberries with a Tomato-Cinnamon Confiture, Balsamic Vinegar, and Tomato Liqueur is on page 172.

WALLY JOE
KC's Restaurant
Cleveland, Mississippi

Wally Joe's culinary career started in his family's restaurant in Mississippi. By the time he completed his teenage years, he had learned the basics of cooking at his parents' stoves and decided to pursue a dual degree in banking and finance at the University of Mississippi.

During college Wally traveled extensively throughout the United States, Puerto Rico, and South America, visiting restaurants and studying ethnic cookbooks and culinary references. The travels heightened and ignited his passion for cooking, and after graduation in 1987 he returned to the family restaurant business to begin his cooking career. It was at this time that he began to experiment with new ideas.

Despite a successful fifteen-year history,

KC's reputation and success rose with the ascension of Wally Joe to the stoves. His exactitude, precise cooking skills, and obsessive quest for quality ingredients garnered rave reviews from every newspaper in the area, and the restaurant was one of the first to achieve an overall four-star rating from Jackson's newspaper, the *Clarion Ledger*. In November 1994, Wally Joe was the first chef from Mississippi to be invited to cook at the James Beard House in New York City. He and his recipes have been featured in *Food Arts*, *USA Today*, and *Chef* magazine of Great Britain.

Still in his mid thirties, Wally feels that he has only scratched the surface of the potential of his abilities. Each day is the beginning of a new experience, a new opportunity to further his craft and refine his skills. He ascribes to the simple and direct philosophy that foods should be used within the season in which they ripen. In keeping with this tradition, he frequently changes his menus. Organic vegetables dominate, and he insists on free range and naturally raised meats. Although he does not completely eschew the use of butter and cream, he increasingly relies on infused oils, vegetable purées and reductions, and low-acid infused vinegars to provide flavor and texture to his recipes. Wally always rewards diners at KC's with his near fanatical insistence on quality and attention to detail.

Wally Joe's recipe for Grilled Yellowfin Tuna with Ratatouille Risotto, Grilled Shallots, and Red Wine-Morel Sauce is on page 72, Grilled Mississippi Quail Marinated in Hoisin, Szechuan Chilies, and Sesame with Sweet Potato Polenta is on page 39, and Crème Brûlée Napoleon with Bourbon Crème Anglaise is on page 132.

ALLEN RUBIN WHITE
The Hermitage Hotel
Nashville, Tennessee

When Allen Rubin White graduated in 1980 from the University of Tennessee with a bachelor of science in botany, he already knew that he would spend a career cooking rather than examining plants. Before graduating, he had been working since 1975 in Knoxville's Hyatt Regency Hotel mastering styles of food presentation from the garde manger to the pastry station. When The Vanderbilt Plaza Hotel opened in Nashville in 1984, they lured Allen away as opening banquet chef. He rose to the executive sous chef position before moving on to the acclaimed Arthur's restaurant.

But White wanted to learn it all—bread baking, chocolate, pulled sugar, as well as quality control, management skills, and equipment maintenance. So in a continuing quest to improve and expand his repertoire, White moved on to stints at Franklin's Café on the Court and Nashville's Riverview Baking Corporation. Continuing to expand his prowess in bread and pastry production, he spent time in Maude's Courtyard Restaurant as pastry chef.

Having determined that his career in the food industry was in bread baking and confection making, White took a job in 1989 as the executive pastry chef at Nashville's Monterey Baking Corporation, where he was responsible for recipe development and production. He returned to the hotel business to work for the Marriott in Nashville as the baker/pastry chef, and then moved on to the executive sous chef and pastry chef position at Service America Corporation. In 1990 White went to work for the Tennessee Christian Medical Center Nutrition Services, where he spent the next five years, solely responsible for quality production of the breads, pastries, and desserts served to the center's patients.

White joined The Hermitage Hotel in April of 1995 as pastry chef, and has been creating spectacular desserts for the hotel's acclaimed Grille Room restaurant as well as the banquet and other hotel facilities ever since.

Allen Rubin White's recipe for White Chocolate Black Jack Ice Cream Sandwiches is on page 160.

HALLMAN WOODS III

Le Rosier
New Iberia, Louisiana

Foodies combing the bayous and back roads of Louisiana for culinary magic could stumble across no greater treasure than Hallman Woods's New Iberia restaurant, Le Rosier. But, these days, people don't often arrive at Le Rosier by accident. Having put New Iberia on the culinary map, hungry travelers now plot their expeditions to Le Rosier.

Woods had completed extensive graduate studies in clinical psychology when he discovered that what he really wanted to do was to return to his first love—cooking. Woods's infatuation was cultivated early on by his father, who often cooked in his spare time. After college Woods went to work cooking in New Orleans kitchens and quickly earned the attention of Gautreau's Larkin Selman.

The beautiful town of New Iberia is located in the heart of Cajun Country or "Acadiana," a close neighbor of Avery Island where the McIlhenny's famous Tabasco sauce is made. In 1990 Woods's parents bought a nineteenth-century home on New Iberia's Main Street, and restored it for use as a restaurant. They also replicated a four-room inn on the property and named both the inn and restaurant Le Rosier—the rosebush. They furnished the rooms with antiques and the gardens with over fifty varieties of flowers. *Saveur* magazine called it "the perfect little inn fantasy."

It was a natural location for Woods to return home to and help create a whole new genre of cooking—New Acadian. Woods was well aware that his prospective customers would anticipate the traditional fare of the region, but Woods had other ideas. Using classic techniques and the abundance of fresh local foods, he created a menu full of inspired new dishes. It wasn't long before the food world took notice and the reviews were all cheers. "It is worth the drive out to LeRosier Country Inn and Restaurant to taste the talent of chef Hallman Woods III," wrote Dana Campbell of *Southern Living* magazine. "An exquisite flower of fine dining on the banks of the Bayou Teche," from food writer Jessie Tirsch. All the recognition brought Woods *Food & Wine* magazine's top honor as one of "America's Best New Chefs" of 1995.

Hallman Woods's recipe for Crawfish Spring Rolls with Root Vegetables and Crawfish Beurre Blanc is on page 15, and Lemon Soufflé is on page 158.

BASIC RECIPES

BASIL OIL

¾ cup fresh basil, stemmed and minced
1 cup olive oil

🌿 In a medium bowl combine the fresh basil with the olive oil. Cover and let sit for a minimum of 48 hours. Pour through a fine-meshed strainer into a glass jar or bottle. Cover.

CLARIFIED BUTTER

🌿 Melt butter over low heat, then cover and refrigerate it. Once the fat has hardened, scoop it off, being careful to leave the bottom layer of milk solids. Cover the clarified butter and refrigerate for up to 2 weeks.

🌿 If you don't have time to let the butter chill, melt the butter gently so that the milk solids settle on the bottom of the pan, forming a creamy white sediment. Carefully pour off the clear yellow butter, and discard the milk solids or add them to soup or sauce.

CRÈME ANGLAISE

MAKES 2 CUPS

4	*egg yolks*
⅓	*sugar*
1½	*cups milk, heated*
1	*vanilla bean, split in half lengthwise, or 2 teaspoons vanilla extract*
1	*tablespoon butter, at room temperature (optional)*

🌿 In a medium heavy saucepan whisk the egg yolks over low heat until they are pale in color. Whisk in the sugar 1 tablespoon at a time, then whisk until the mixture reaches the consistency of cake batter.

🌿 Whisk in the milk and vanilla bean, if using, then stir continuously with a wooden spoon until the custard coats the spoon and a line drawn down the back of the spoon remains visible. Remove the pan from the heat and stir in the vanilla extract, if using, or remove vanilla bean pods.

🌿 If the custard is to be chilled, press a sheet of plastic wrap directly onto the surface to prevent a skin from forming, or dot the top with bits of optional butter. Chill the custard for up to 2 days.

❧ *Note:* If the custard begins to overheat and the egg yolks are forming lumps, remove it immediately from the heat and whisk briskly to cool the mixture. Push the custard through a fine meshed sieve with the back of a spoon to remove the lumps. If it has not sufficiently thickened, return it to heat to complete cooking.

Crème Fraîche

❧ Crème fraîche is now widely available in specialty food stores; however, it is also easy to make by combining 1 cup of heavy (whipping) cream (preferably not ultra-pasteurized) with 1 tablespoon of buttermilk in a small saucepan. Slowly heat the cream to warm, 105°F to 115°F. Pour the mixture into a clean glass container and cover it loosely. Set in a warm place (70°F to 80°F) until thickened, about 24 to 36 hours. Cover tightly and refrigerate for 1 more day to develop the tangy flavor.

Cooked Fruit Purée or Sauce

MAKES 2 CUPS

4	*cups fresh berries or fruit*
1/4	*cup sugar (or to taste)*
1/4	*cup water*
2	*tablespoons raspberry liqueur (or eau-de-vie) (optional)*
1	*tablespoon fresh lemon juice (or more to taste)*
1/2	*teaspoon ground cinnamon (or more to taste)*

❧ Put the berries in a large sauté pan or skillet with the sugar, water, and optional liqueur or eau-de vie. Cook over medium heat for 15 minutes, or until the fruit is soft enough to mash with a spoon and most of the liquid has evaporated. Add the lemon juice and cinnamon, then taste and adjust the flavor with additional sugar, lemon juice, or cinnamon as needed.

❧ Transfer the mixture to a blender or food processor and purée until smooth. Strain the fruit through a fine-meshed sieve, cover, and refrigerate until cold, about 2 hours; this should be a very thick purée. It may be used as an ingredient in another recipe, or by itself as a sauce.

Variations:

❧ *Plum, Prune, Apple, or Pear Purée or Sauce:* Substitute 12 chopped pitted large plums or dried prunes, or 8 peeled, cored, and chopped large apples or pears for the berries.

Apricot Purée

MAKES ABOUT 2 CUPS

1 1/4	*cups apricot nectar*
1	*6-ounce package dried apricots*
6	*tablespoons sugar*

❧ In a heavy, medium saucepan combine the apricot nectar, dried apricots, and sugar, and cook over medium heat, stirring constantly, until the sugar dissolves and the mixture simmers. Cover and cook about 6 minutes until the apricots soften. Cool. Transfer the mixture to a food processor and purée until almost smooth. Some apricot bits will remain. Cover and refrigerate until needed. May be prepared 1 week in advance.

Uncooked Fruit Purée (Coulis)

MAKES ABOUT 2 CUPS

4   *cups fresh berries (or 2 cups diced fresh fruit)*
2   *tablespoons sugar or more to taste*
1   *teaspoon fresh lemon juice*

🍃 Purée the berries or fruit in a blender or food processor. Strain the purée through a fine-meshed sieve. Stir in the sugar and lemon juice. Adjust the amount of sugar if necessary. Cover and refrigerate until needed. This purée may be used as an ingredient in another recipe, or by itself as a sauce.

Simple Syrup

2   *cups sugar*
1   *cup water*

🍃 In a medium saucepan combine the sugar and water and cook over high heat, stirring constantly, until the sugar dissolves and the mixture reaches a full boil. Remove the pan from the heat and cool to room temperature. Strain, cover, and refrigerate until needed.

Peppers

Handling Bell Peppers and Chilis
🍃 Bell peppers now come in a rainbow of colors, and there are literally hundreds of varieties of chilies. Here are some general rules common to all:

🍃 **Handling fresh chilies:** Precautions should be exercised in handling fresh hot chilies, since they contain potent oils. Either wear rubber gloves, or wash your hands thoroughly with soap and hot water after handling chilies. Never touch your skin until you've washed your hands. Also, wash the knife and cutting board in hot soapy water. Do not handle hot chilies under running water, since that spreads the oil vapors upward to your eyes.

🍃 **Seeding and deribbing:** Either cut out the ribs and seeds with a paring knife, or cut away the flesh, leaving a skeleton of ribs and seeds to discard. For the second method, cut a slice off the bottom of the pepper or chili so that it will stand up on the cutting board. Holding the pepper or chili with your free hand, slice its natural curvature in sections. You will be left with all the flesh and none of the seeds and ribs. The flesh may now be cut as indicated in the recipe.

Roasting and peeling: Cut a small slit near the stem end of each whole pepper or chili to ensure that it will not explode. Roast the peppers or chilies in one of the following ways:

🍃 For a large number of peppers or chilies, and to retain the most texture, lower them gently into 375°F (almost smoking) oil and fry until the skin blisters. Turn them with tongs when one side is blistered, since they will float to the surface of the oil. This method is also the most effective if the vegetables are not perfectly shaped, since it is difficult to get the heat from the broiler into the folds of peppers and some chilies.

🍃 Place the peppers or chilies 6 inches from the preheated broiler, turning them with tongs until all surfaces are charred.

🍃 Place the peppers or chilies on the cooking rack of a hot charcoal or gas grill and turn them until the skin is charred.

🍃 Place a wire cake rack over a gas or

electric burner set at the highest temperature and turn the peppers or chilies with tongs until all surfaces are charred.

🍃 Place the peppers or chilies on a rack on a baking sheet in a preheated 550°F oven until they are totally blistered. Use this method only for a sauce or a recipe in which the peppers or chilies are to be puréed.

🍃 *Cool the peppers or chilies by one of the following methods:*
🍃 Place them in ice water. This stops the cooking action immediately and cools them enough to peel them within 1 minute. The peppers or chilies will stay relatively firm.

🍃 Place the peppers or chilies in a paper bag, close it, and let them cool. This also effectively separates the flesh from the skin, but it will be about 20 minutes before they are cool enough to handle, and they will soften somewhat during that time.

🍃 Finally, pull the skin off and remove the seeds.

🍃 *Cleaning dried chilies:* Remove the stem, then pull the chili apart lengthwise, splitting it in half. Brush the seeds from both halves and the chili is ready to cook. If it is dusty, rinse it under cold water.

ROASTED GARLIC PURÉE

1   whole head garlic
1   tablespoon olive oil
     Salt and pepper to taste

🍃 Preheat the oven to 400°. With a serrated knife, remove the top third of the garlic head with a sawing motion, exposing the cloves. Brush the cut side with the olive oil

and loosely wrap the garlic in aluminum foil. Set the garlic on a baking sheet and roast about 1 hour until soft. Remove the garlic from the oven, unwrap and separate the garlic cloves. Squeeze the garlic from its paper by pinching the bottom of the clove. Put the garlic cloves in a small bowl, season to taste with salt and pepper, and mash with a fork or pestle until puréed.

CHICKEN STOCK

MAKES 12 CUPS

6   quarts water
5   pounds chicken bones, skin, and trimmings
2   carrots, peeled and cut into chunks
1   large onion, halved
3   garlic cloves, halved
3   celery stalks, halved
3   fresh thyme sprigs, or 1 teaspoon dried
     thyme
6   fresh parsley sprigs
3   bay leaves
12   black peppercorns

🍃 In a large stockpot combine the water and the chicken bones, skin, and trimmings. Bring to a boil, then reduce the heat to a simmer, skimming off the foam that rises for the first 10 to 15 minutes. Cook for 1 hour, then add the remaining ingredients. Increase the heat to bring the liquid to a boil, reduce heat to low, and simmer the stock for 3 hours.

🍃 Strain the stock through a fine-meshed sieve and let cool to room temperature, then refrigerate. Remove and discard the congealed layer of fat on the surface. Store in the refrigerator up to 3 days. To keep longer, bring the stock to a boil every 3 days, or freeze it for up to 3 months.

✍ **To clarify the stock:** Let the stock cool until lukewarm. Blend 3 egg whites together and pour into the warm stock; as the whites coagulate and rise they will trap bits still floating in the stock. When the egg whites have risen to the top and the stock is clear, skim the eggs off the top with a slotted spoon. Repeat the process if necessary to obtain clear stock.

VEAL OR BEEF STOCK

MAKES 12 CUPS

8	pounds veal or beef bones and trimmings
2	onions, halved
2	carrots, peeled and cut into chunks
2	celery stalks, halved
3	garlic cloves, halved
8	quarts water
3	fresh thyme sprigs, or 1 teaspoon dried thyme
6	fresh parsley sprigs
2	bay leaves
12	black peppercorns

✍ Preheat the oven to 400°F. Put the bones and trimmings in a roasting pan and roast until they are browned, about 45 minutes, turning occasionally. Add the vegetables to the pan and roast 20 minutes longer or until the vegetables are browned. Pour off any fat.

✍ Place the bones and vegetables in a large stockpot. Add 1 quart of the water to the pan and place on the stove over high heat. Stir to scrape up the brown bits, clinging to the bottom of the pan. Pour this liquid into the stockpot with the remaining 7 quarts of water and the herbs and spices. Bring to a boil, then reduce the heat to a simmer, skimming off the foam that rises for the first 10 to 15 minutes. Simmer for 5 to 6 hours.

✍ Strain the stock through a fine-meshed sieve and discard the solids. Let cool, then refrigerate. Remove and discard the congealed layer of fat on the surface. Store the stock in the refrigerator up to 3 days. To keep longer, bring the stock to a boil every 3 days or freeze it for up to 3 months.

FISH STOCK

MAKES 12 CUPS

4	quarts water
1	cup dry white wine
4	pounds fish trimmings such as skin, bones, and heads
2	tablespoons fresh lemon juice
1	onion, halved
2	celery stalks, halved
4	fresh parsley sprigs
2	fresh thyme sprigs, or 1 teaspoon dried thyme
2	bay leaves
6	black peppercorns

In a large stockpot bring the water and wine to a boil. Rinse all the fish trimmings under cold running water, add to the stockpot, and return to a boil. Reduce the heat to a simmer, skimming off the foam that rises for the first 10 to 15 minutes. Simmer for 1 hour.

Add the remaining ingredients to the pot. Bring the mixture to a boil, then reduce the heat and simmer for 1 hour and 30 minutes to 2 hours. Strain the stock through a fine-meshed sieve, pressing on the solids with the back of a large spoon. Discard the solids. Let cool, then cover and refrigerate up to 3 days. To keep longer, bring the stock of a boil every 3 days, or freeze it for up to 3 months.

❧ *Shrimp or lobster stock:* Follow the preceding recipe, using 4 pounds shrimp shells or lobsster shells in place of the fish trimmings.

VEGETABLE STOCK

MAKES 12 CUPS

4	large leeks, carefully washed
2	large carrots, peeled and sliced
4	large celery stalks, sliced
4	large yellow onions, sliced
5	garlic cloves
6	fresh parsley sprigs
4	fresh thyme sprigs, or 1 teaspoon dried thyme
2	bay leaves
16	cups water
½	teaspoon white peppercorns
1	teaspoon black peppercorns
	Salt to taste

❧ Place all the ingredients except the salt in a large stockpot. Slowly bring the liquid to a boil over medium heat, reduce heat to a simmer, and cook, partially covered for 1 hour and 30 minutes. Strain through a fine-meshed sieve, pressing the liquid from the solids with the back of a large spoon. Let cool, then cover and refrigerate for up to 3 days. To keep longer, bring to a boil every 3 days or freeze for up to 3 months.

DUCK, RABBIT, LAMB, OR VENISON STOCK

3	pounds duck, rabbit, lamb, or venison trimmings (bones, skin, fat, and/or anything else you can trim away) and meat
4	quarts (16 cups) water
1	onion, halved
1	carrot, peeled and halved
2	celery stalks, including leaves, cut into sections
3	fresh thyme sprigs, or 1 teaspoon dried thyme
3	fresh parsley sprigs
6	black peppercorns

❧ Preheat the oven to 450°F. Put the trimmings and meat in a shallow roasting pan and roast for 30 minutes, or until browned.

❧ Bring the water to a boil over high heat. Add the trimmings and meat to the water and reduce the heat to medium. When the water comes back to a boil, skim frequently until the scum stops rising, then add the remaining ingredients and simmer, uncovered, for at least 6 hours. Add additional water if the stock level falls below the level of the ingredients.

❧ Strain the stock and discard the solids. Let the stock cool to room temperature, then refrigerate. remove and discard the congealed fat layer from the top. Store in the refrigerator for up to 3 days. To keep longer, bring to a boil every 3 days or refrigerate for up to 3 months.

❧ *Rich Stock:* Multiply the amount of rich stock specified in the recipe by 1½, and pour that amount of the kind of stock specified into a small saucepan. Bring to a boil over high heat. Cook the stock to reduce it by one third. If the stock was not salt-free, add a few slices of raw potato or some uncooked rice before reducing the stock; the starchy substance will absorb much of the salt.

VEAL OR BEEF DEMI-GLACE

MAKES 2 CUPS

Demi-glace is unsalted meat stock that has been degreased and then reduced over medium low heat until it becomes rich and syrupy. The concentrated flavor adds richness and depth to sauces and stews. Traditional demi-glace is thickened with flour and must simmer gently with much tending, but this quick version is lighter and can be made more quickly because it is thickened at the end with arrowroot or cornstarch.

2   *tablespoons vegetable oil*
1   *large onion, diced*
2   *celery stalks, diced*
1   *carrot, peeled and sliced*
½   *cup diced ham*
3   *tablespoons tomato paste*
1   *fresh thyme sprig*
1   *bay leaf*
6   *peppercorns*
10   *cups Veal or Beef stock (see page xxx)*
½   *cup Madeira*
2   *to 3 teaspoons arrowroot or cornstarch mixed with 2 tablespoons cold water*
     Salt and freshly ground black pepper to taste
1   *tablespoon unsalted butter*

❧ In a large saucepan heat the oil over medium heat. Stir in the onion, celery, carrot, and ham. Cover and cook over low heat for 10 minutes. Uncover the pan and stir in the tomato paste, thyme, bay leaf, and peppercorns. Whisk in the stock and Madeira, and bring to a boil over high heat.

❧ Once the mixture has started to boil, reduce heat to medium high and cook the sauce to reduce to 2 cups. Depending on the rate at which the liquid is boiling, this may take anywhere from 30 minutes to 1 hour. Strain the liquid through a fine-meshed sieve into a 2-cup measuring cup. If it has not reduced enough, pour the liquid back into the pan and keep boiling. If it has reduced too much, add enough water to make 2 cups.

❧ Pour the liquid back into the pan and bring it back to a simmer. Whisk in the arrowroot or cornstarch mixture 1 teaspoon at a time, returning the sauce to a simmer after each addition, until the sauce reaches the desired consistency. Add salt and pepper. If using the sauce immediately, swirl in the butter. If not serving immediately, do not whisk in the butter, but remove the pan from heat and place dots of butter on the surface of the sauce to prevent a skin from forming. Whisk in the butter when reheating the sauce. To store, cover and refrigerate for up to 5 days or freeze for up to 3 months.

TOMATOES

❧ **To peel and seed tomatoes:** Cut out the core of the tomato. With a knife, make an X on the bottom of the tomato. Plunge the tomato into boiling water for exactly 10 seconds. Remove with a slotted spoon and plunge into a bowl of cold water, then drain. Peel off the skin. Cut the tomato in half crosswise. Squeeze and shake the tomato gently over a bowl or sink to remove the seeds. Any clinging seeds may be removed with the tip of a paring knife or your fingers.

🍂 *Oven-dried tomatoes:* Preheat the oven to 250°. Cut plum (Roma) tomatoes in half lengthwise and sprinkle with salt and pepper. Place on a baking sheet cut side up and bake 45 to 60 minutes until almost dry.

🍂 *Smoked tomatoes:* Arrange your smoker or charcoal grill for smoking: place the charcoal to one side of the grill, ignite it and let it burn until white ash forms on the briquettes, and add selected wood for smoke flavor (hickory, mesquite, apple, etc.). In a gas grill, light the gas, turn to low flame, and place the wood chips over the fire area. Place a rack over the fire area. Cut plum (Roma) tomatoes in half lengthwise, sprinkle with salt, and place on the rack cut side up on the side away from the fire. Cover, open the air vents in the bottom of the grill, and nearly close the vents in the top of the grill. Smoke for 45 to 60 minutes or until the tomatoes are almost dry and have absorbed the smoky flavor.

Vegetable Curls

To curl carrots, beets, and radishes for garnish, grate or pare the cleaned vegetable in long thin strips and immediately place the strips in ice water. To curl green onions (scallions), with a small sharp knife, cut in half lengthwise through the bulb. Trim the stems 4 to 5 inches above the bulb. Cut the green stems into lengthwise strips, leaving attached at the bulb, and place in ice water.

Great Chefs®
Glossary of Ingredients©

A

Achiote: Annatto, the dark, brick-red seeds from the annatto tree that are often made into a paste; these are especially popular in the Yucatán for adding color and an earthy flavor to food. They must be soaked in water overnight before grinding, or you can bring them to a simmer, let them soak for an hour, and then grind them.

Almond paste: A thick paste made of finely ground almonds, sugar, and water. Almond paste can be formed into sheets or molded into shapes. It is similar to marzipan, but marzipan is made from almond paste, confectioners' sugar, flavoring, and sometimes egg white.

Anaheim chili: Long green narrow chili used often in Southwest cuisines.

Ancho chili: The dried poblano chili, dark red and usually 4 to 6 inches long.

Anise: Two types of unrelated spices that impart a licorice flavor to food: European or green anise is in the form of small seeds from a bush related to parsley, and star, badian, or Chinese anise takes the form of small brown star-shaped pods. In South-western cooking the European type is used, although the two can be interchanged.

Annato: *See achiote.*

Arborio rice: Imported Italian rice with a short, fat grain and high starch content that makes it ideal for risotto.

Avocado: A light- to dark-skinned fruit, roughly the shape of a pear, with creamy light green flesh. The pale green flesh is eaten as a vegetable, dip, garnish, or butter substitute. The skin of the avocado may be smooth and green or dark and rough; a ripe avocado should be soft when touched, but not mushy unless it is to be mashed. Do not allow the flesh of any avocado to be exposed to air or it will turn brown. Sprinkle cut surfaces with lemon juice or acidulated water, and for dips such as guacamole, press plastic wrap directly onto the surface of the food until ready to serve.

B

Balsamic vinegar: Imported from Italy and prized for its mild, almost sweet flavor, balsamic vinegar is made from unfermented grape juice that has been aged for at least ten years. Balsamic vinegar may be used in sauces and salad dressings, and as a topping for fresh fruit.

Bay leaves: Flavorful leaves of the laurel tree, used as a seasoning in many dishes. The leaves should always be removed before serving.

Beans, black: Also called frijoles negros, or turtle beans, these small black kidney-shaped beans are from the Yucatán and central Mexico and have a smoky mushroom flavor stronger than pinto beans. They are used for black bean soup, and have a black-purplish cast when cooked.

Beurre blanc: A white butter sauce made of a reduction of white wine and shallots thickened withbutter, and possibly finished with fresh herbs or other seasonings.

Black-eyed peas: Each of these little, slightly kidney-shaped beans is marked with one black spot, or "eye." Black-eyed peas are sold dried or canned, and are now available fresh.

Bouquet garni: A small bundle of herbs, usually bay leaf, parsley, and thyme, used to flavor stocks, braises, and other preparations.

C

Capers: The small picked flower buds of a shrub thought to have originated in the Orient or the Sahara region. Mexican capers are large; large Italian capers are widely available and may be substituted.

Caul fat: A lacy fat from the belly of animals. It is used as a covering or binding for foods to be cooked, especially small sausages.

Celery root: Available September through May, celeriac is a brown, gnarled root prized for its flavor, which is more intene than celery. It should be placed in acidulated water after peeling to prevent discoloration. It can be eaten raw in salads, or braised, sautéed, or boiled and pureed. Store, wrapped in plastic, in the refrigerator for seven to ten days.

Chayote squash: Also called mirliton or christophene, chayote was originally a staple of the Mayas and the Aztecs. The pear-shaped gourd with pale green furrowed skin is grown in the southern states, from California to Florida. Widely available in supermarkets, chayote may be stored in the refrigerator, wrapped in plastic, for up to 30 days. It can be boiled, sautéed, baked and stuffed, or used raw in salads.

Chili paste: A thick chili sauce produced and used in many Asian cuisines such as Thai, Vietnamese, Indonesian, and Filipino. It is made of chilis, onions, sugar, and tamarind.

Chocolate
Unsweetened: Also referred to as baking or bitter chocolate, this is the purest of all cooking chocolates. A hardened chocolate liquor (which is the essence of the cocoa bean, not an alcohol), it contains no sugar and is usually packaged in a bar or eight blocks weighing 1 ounce each. Unsweetened chocolate must contain 50 to 58 percent cocoa butter.
Bittersweet: This chocolate is slightly sweetened with sugar, in amounts that vary depending on the manufacturer. It must contain 35 percent chocolate liquor and is used whenever an intense chocolate taste is desired. Bittersweet chocolate may be used interchangeably with semisweet chocolate in cooking and baking.
Semisweet: Sweetened with sugar, semi-

sweet chocolate, unlike bittersweet, may have flavorings such as vanilla added to it. It is available in bar form as well as in chips and pieces.

Milk: A mild-flavored chocolate used primarily for candy bars but rarely (except for milk chocolate chips) in cooking. It may have as little as 10 percent chocolate liquor, but must contain 1 percent milk solids.

Unsweetened cocoa powder: Powdered chocolate that has had a portion of the cocoa butter removed.

Dutch process cocoa powder: Cocoa powder that has been treated to reduce its acidity. It has a more mellow flavor than regular cocoa, but it burns at a lower temperature.

White chocolate: Ivory in color, white chocolate is technically not chocolate at all: It is made from cocoa butter, sugar, and flavoring. It is difficult to work with, and should be used only in recipes that are specifically designed for it.

Christophene: *See chayote squash.*

Cilantro: A pungent flat-leaf herb resembling parsley; also called fresh coriander or Chinese parsley. The flavor is pungently sweet, and the scent has been compared to that or orange or lemon peel; a combination of caraway and cumin, or honey. Look for crisp, green, unwilted leaves. Although much less interesting, parsley may be substituted.

Cinnamon: The inner bark from shoots of a tree called Cinnamomum zeylanicum. Cinnamon was originally imported from Spain and Mexico, where it continues to be heavily used; however, the Mexican variety of cinnamon, originally from Sri Lanka, is a lighter brown, is softer in texture, and has a milder taste than the American variety.

Clarified butter: Butter from which the milk solids and water have been removed, leaving pure butterfat that can be heated to a higher temperature without smoking or scorching.

Cloves: Originally from the Spice Islands and now grown in Madagascar and Zanzibar, supposedly all clove trees are descended from one tree saved when Frenchman Pierre Poivre's collection was destroyed by members of Louis XV's court for political reasons. Cloves are a labor-intensive and expensive spice, as clove buds must be hand-picked from the trees just before they are ready to bloom. Ground cloves will impart a brown shade along with their flavor.

Coco Lopez: *See cream of coconut.*

Coconut milk: A liquid extracted from shredded coconut meat by soaking it with hot water and straining. Available in cans from Southeast Asia.

Conch: A shellfish native to the warm waters of the Caribbean and used in the cuisine of south Florida. Conch meat must be tenderized by being pounded before it is cooked.

Coriander: The seed of cilantro, or Chinese parsley. See cilantro.

Corn husks: Dried husks are used for encasing tamale dough before steaming the tamales. Before using, the husks are soaked in hot water for at least several hours, or even overnight, and the inner corn silk is removed.

Crab meat: The crab meat called for in Cajun seafood recipes is lump crab meat from the blue crab. Lump meat distinguishes the large pieces of white body meat from flaked crab meat, or small pieces of dark and white body meat from the body and claws. Crab meat is sold fresh, frozen, pasteurized, and canned.

Crawfish: Variously known as crawfish, crayfish, mudbugs, and crawdaddies, these fresh-water crustaceans resemble little lobsters, and are sold fresh and frozen, whole and raw, or whole and cooked. Tails are also sold blanched and peeled, and blanched, peeled, and frozen.

Cream of coconut: The thick sweetened "milk" extracted from coconut flesh and used in desserts and drinks such as piña colada. Coco Lopez is the most widely available brand.

Crème fraîche: While its tangy, tart flavor is similar to that of sour cream, crème fraîche is thinner and is used in cooking because it does not curdle when heated as do sour cream and yogurt.

Cumin: Seeds from pods of the indigenous and plentiful Southwestern cumin plant. Used whole and ground, they are mixed with ground chilies to make commercial chili powder, and are also used in curry powder. If a recipe calls for ground red chilies and cumin, do not add additional cumin if substituting chili powder.

E

Escabeche: Spanish for pickled; a technique usually applied to various fish dishes.

F

Five-spice powder: A spice mix of anise, cinnamon, cloves, fennel, and star anise. Available in Asian markets.

Flat-leaf (Italian) parsley: A variety of parsley with large leaves and a stronger, more pungent flavor than curly-leaf parsley.

Foie gras: The oversized liver of force-fed geese or ducks, foie gras is considered one of the most luxurious of foods. Fresh foie gras should be soaked in tepid water for 1 hour. Then it should be patted dry, the lobes gently separated, and any connecting tubes and visible blood vessels removed and discarded.

Frisée: A green with decorative curley edges, frisée is used in salads and as a garnish.

G

Ganache: A filling or coating made from heavy cream and chocolate. It is also used to make chocolate truffles.

Ginger: Fresh ginger is a brown, fibrous, knobby rhizome. It keeps for long periods of time. To use, peel the brown outside skin and slice, chop, or puree. It will keep indefinitely placed in a jar with sherry and refrigerated.

Goat cheese: Called chèvre in French, goat cheese ranges in flavor from mild and tangy in its fresh form to sharp when it is aged.

Green papaya: The unripe form of the papaya, usually shredded and used in salads and stir-fries in Southeast Asian cuisines.

Grits: Ground white hominy, eaten as a cereal that is similar in texture to pudding.

H

Haricots verts: Tender, long, and very thin green beans used in French cuisine and now becoming popular in America. They are available in specialty produce markets. Baby Blue Lake beans may be substituted.

Hearts of palm: Tender palm shoots, sometimes available fresh, but most often found in cans in Asian markets. Used mostly in salads and stir-fries.

Hoisin sauce: A thick, brownish sweet sauce made from soybean paste, sugar, and spices. Can be purchased bottled.

J

Japanese eggplant: A long, narrow purple, eggplant. Substitute Italian eggplant.

Jícama: A bulbous, turniplike root vegetable with a taste similar to a very mild and slightly sweet radish. Jícama is crisp and white with a thick brown skin. Choose jícamas that are small, firm, and not visibly damaged. Peel both the brown skin and the woody layer underneath, and use raw or slightly cooked as a vegetable. Fresh water chestnuts have a similar flavor. Available in Asian and Latino markets.

K

Kiwi: Kiwis hide their sweet green flesh in a fuzzy brown skin. Select fruit with few imperfections in the skin, and no very soft bruised spots. Peel the kiwi and slice; the seeds are edible.

Kosher salt: Also known as coarse salt or pickling salt, kosher salt is pure refined rock salt that does not contain magnesium carbonate. It is less salty than table salt and has larger grains. Use $\frac{1}{2}$ to 1 teaspoon of table salt for each tablespoon of kosher salt specified.

L

Lemongrass: Long greenish stalks with a pungent lemony flavor. Also called citronella. Substitute grated lemon zest.

Lobster: The American, Atlantic, or Maine lobster is a crustacean with a jointed body and two large pincer claws. The larger claw is used for crushing and the smaller one is used for catching its prey. The spiny, or rock, lobster, found in warmer waters from South Africa to the eastern Pacific, lacks the large claws of its northern relative.

M

Mahimahi: Also called dolphinfish, with a firm pink flesh. Best fresh, but often available frozen. A standard in island restaurants and markets. Substitute snapper, catfish, or halibut.

Mango: Gold and green tropical fruit available in many supermarkets. A ripe mango has a smooth yellow to red skin and smells sweet, with the pale to bright orange-yellow flesh tender to the touch and having a very pleasant but complex taste, simultaneously sweet and tart. A fibrous but gracefully shaped fruit, the mango looks something like a smooth, elongated curved disk or partial kidney bean that is 5 to 6 inches long and 3 to 4 inches wide. The skin should be peeled and the flesh cut away from the stone in strips. Substitute fresh peaches or papaya. Available fresh June through September in the tropics.

Marjoram: Often confused with and substituted for oregano. Sometimes called the "wild oregano," marjoram is an herb in the mint family and is related to thyme. Though similar to oregano, marjoram is sometimes called sweet marjoram becausse it tastes sweeter and milder. Marjoram grows up to 2 feet high, with closely bunched purple and white flowers that resemble knots. It is used to season pork and game.

Marzipan: A confection made from almond paste, confectioners' sugar, flavoring, and sometimes egg white. Marzipan is often used for shaped candies, such as fruit or flowers, or as a coating for cakes.

Masa: A cornmeal dough used to make tortillas and tamales.

Masa harina: Finely ground cornmeal that is usually commercially prepared and used to make the dough for tamales and corn tortillas.

Mascarpone: A soft, fresh Italian cheese with a high fat content used primarily in desserts and for cheese tortas. If it is not available, combining equal parts of cream cheese and unsalted butter will produce a similar product.

Miso: A soybean paste made by salting and fermenting soybeans and rice. Shiro miso, or white miso, is the mildest of several different types. Available shrink-wrapped, and in cans and jars, in Asian markets. Can be stored for months in a refrigerator.

Mushrooms
 Black trumpet mushrooms: Also called black chanterelles, these have the same shape and size as their orange cousins, and must be cooked before eating.
 Cèpes: See porcini mushrooms.
 Cremini mushrooms: These mushrooms resemble white, or common, mushrooms but are a medium brown in color and have a dense, earthy flavor. They may be used interchangeably with white mushrooms in almost all dishes.
 Enoki mushrooms: These Japanese mushrooms have thin pale stems, about 3 inches long, and small ivory buttonlike heads. Available year round, they may be used without washing or other preparation, but the base holding the mushroom stalks together should be trimmed away.
 Morels: These spring mushrooms are about 1 inch long with a tall, hollow, pitted cap. The colors range from grey to brown to black, depending on where they are found. Their flavor is rich, nutty, and meaty when cooked, and they should never be eaten raw. Morels are also available dried.
 Oyster mushrooms: The oyster mushroom is now widely cultivated. Shaped like a fan, it ranges in color from pale to dark brownish grey. It is prized for its mild flavor once cooked (tasted raw, it is peppery), and for its firm texture.
 Porcini mushrooms: Also known as cèpes and crowned by culinary consensus as the king of mushrooms, porcinis (as they are known in Italy) are prized for their earthy, woodsy flavor and meaty texture. It is possible to find them fresh in fancy food markets in spring and fall; however, they are most widely available dried. Dried porcini should be soaked in hot water for about thirty minutes before using.
 Portobello mushrooms: Huge mushrooms with caps from 3 to 6 inches in diameter. The brown gills underneath the cap should be cut away before the mushrooms are cooked or they will give a dark brown color

to the dish.

Shiitake mushrooms: Although they originated in Japan and Korea, shiitake mushrooms are now cultivated in the U.S. They have a meaty flavor and texture and average from three to six inches in diameter. Widely available year-round both fresh and dried, the fresh ones tend to be expensive. They are most plentiful in spring and fall.

N

Nori: Sheets of dried and compressed seaweed used in making rolled sushi. Available in Japanese markets.

N

Old Bay Seasoning: This brand-name seasoning is available in most groceries. It contains celery salt, mustard, red and black pepper, bay leaf, cloves, allspice, ginger, mace, cardamom, cinnamon, and paprika, and is used on seafood, meats, and vegetables.

Opal basil: A purple-tinged basil used in Asian cooking.

Oregano: Also called wild, bastard, or dwarf marjoram, oregano is used to season many foods, especially sauces and soups. Though similar to marjoram, oregano plants grow wild in the Southwest and are shorter, heartier, huskier, and more potent than marjoram. The best substitute for oregano is marjoram or, if preferred, sage.

P

Panko: A crispy large-flaked Japanese bread crumb that adds more texture than ordinary breadcrumbs. Found in Asian markets.

Papaya: An attractive fruit with shiny round black seeds surrounded by bright orange or pink flesh. It is tender to the touch, shaped like a gourd or a large, elongated pear, and has a mottled yellow-green skin. Papayas are available year-round. They have a sweet, musky flavor with a slight citrus tang and are used primarily for dessert. They must be ripe when used or they will be bitter and acid. The skion of the papaya contains a natural enzyme that tenderizes meat, and is frequently included in marinades for that reason. In Hawaii, the most common papaya used is the solo papaya, a tropical fruit with a yellow flesh, black seeds, and a perfumey scent. Other types are larger, and may have pink flesh; all are suitable for island recipes. Also see green papaya.

Parchment paper: A white heat-resistant paper sold in rolls at cookware stores. It is used in cooking to line baking pans and baking sheets, to cook foods en papillote, and to loosely cover delicate foods like fish fillets during poaching.

Passion fruit: A small yellow, purple, or brown oval fruit of the passion fruit vine. The "passion" in passion fruit comes from the fact that its flower resembles a Maltese cross and refers to Christ's crucifixion, not to aphrodesiac qualities. The flavor is delicate but somewhat sharp, and perfumelike. Passion fruit is a natural substitute for lemon juice. Passion fruit concentrate can be found in the frozen juice section of many markets. Substitute oranges.

Paste food coloring: Available from confectioners' supply stores, paste food colors are more intense than the liquid food colors commonly found in supermarkets and can be used like paints to obtain bright colors.

Patis fish sauce: A strong-flavored seasoning sauce used in Southeast Asian cuisines. Tiparos is one brand name.

Pecans: Native to the U.S., pecans probably originated in Texas. The elongated oval nut hulls each contain two nutmeat pieces. Pre-Columbian Indians used ground pecans as a thickener and flavoring, and pressed whole pecans for oil. Today they are used in salads, entrées, and desserts, for oil, and straight from the hand.

Peppers (chilis): Indigenous to South American and cultiaved by the Incas and Aztecs, chilis were used as a seasoning and spread north through Mexico City to the Pueblo Indians in New Mexico. In lore, chilies are credited with everything from increasing sexual potency to aiding digestion. We do know they are high in vitamins A and C, and cause a secretion in the stomach that may aid in digestion. Chilies may be named for their use, appearance, flavor, creator, or potency. Chili potency is commercially rated from 1 (for the weakest) to 120 (for the strongest), with jalapeños rated at 15. When shopping, look for firm, unblemished, and fairly straight chilies with smooth skinds. Dried chilies should be free from mold and unbroken.

Anaheim: Also called California, California greens, chiles verdes, or, when canned, mild green chilies, Anaheim chilies are dark green, about 7 inches long, 1½ inches wide, and mild to hot in flavor. When the chilies ripen completely in the fall, they turn red and are sweeter and milder. Their large size makes Anaheim chilies ideal for stuffing.

Ancho: Dried poblano chilies, anchos come from California (where they're sometimes incorrectly called pasilla chilies) and Mexico, and range from dark red to almost black. They are about 4½ inches long and 3 inches wide and are moderately hot, with a smoky undertaste. They are wrinkled and should still be pliable if fresh. Pasilla chilies, though difficult to find, may be substituted.

Cayenne: Also called finger or ginnie peppers, cayenne chilies are long (3 to 8 inches) and slender. The bright green chilies turn red when ripe and are very hot. Cayennes are usually dried and ground; the powder may be used interchangeably with pure red New Mexico chili powder. Cayenne pepper is a staple in Louisiana cuisine.

Chipotle: Jalapeño chilies that have been dried, smoked, and very often picked, chipotles are usually a dark shade of brown and have a very hot smoky taste. If packed in tomato sauce, chipotles may be called mara and are a dark brick red.

Jalapeño: A fairly small, dark green hot chili approximately 2 inches long and 1 inch wide. One of the most widely available fresh chilies. Serrano is a common substitution, although the heat from jalapeños is immediate while the serrano provides more of an afterburn. Jalapeños can vary in the level of hotness, and those with striations on the skin are older and usually hotter. It's better to start with less than the required amount, and add to suit personal taste.

Pasilla: Named for pasa, which means "raisin" in Spanish, the chili is also called chilaca when fresh, brown, and ripe, and negro when dried and black. Pasillas are mild to hot in temperature, are used in mole, and may be substituted with ancho or mulatto chilies.

Poblano: A shiny dark green chili pepper, about three inches wide and five inches long, poblanos are mild to hot. They are widely availabe fresh in supermarkets, and are also sold canned. They are the chili used in chiles relleños. When used in sauces, they may be interchanged with

Anaheim chilies, though the flavor will be different. In their dried form, they are known as ancho peppers.

Scotch bonnet (habañero): The hottest of all chilies, these tiny crinkled red or yellow peppers are available in supermarkets and specialty produce markets.

Serrano: A tapered, thin, bright-green chili that is similar to but smaller than a jalapeño and often pickled or canned in oil. Good for cooking or as a garnish, it varies in hotness as much as a jalapeño. Jalapeño chilies may be substituted.

Thai: Very powerful chilies that are about 1 inch long, slender, and dark green or deep red. Cayennes or pequins may be substituted.

Phyllo (filo) dough: This tissue-paper-thin pastry is made from a flour and water dough. Phyllo sheets are used in layers, and brushed with butter or oil before baking. They are widely available in packages in the frozen section of supermarkets.

Pineapple: Fresh pineapples are covered with a prickly brown skin, and topped with sharp, pointed leaves. To select a fresh ripe pineapple, give the tiny center leaves at the top a light tug: The leaves will easily pluck out of a ripe pineapple. Fresh pineapple contains an enzyme which will break down protein; rinse well and add as close to serving time as possible when using in dishes containing gelatin.

Plantains: Similar to a banana in both shape and texture, plantains are a member of the same family. The green skin will develop black spots as it ripens, and the slightly pink flesh must be cooked to be edible. Most commonly sliced thin and fried.

Plum (Roma) tomatoes: Small plum-sized red tomatoes frequently used in Italian cuisine because their thick, meaty flesh is excellent for drying and for making sauces. Regular red tomatoes may be substituted.

Plum sauce: Also called Chinese plum sauce. A sweet and sour sauce available in most Asian markets.

Plum wine: Wine made from the Japanese plum, or ume, and available in Asian and specialty foods stores.

Polenta: Coarsely ground yellow or white cornmeal. Polenta is traditoinally combined with stock or water and cooked slowly until thick. It may be served creamy, or it may be chilled, cut into shapes, and grilled.

Praline: A candy eaten in the South and Southwest; made from brown sugar and pecans.

Puff pastry: Flaky pastry that rises up to ten times its original height when baked. It is made from flour, water, butter, and salt. The distinctive flakiness results from adding the butter during a series of at least six rollings, turnings, and foldings that trap layers of butter and air between the layers of the pastry; when baked, the butter melts and the air expands as steam, puffing up the pastry. It can be prepared at home, or purchased frozen.

Q

Quail: The American quail or bobwhite quail is a Galliformes, a different family than the European quail. There is some possibility that the bird in this hemisphere is named for its resemblance to European species and is not a quail at all; however, the name has stuck. Quail have pale meat, usually weigh about 4 ounces, and are subtly flavored.

R

Radicchio: A member of the chicory family developed in Italy. The head ranges in size from that of a golf ball to that of a grapefruit. The beautifully white-veined leaves may be any shade from bright red to dark maroon, and the flavor is rather bitter. In Italy radicchio is served as a salad, or is braised, brilled, or wilted and often served with a splash of vinegar and oil.

Rice paper: Thin sheets of noodles made from rice flour and water. Soften the sheets in water before wrapping food with them.

Rice wine vinegar: A light vinegar made from fermented rice.

S

Saffron: Saffron is the most expensive food in the world. It is made up of the dried stigmas of the Crocus sativus, which are laboriously hand-picked from each flower. One acre of crocus plants produces about four-four pounds of saffron. Unique and slightly medicinal in taste, saffron is used both as a flavoring and to impart its characteristic yellow color to food. It takes only a few threads to achieve the desired flavor and color.

Sake: Clear Japanese rice wine. Other strong clear liquors, such as tequila or vodka, can be substituted.

Salsa: Spanish for sauce. Usually refers to a fresh tomato and onion sauce used for dipping tortilla chips.

Sesame seeds: Small flat oval white or black seeds used to flavor or garnish main dishes and desserts.

Shallots: A member of the onion family, their flavor is milder than that of the onion and less pungent than garlic. Shallots are usually about $\frac{1}{2}$ to 1 inch long, oval in shape and may come as one bulb or a pair. They are excellent in sauces, salad dressing, and roasted whole.

Shiitake mushrooms: The second most widely cultivated mushroom in the world, medium to large with umbrella-shaped, flopped tan to dark brown caps with edges that tend to roll under. Shiitakes have a woodsy, smoky flavor. Can be purchased fresh or dried in Asian groceries. To reconstitute the dried variety, soak in warm water for 30 minutes before using. Stem both fresh and dried shiitakes.

Soft-shell crabs: When the crab sheds its old shell in order to grow, there is a period of a few days before the new shell hardens. Crabs are harvested during this time when the new shell is tissue thin and edible. The crab most commonly harvested for consumption as soft-shell crab in the U.S. is the blue crab.

Soy sauce: A dark salty liquid made from soybeans, flour, salt, and water. Dark soy sauce is stronger than light soy sauce. A staple in most Asian cuisines.

Star anise: Brownish seeds with eight points that taste like licorice.

Star fruit: A waxy, light green fruit; also called carambola. Cut in cross section, it reveals a five-pointed star shape. Trim the points off the stars if the points are too dark for your taste.

Stone crab: A south Florida favorite, the stone crab is an ivory-colored crab with an extremely hard shell. The large dark-tipped claws are used in many regional dishes.

Sweet chili sauce: *See Thai chili paste.*

Szechuan chili paste: A Northern Chinese spicy chili paste using chilies, garlic, oil, and salt.

T

Tamale: Cornmeal dough stuffed with either sweet or savory fillings, and wrapped in corn husks, then steamed.

Tamarind: A brown, bean-shaped pod from the tamarind tree. The fruit is sweet-sour, and is made into sauces, candy, and pastes.

Tasso: Highly spiced, heavily smoked ham, a Cajun specialty. Usually used as a seasoning.

Thai basil: A green and red variety of basil. Substitute fresh sweet basil.

Thai chili paste: A slightly sweet, thick, hot bottledpaste of garlic, vinegar, and chilies. Sriracha is a brand name.

Thai curry paste: Yellow, red, and green curry pastes used in many Thai and Southeast Asian sauces. Yellow is generally the mildest and green the hottest. Thai ginger: See galangal.

Tomatillos: Related to red tomatoes, tomatillos are small and dark green (even when ripe), with a protective brown paper-like husk. Also called frescadillas or green tomatoes, tomatillos belong to the nightshade family and were originally eaten by the Aztecs. Fresh tomatillos should be green and firm, with dry husks. The best substitution is small green tomatoes.

Tortilla: Round flat breads made from either wheat flour or cornmeal and lard. The tortilla is the staple of all Latin American cooking.

V

Vanilla beans: The pods of a relative of the orchid, vanilla beans are green and have no flavor when picked, they are then cured by a process of sweating and drying. Once cured, the long, wrinkled black beans are either bundled whole for export or processed into extract.

Vidalia onions: These alrge sweet onions, named for the Vidalia, Georgia, area in which they are grown, are so mild they can be eaten raw like an apple. They are similar to Maui onions, with which they are interchangeable. Other mild onions may be substituted, but reduce the amount used in the recipe.

Y

Yams: A sweet root vegetable similar in appearance to the sweet potato, but with pointed ends and a subdued yellow-orange color. Though Dioscorea sativa is the most popular commercial type, the darker variety called yampee, or cush-cush (D. trifida) grows in the southern U.S. and Mexico and produces clusters of smaller, tastier yams. Yams are often candied. They should be firm, unwithered, and umblemished when purchased.

Yuca: A plant native to Latin America and the Southwest. The petals, fruit, and root can all be eaten, and the root is also used as a thickener for soups and stews.

Z

Zest: The thin, brightly colored outer part of citrus rind. It contains volatile oils, making it ideal for use as a flavoring.

© 1977 Great Chefs Television/Publishing, Div. GCI Inc.

Index

A

Appetizers, 1–44

apples

Caramelized Bourbon Apples, 144

Maine Lobster with Celery Root and Apple Salad, 48

Morel-crusted Trout Salad with Apple and Walnut Vinaigrette, 51

Roasted Game Hen with Goat Cheese and Spinach, 96

Strawberry Apple Cheese Strudel, 162

Apricot Purée, 216

artichokes

Panfried Mountain Rainbow Trout with Green Tomato and Lime Butter Salsa on Sweet Potato, Artichoke, and Crayfish Hash, 83

Arugula Creamy Tartar Sauce, Tempura-battered Frog Legs with, 36

asparagus

Asparagus Charlotte, 1

Crepinette of Turbot and Foie Gras on Salsify Mousselline with White Asparagus and Morel Jus, 32

Herb-crusted Red Snapper with Pine Nut-Herb Sauce, 70

Grilled Vegetable Terrine with Lobster and Red Pepper Coulis, 2

Pecan Flour-dusted Softshell Crab with Roasted Garlic Tomato Butter, 83

Shrimp with Sugar Cane and Papaya Ketchup, 22

Aunt Irma's Banana-Pecan Beignets, 119

B

bacon

Bacon-wrapped Trout Stuffed with Crawfish, 86

Coq au Vin, 94

Grilled and Braised Rabbit with Molasses, Bourbon, Slab Bacon, and Stone-ground Grits, 106

Pork Tenderloin "au Poivre," 110

Risotto with Bacon, Silver Queen Corn, and Catfish, 9

Smoked Scotch Bonnet Jerk Spice Mahimahi Stuffed with Christophene, Carrot, and Pepper with Mofongo Broth, 66

Wild and Exotic Mushroom Salad on Marinated Tomatoes with Warm Sherry Bacon Vinaigrette, 46

Baked Creams with Orange Custard Sauce, 127

balsamic vinegar

Brioche Pain Perdu with Orange-Balsamic Syrup, 116

Grilled Mississippi Quail, Marinated in Hoisin, Szechuan Chilies, and Sesame with Sweet Potato Polenta, 39

Poached Vidalia Onions with Foie Gras and Marmalade, 44

Stuffed Collard Greens with Roasted Chicken, Carolina Goat Cheese, and Black-eyed Pea Salad, 6

Stuffed Strawberries with a Tomato-Cinnamon Confiture, Balsamic Vinegar, and Tomato Liqueur, 172

bananas

Aunt Irma's Banana-Pecan Beignets, 119

Bananas Foster Chimichanga, 148

Chocolate Banana Foster Cake with Orange Foster Caramel Sauce, 146

Havana Bananas with Rum, Chilies, and Chocolate Sauce, 150

Barbecued Breast of Duck with Crushed Pepper, Plums and Plum Wine, 103

Barbecued Duck with Wilted Greens, 101

Barbecued Spiced Oysters on Creamy Succotash, 31
Basil Oil, 215
Bayona Crispy Smoked Quail Salad, 52
beans, *also see* black beans
    Barbecued Spiced Oysters on Creamy Succotash, 31
    Salad Niçoise, 49
    Salmon South by Southwest, 88
Beef Tenderloin Stuffed with Herb Cream Cheese, with Sauce Bordelaise, 108
Beignets, Aunt Irma's Banana-Pecan, 119
Berry Cobbler, 140
beurre blanc
    Crawfish Spring Rolls with Root Vegetables and Crawfish Beurre Blanc, 15
    Roulade of Salmon with Egg and Capers, 34
black beans
    Fresh Cracked Conch with Vanilla Rum Sauce and Spicy Black Bean Salad, 27
    Spicy Crawfish and Black Bean Phyllo Burritos with Cilantro Cream and Fresh Salsa, 29
    Whole Sizzling Catfish with Chili-Black Bean Sauce, 82
    Yellowtail Snapper Encrusted in Yuca with Roasted Pepper-Orange Salsa and Sizzling Black Beans, 68
Blackberry-glazed Quail, 41
black-eyed peas
    Blackberry-glazed Quail, 41
    Stuffed Collard Greens with Roasted Chicken, Carolina Goat Cheese, and Black-eyed Pea Salad, 6
bourbon
    Bayona Crispy Smoked Quail Salad, 52
    Caramelized Bourbon Apples, 144
    Chocolate Soufflé, 126
    Crème Brûlée with Bourbon Crème Anglaise, 132
    Fearrington House Chocolate Refresh-Mint, 124
    Grilled and Braised Rabbit with Molasses, Bourbon, Slab Bacon, and Stone-ground Grits, 106
    Pork Tenderloin "au Poivre," 110
Brioche Pain Perdu with Orange-Balsamic Syrup, 116
Burritos, Spicy Crawfish and Black Bean Phyllo, with Cilantro Cream and Fresh Salsa, 29

C

cabbage
    Crawfish Spring Rolls with Root Vegetables and Crawfish Beurre Blanc, 15

Spicy Scallops with Chile Sauce, 21
cake
    Cardamom Cake with Saffron Ice Cream, 164
    Chocolate Banana Foster Cake with Orange Foster Caramel Sauce, 146
    Fearrington House Chocolate Refresh-Mint, 124
    Warm Center Chocolate Pyramid Cake, 168
calabaza
    Creole Spiny Lobster, 64
    Grouper Pibil, 75
capers
    Herb-crusted Red Snapper with Pine Nut-Herb Sauce, 70
    Roulade of Salmon with Egg and Capers, 34
caramel
    Caramelized Bourbon Apples, 144
    Cardamom Cake with Saffron Ice Cream, 164
    Chocolate Banana Foster Cake with Orange Foster Caramel Sauce, 146
Cardamom Cake with Saffron Ice Cream, 164
catfish
    Panéed Catfish with Crayfish Stuffing in an Herb Butter Sauce, 80
    Risotto with Bacon, Silver Queen Corn, and Catfish, 9
    Whole Sizzling Catfish with Chili-Black Bean Sauce, 82
Celery Root and Apple Salad, Maine Lobster with, 48
Charlotte, Asparagus, 1
cheese, *also see* goat cheese
    Gnocchi Stuffed with Fonduta in Parmesan Cheese-Cream Sauce, 11
    Pan-seared Scallops with Zucchini and Summer Squash, Cheddar Grits Soufflé, and Salmon Roe Butter Sauce, 56
Cheesecake, Lemon, 158
chicken
    Chicken Stock, 218
    Coq au Vin, 94
    Roasted Chicken with Collards, Red Onion, and Sweet Potato Chips, 92
    Stuffed Collard Greens with Roasted Chicken, Carolina Goat Cheese, and Black-eyed Pea Salad, 6
Chili-Black Bean Sauce, Whole Sizzling Catfish with, 82
Chimichangas, Bananas Foster, 148
chocolate
    Chocolate Banana Foster Cake with Orange Foster Caramel Sauce, 146
    Chocolate Crème Bruleé with a Sweet Basil Vanilla Sauce, 122

Chocolate Genoise Truffle Torte with Fresh
  Berries
Chocolate Soufflé, 126
Fearrington House Chocolate Refresh-Mint,
  124
Frozen Lime-Ganache Parfait with Chocolate
  Tuiles, 154
Havana Bananas with Rum, Chilies, and
  Chocolate Sauce, 150
Mocha Toffee Meringue, 152
Praline Mousse Served with Chocolate
  Meringue, 133
Rich Dense Chocolate Pecan Torte, 166
Warm Center Chocolate Pyramid Cake, 168
White Chocolate Black Jack Ice Cream Sand-
  wiches, 160
cilantro
  Spicy Crawfish and Black Bean Phyllo Burritos
    with Cilantro Cream and Fresh Salsa, 29
Clarified Butter, 215
cobblers
  Berry Cobbler, 140
  Stone Crab Cobbler with Coconut Milk,
    Chilies, Key Lime, and Coriander, 26
Cobb Salad, Fruited, 54
coconut
  Grouper Pibil, 75
  Stone Crab Cobbler with Coconut Milk,
    Chilies, Key Lime, and Coriander, 26
  Sugar Cane-speared Gulf Shrimp with
    Tamarind-Orange Honey Glaze, 17
  Tropical Tiramisu, 135
Coffee Cup with Sabayon, 129
collard greens
  Roasted Chicken with Collards, Red Onion,
    and Sweet Potato Chips, 92
  Stuffed Collard Greens with Roasted Chicken,
    Carolina Goat Cheese, and Black-eyed Pea
    Salad, 6
Conch, Fresh Cracked, with Vanilla Rum Sauce
    and Spicy Black Bean Salad, 27
Cooked Fruit Purée or Sauce, 216
Coq au Vin, 94
corn
  Barbecued Duck with Wilted Greens, 101
  Barbecued Spiced Oysters on Creamy Succo-
    tash, 31
  Creole Spiny Lobster, 64
  Risotto with Bacon, Silver Queen Corn, and
    Catfish, 9
crab
  Pecan Flour-dusted Softshell Crab with Roasted
    Garlic Tomato Butter, 61
  Stone Crab Cakes with Curried Potatoes and

Thai Butter, 25
  Stone Crab Cakes with Red Pepper
    Remoulade, 24
  Stone Crab Cobbler with Coconut Milk,
    Chilies, Key Lime, and Coriander, 26
crawfish (crayfish)
  Bacon-wrapped Trout Stuffed with Crawfish,
    86
  Crawfish Spring Rolls with Root Vegetables
    and Crawfish Beurre Blanc, 15
  Panéed Catfish with Crayfish Stuffing in an
    Herb Butter Sauce, 80
  Panfried Mountain Rainbow Trout with Green
    Tomato and Lime Butter Salsa on Sweet
    Potato, Artichoke, and Crayfish Hash, 83
  Spicy Crawfish and Black Bean Phyllo Burritos
    with Cilantro Cream and Fresh Salsa, 29
Creams, Baked, with Orange Custard Sauce, 127
crème Anglaise
  Crème Anglaise, 215
  Crème Brûlée Napoleon with Bourbon Crème
    Anglaise, 132
crème bruleé
  Chocolate Crème Bruleé with a Sweet Basil
    Vanilla Sauce, 122
  Crème Brûlée Napoleon with Bourbon Crème
    Anglaise, 132
Creole Spiny Lobster, 64
Crêpes, Galliano, with Seasonal Berries, 120
Crepinette of Turbot and Foie Gras on Salsify
    Mousseline with White Asparagus and
    Morel Jus, 32
Cuban French Toast, 117
curry
  Barbecued Spiced Oysters on Creamy Succo-
    tash, 31
  Creole Spiny Lobster, 64
  Stone Crab Cakes with Curried Potatoes and
    Thai Butter, 25
  Stone Crab Cobbler with Coconut Milk,
    Chilies, Key Lime, and Coriander, 26
  Sugar Cane-speared Gulf Shrimp with
    Tamarind-Orange Honey Glaze, 17

D

Desserts, 115–172
Dover Sole Riviera, Nage of, 78
duck
  Barbecued Breast of Duck with Crushed Pep-
    per, Plums, and Plum Wine, 103
  Barbecued Duck with Wilted Greens, 101
  Duck and Sweet Potato Hash with Quail Eggs,
    Sunny Side Up, 38

Duck, Rabbit, Lamb, or Venison Stock, 220
Pressed Duck, 105

E

eggplant
Grilled Yellowfin Tuna with Ratatouille, Risotto, Grilled Shallots, and Red Wine-Morel Sauce, 72
Yellowtail Snapper Encrusted in Yuca with Roasted Pepper-Orange Salsa and Sizzling Black Beans, 68
eggs
Asparagus Charlotte, 1
Duck and Sweet Potato Hash with Quail Eggs, Sunny Side Up, 38
Roulade of Salmon with Egg and Capers, 34
Salad Niçoise, 49
Escabeche, Scallop, 4

F

Fearrington House Chocolate Refresh-Mint, 124
Fish and Seafood, 55–90
Fish Stock, 219
foie gras
Crepinette of Turbot and Foie Gras on Salsify Mousselline with White Asparagus and Morel Jus, 32
Guinea Hen "Souva Roff" Modern with Foie Gras, Truffles, and Morels, 99
Poached Vidalia Onions with Foie Gras and Marmalade, 44
French Toast, Cuban, 117
Fresh Cracked Conch with Vanilla Rum Sauce and Spicy Black Bean Salad, 27
Frog Legs, Tempura-battered, with Arugula Creamy Tartar Sauce, 36
Frozen Lime-Ganache Parfait with Chocolate Tuiles, 154
Fruited Cobb Salad, 54

G

Galliano
Barbecued Breast of Duck with Crushed Pepper, Plums, and Plum Wine, 103
Galliano Crêpes with Seasonal Berries, 120
Game Hen, Roasted, with Goat Cheese and Spinach, 96
garlic
Bacon-wrapped Trout Stuffed with Crawfish, 86
Barbecued Duck with Wilted Greens, 101
Blackberry-glazed Quail, 41
Beef Tenderloin Stuffed with Herb Cream Cheese, with Sauce Bordelaise, 108

Coq au Vin, 94
Crawfish Spring Rolls with Root Vegetables and Crawfish Beurre Blanc, 15
Creole Spiny Lobster, 64
Fresh Cracked Conch with Vanilla Rum Sauce and Spicy Black Bean Salad, 27
Fruited Cobb Salad, 54
Greenhouse Grill Rack of Lamb, 112
Grilled and Braised Rabbit with Molasses, Bourbon, Slab Bacon, and Stone-ground Grits, 106
Grilled Vegetable Terrine with Lobster and Red Pepper Coulis, 2
Grilled Yellowfin Tuna with Ratatouille, Risotto, Grilled Shallots, and Red Wine-Morel Sauce, 72
Grouper Pibil, 75
Herb-crusted Red snapper with Pine Nut-Herb Sauce, 70
Lamb Ribs with Shallot Pepper Butter Sauce, 42
Pork Tenderloin "au Poivre," 110
Panéed Catfish with Crayfish Stuffing in an Herb Butter Sauce, 80
Panfried Mountain Rainbow Trout with Green Tomato and Lime Butter Salsa on Sweet Potato, Artichoke, and Crayfish Hash, 83
Pan-seared Scallops with Zucchini and Summer Squash, Cheddar Grits Soufflé, and Salmon Roe Butter Sauce, 80
Pecan Flour-dusted Softshell Crab with Roasted Garlic Tomato Butter, 61
Pressed Duck, 105
Rice Paper-wrapped Tuna Loin with Ginger Sauce, 84
Risotto with Bacon, Silver Queen Corn, and Catfish, 9
Roasted Chicken with Collards, Red Onion, and Sweet Potato Chips, 92
Roasted Game Hen with Goat Cheese and Spinach, 96
Roasted Garlic Purée, 218
Roasted Portabello Caps, 8
Salmon South by Southwest, 88
Shad Stuffed with Shad Roe, 87
Shrimp and Plantain Torte, 13
Smoked Scotch Bonnet Jerk Spice Mahimahi Stuffed with Christophene, Carrot, and Pepper with Mofongo Broth, 66
Spicy Crawfish and Black Bean Phyllo Burritos with Cilantro Cream and Fresh Salsa, 29
Stuffed Collard Greens with Roasted Chicken, Carolina Goat Cheese, and Black-eyed Pea Salad, 6

Sugar Cane-speared Gulf Shrimp with Tamarind-Orange Honey Glaze, 17

Whole Sizzling Catfish with Chili-Black Bean Sauce, 82

Wild and Exotic Mushroom Salad on Marinated Tomatoes and Warm Sherry Bacon Vinaigrette, 46

Yuca-stuffed Shrimp with a Sour Orange Mojo and Scotch Bonnet Tartar Salsa, 19

ginger
Rice Paper-wrapped Tuna Loin with Ginger Sauce, 84

Roasted Game Hen with Goat Cheese and Spinach, 96

Sugar Cane-speared Gulf Shrimp with Tamarind-Orange Honey Glaze, 17

Gnocchi Stuffed with Fonduta in Parmesan Cheese-Cream Sauce, 11

goat cheese
Greenhouse Grill Rack of Lamb, 112

Roasted Game Hen with Goat Cheese and Spinach, 96

Roasted Portabello Caps, 8

Stuffed Collard Greens with Roasted Chicken, Carolina Goat Cheese, and Black-eyed Pea Salad, 6

Grand Marnier
Chocolate Banana Foster Cake with Orange Foster Caramel Sauce, 146

Praline Mousse Served with Chocolate Meringue, 133

Greenhouse Grill Rack of Lamb, 112

Grilled and Braised Rabbit with Molasses, Bourbon, Slab Bacon, and Stone-ground Grits, 106

Grilled Barbecued Tuna, 74

Grilled Mississippi Quail, Marinated in Hoisin, Szechuan Chilies, and Sesame with Sweet Potato Polenta, 39

Grilled Vegetable Terrine with Lobster and Red Pepper Coulis, 2

Grilled Yellowfin Tuna with Ratatouille, Risotto, Grilled Shallots, and Red Wine-Morel Sauce, 72

grits
Grilled and Braised Rabbit with Molasses, Bourbon, Slab Bacon, and Stone-ground Grits, 106

Pan-seared Scallops with Zucchini and Summer Squash, Cheddar Grits Souffle, and Salmon Roe Butter Sauce, 56

Spicy Shrimp, Sausage, and Tasso Gravy over White Grits, 59

Grouper Pibil, 75

Guinea Hen "Souva Roff" Modern with Foie Gras, Truffles, and Morels, 99

H

hash
Duck and Sweet Potato Hash with Quail Eggs, Sunny Side Up, 38

Panfried Mountain Rainbow Trout with Green Tomato and Lime Butter Salsa on Sweet Potato, Artichoke, and Crayfish Hash, 83

Havana Bananas with Rum, Chilies, and Chocolate Sauce, 150

Herb Cream Cheese, with Sauce Bordelaise, Beef Tenderloin Stuffed with, 108

Herb-crusted Red Snapper with Pine Nut-Herb Sauce, 70

horseradish
Horseradish-Crusted Sea Bass with Roast Shiitake Mushrooms and Miso, 77

Stuffed Collard Greens with Roasted Chicken, Carolina Goat Cheese, and Black-eyed Pea Salad, 6

I

ice cream
Cardamom Cake with Saffron Ice Cream, 164

White Chocolate Black Jack Ice Cream Sandwiches, 160

J

jerk spice
Grouper Pibil, 75

Smoked Scotch Bonnet Jerk Spice Mahimahi Stuffed with Christophene, Carrot, and Pepper with Mofongo Broth, 66

K

key lime, *see* lime
Key Lime Pie, Stacked, 156

L

lamb
Duck, Rabbit, Lamb, or Venison Stock, 220

Greenhouse Grill Rack of Lamb, 112

Lamb Ribs with Shallot Pepper Butter Sauce, 42

lemon
Lemon Cheesecake, 158

Lemon Parfait with Fruits and Sauces, 138

Lemon Soufflé, 137

lime
Frozen Lime-Ganache Parfait with Chocolate Tuiles, 154

Panfried Mountain Rainbow Trout with Green
    Tomato and Lime Butter Salsa on Sweet
    Potato, Artichoke, and Crayfish Hash, 83
Stacked Key Lime Pie, 156
Stone Crab Cobbler with Coconut Milk,
    Chilies, Key Lime, and Coriander, 26
lobster
    Creole Spiny Lobster, 64
    Grilled Vegetable Terrine with Lobster and Red
        Pepper Coulis, 2
    Maine Lobster with Celery Root and Apple
        Salad, 48
    Roast Bahamian Lobster with Chili, Saffron,
        Vanilla, and Rum, 63

M

Mahimahi, Smoked Scotch Bonnet Jerk Spice,
    Stuffed with Christophene, Carrot, and Pep-
    per with Mofongo Broth, 66
Maine Lobster with Celery Root and Apple Salad,
    48
mango
    Havana Bananas with Rum, Chilies, and
        Chocolate Sauce, 150
    Lemon Parfait with Fruits and Sauces, 138
    Maine Lobster with Celery Root and Apple
        Salad, 48
    Sea Scallops with Mango and Jalapeños, 58
mascarpone
    Cuban French Toast, 117
    Tropical Tiramisu, 135
Meats and Poultry, 91–115
Miso, Horseradish-Crusted Sea Bass with Roast
    Shiitake Mushrooms and, 77
Mocha Toffee Meringue, 152
Mofongo Broth, Smoked Scotch Bonnet Jerk Spice
    Mahimahi Stuffed with Christophene, Car-
    rot, and Pepper with, 66
molasses
    Bananas Foster Chimichanga, 148
    Bayona Crispy Smoked Quail Salad, 52
    Grilled and Braised Rabbit with Molasses,
        Bourbon, Slab Bacon, and Stone-ground
        Grits, 106
    Pork Tenderloin "au Poivre," 110
    Roast Chicken with Collards, Red Onion, and
        Sweet Potato Chips, 92
morels
    Crepinette of Turbot and Foie Gras on Salsify
        Mousseline with White Asparagus and Morel
        Jus, 32
    Grilled Yellowfin Tuna with Ratatouille,
        Risotto, Grilled Shallots, and Red Wine-
        Morel Sauce, 72
    Guinea Hen "Souva Roff" Modern with Foie

Gras, Truffles, and Morels, 99
    Morel-crusted Trout Salad with Apple and Wal-
        nut Vinaigrette, 51
Mousse, Praline, Served with Chocolate Meringue,
    133
mushrooms
    Coq au Vin, 94
    Crepinette of Turbot and Foie Gras on Salsify
        Mousseline with White Asparagus and Morel
        Jus, 32
    Grilled Yellowfin Tuna with Ratatouille,
        Risotto, Grilled Shallots, and Red Wine-
        Morel Sauce, 72
    Guinea Hen "Souva Roff" Modern with Foie
        Gras, Truffles, and Morels, 99
    Horseradish-Crusted Sea Bass with Roast Shi-
        itake Mushrooms and Miso, 77
    Morel-crusted Trout Salad with Apple and Wal-
        nut Vinaigrette, 51
    Potato Crisp Pizza, 10
    Roasted Portabello Caps, 8
    Wild and Exotic Mushroom Salad on Mari-
        nated Tomatoes and Warm Sherry Bacon
        Vinaigrette, 46

N

Nage of Dover Sole Riveria, 78
napoleon
    Crème Brûlée Napoleon with Bourbon Crème
        Anglaise, 132
    Strawberry Napoleon, 142

O

orange
    Baked Creams with Orange Custard Sauce, 127
    Brioche Pain Perdu with Orange-Balsamic
        Syrup, 116
    Chocolate Banana Foster Cake with Orange
        Foster Caramel Sauce, 146
    Sugar Cane-speared Gulf Shrimp with
        Tamarind-Orange Honey Glaze, 17
    Yellowtail Snapper Encrusted in Yuca with
        Roasted Pepper-Orange Salsa and Sizzling
        Black Beans, 68
    Yuca-stuffed Shrimp with a Sour Orange Mojo
        and Scotch Bonnet Tartar Salsa, 19
oysters
    Barbecued Spiced Oysters on Creamy Succo-
        tash, 31
    Grilled Barbecued Tuna, 74

P

Pain Perdu, Brioche, with Orange-Balsamic Syrup,
    116

Panéed Catfish with Crayfish Stuffing in an Herb Butter Sauce, 80

Panfried Mountain Rainbow Trout with Green Tomato and Lime Butter Salsa on Sweet Potato, Artichoke, and Crayfish Hash, 83

Pan-seared Scallops with Zucchini and Summer Squash, Cheddar Grits Soufflé, and Salmon Roe Butter Sauce, 80

papayas
    Roast Bahamian Lobster with Chili, Saffron, Vanilla, and Rum, 63
    Scallop Escabeche, 4
    Shrimp with Sugar Cane and Papaya Ketchup, 22

parfaits
    Frozen Lime-Ganache Parfait with Chocolate Tuiles, 154
    Lemon Parfait with Fruits and Sauces, 138

pasta
    Nage of Dover Sole Riveria, 78
    Salmon South by Southwest, 88

pecans
    Aunt Irma's Banana-Pecan Beignets, 119
    Bayona Crispy Smoked Quail Salad, 52
    Pecan Flour-dusted Softshell Crab with Roasted Garlic Tomato Butter, 61
    Rich Dense Chocolate Pecan Torte, 166
    Roasted Game Hen with Goat Cheese and Spinach, 96

peppers, basics, 217

Pie, Stacked Key Lime, 156

Pine Nut-Herb Sauce, Herb Crusted Red Snapper with, 70

Pizza, Potato Crisp, 10

plantains
    Creole Spiny Lobster, 64
    Scallop Escabeche, 4
    Shrimp and Plantain Torte, 13
    Smoked Scotch Bonnet Jerk Spice Mahimahi Stuffed with Christophene, Carrot, and Pepper with Mofongo Broth, 66

Plums, and Plum Wine, Barbecued Breast of Duck with Crushed Pepper, 103

Poached Vidalia Onions with Foie Gras and Marmalade. 44

Polenta, Sweet Potato, Grilled Mississippi Quail, Marinated in Hoisin, Szechuan Chilies, and Sesame with, 39

Pork Tenderloin "au Poivre," 110

Portabello Caps, Roasted, 8

potatoes, also see sweet potatoes
    Coq au Vin, 94
    Gnocchi Stuffed with Fonduta in Parmesan Cheese-Cream Sauce, 11
    Greenhouse Grill Rack of Lamb, 112

Potato Crisp Pizza, 10

Salad Niçoise, 49

Sea Scallops with Mango and Jalapeños, 58

Stone Crab Cakes with Curried Potatoes and Thai Butter, 25

Praline Mousse Served with Chocolate Meringue, 133

Pressed Duck, 105

Q

quail
    Bayona Crispy Smoked Quail Salad, 52
    Blackberry-glazed Quail, 41
    Duck and Sweet Potato Hash with Quail Eggs, Sunny Side Up, 38
    Grilled Mississippi Quail, Marinated in Hoisin, Szechuan Chilies, and Sesame with Sweet Potato Polenta, 39

R

rabbit
    Duck, Rabbit, Lamb, or Venison Stock, 220
    Grilled and Braised Rabbit with Molasses, Bourbon, Slab Bacon, and Stone Ground Grits, 106

Rack of Lamb, Greenhouse Grill, 112

rainbow trout
    Panfried Mountain Rainbow Trout with Green Tomato and Lime Butter Salsa on Sweet Potato, Artichoke, and Crayfish Hash, 83

Red Pepper Remoulade, Stone Crab Cakes with, 24

Refresh-Mint, Fearrington House Chocolate, 124

Remoulade, Red Pepper, Stone Crab Cakes with, 24

Ribs, Lamb, with Shallot Pepper Butter Sauce, 42

rice
    Grilled Yellowfin Tuna with Ratatouille, Risotto, Grilled Shallots, and Red Wine-Morel Sauce, 72
    Rice Paper-wrapped Tuna Loin with Ginger Sauce, 84
    Risotto with Bacon, Silver Queen Corn, and Catfish, 9

Rice Paper-wrapped Tuna Loin with Ginger Sauce, 84

Rich Dense Chocolate Pecan Torte, 166

risotto
    Grilled Yellowfin Tuna with Ratatouille, Risotto, Grilled Shallots, and Red Wine-Morel Sauce, 72
    Risotto with Bacon, Silver Queen Corn, and Catfish, 9

Roast Bahamian Lobster with Chili, Saffron, Vanilla, and Rum, 63

Roasted Chicken with Collards, Red Onion, and Sweet Potato Chips, 92
Roasted Game Hen with Goat Cheese and Spinach, 96
Roasted Garlic Purée, 218
Roasted Portabello Caps, 8
roe
    Pan-seared Scallops with Zucchini and Summer Squash, Cheddar Grits Soufflé, and Salmon Roe Butter Sauce, 56
    Shad Stuffed with Shad Roe, 87
rosemary
    Greenhouse Grill Rack of Lamb, 112
    Lamb Ribs with Shallot Pepper Butter Sauce, 42
    Pork Tenderloin "au Poivre," 110
Roulade of Salmon with Egg and Capers, 34
rum
    Bananas Foster Chimichanga, 148
    Fresh Cracked Conch with Vanilla Rum Sauce and Spicy Black Bean Salad, 27
    Havana Bananas with Rum, Chilies, and Chocolate Sauce, 150
    Roast Bahamian Lobster with Chili, Saffron, Vanilla, and Rum, 63

S

Sabayon, Coffee Cup with, 129
saffron
    Cardamom Cake with Saffron Ice Cream, 164
    Nage of Dover Sole Riviera, 78
    Roast Bahamian Lobster with Chili, Saffron, Vanilla, and Rum, 63
Salade Niçoise, 49
Salads, 45–54
salmon
    Pan-seared Scallops with Zucchini and Summer Squash, Cheddar Grits Soufflé, and Salmon Roe Butter Sauce, 80
    Roulade of Salmon with Egg and Capers, 34
    Salmon South by Southwest, 88
salsa
    Panfried Mountain Rainbow Trout with Green Tomato and Lime Butter Salsa on Sweet Potato, Artichoke, and Crayfish Hash, 83
    Spicy Crawfish and Black Bean Phyllo Burritos with Cilantro Cream and Fresh Salsa, 29
    Yellowtail Snapper Encrusted in Yuca with Roasted Pepper-Orange Salsa and Sizzling Black Beans, 68
    Yuca-stuffed Shrimp with a Sour Orange Mojo and Scotch Bonnet Tartar Salsa, 19
Salsify Mousseline, Crepinette of Turbot and Foie Gras on, with White Asparagus and Morel Jus, 32

Sausage, Spicy Shrimp, and Tasso Gravy over White Grits, 59
scallops
    Pan-seared Scallops with Zucchini and Summer Squash, Cheddar Grits Soufflé, and Salmon Roe Butter Sauce, 80
    Scallop Escabeche, 4
    Spicy Scallops with Chile Sauce, 21
scotch bonnet (habañero) peppers
    Creole Spiny Lobster, 64
    Fresh Cracked Conch with Vanilla Rum Sauce and Spicy Black Bean Salad, 27
    Grouper Pibil, 75
    Roast Bahamian Lobster with Chili, Saffron, Vanilla, and Rum, 63
    Scallop Escabeche, 4
    Sea Scallops with Mango and Jalapeños, 58
    Smoked Scotch Bonnet Jerk Spice Mahimahi Stuffed with Christophene, Carrot, and Pepper with Mofongo Broth, 66
    Sugar Cane-speared Gulf Shrimp with Tamarind-Orange Honey Glaze, 17
    Yuca-stuffed Shrimp with a Sour Orange Mojo and Scotch Bonnet Tartar Salsa, 19
Sea Bass, Horseradish-crusted, with Roast Shiitake Mushrooms and Miso, 77
Sea Scallops with Mango and Jalapeños, 58
Shad Stuffed with Shad Roe, 87
Shallot Pepper Sauce, Lamb Ribs with, 42
shrimp
    Shrimp and Plantain Torte, 13
    Shrimp with Sugar Cane and Papaya Ketchup, 22
    Spicy Shrimp, Sausage, and Tasso Gravy over White Grits, 59
    Sugar Cane-speared Gulf Shrimp with Tamarind-Orange Honey Glaze, 17
    Yuca-stuffed Shrimp with a Sour Orange Mojo and Scotch Bonnet Tartar Salsa, 19
Simple Syrup, 217
Smoked Scotch Bonnet Jerk Spice Mahimahi Stuffed with Christophene, Carrot, and Pepper with Mofongo Broth, 66
snapper
    Herb-crusted Red Snapper with Pine Nut-Herb Sauce, 70
    Yellowtail Snapper Encrusted in Yuca with Roasted Pepper-Orange Salsa and Sizzling Black Beans, 68
soufflé
    Chocolate Souffé, 126
    Lemon Soufflé, 137
    Pan-seared Scallops with Zucchini and Summer Squash, Cheddar Grits Soufflé, and Salmon Roe Butter Sauce, 80

Spicy Crawfish and Black Bean Phyllo Burritos with Cilantro Cream and Fresh Salsa, 29
Spicy Scallops with Chile Sauce, 21
Spicy Shrimp, Sausage and Tasso Gravy over White Grits, 59
spinach
    Grouper Pibil, 75
    Roasted Game Hen with Goat Cheese and Spinach, 96
Spring Rolls, Crawfish, with Root Vegetables and Crawfish Beurre Blanc, 15
Strawberry Napoleon, 142
Stacked Key Lime Pie, 156
stock
    Chicken Stock, 218
    Duck, Rabbit, Lamb, or Venison Stock, 220
    Fish Stock, 219
    Veal or Beef Stock, 219
    Vegetable Stock, 220
Stone Crab Cakes with Red Pepper Remoulade, 24
Stone Crab Cakes with Curried Potatoes and Thai Butter, 25
Stone Crab Cobbler with Coconut Milk, Chilis, Key Lime and Coriander, 26
strawberries
    Strawberry Apple Cheese Strudel, 162
    Stuffed Strawberries with a Tomato-Cinnamon Confiture, Balsamic Vinegar, and Tomato Liqueur, 172
Strudel, Strawberry Apple Cheese, 162
Stuffed Collard Greens with Roasted Chicken, Carolina Goat Cheese, and Black-eyed Pea Salad, 6
Stuffed Strawberries with a Tomato-Cinnamon Confiture, Balsamic Vinegar, and Tomato Liqueur, 172
Succotash, Creamy, Barbecued Spiced Oysters on, 31
sugar cane
    Shrimp with Sugar Cane and Papaya Ketchup, 22
    Sugar Cane-speared Gulf Shrimp with Tamarind-Orange Honey Glaze, 17
sweet potatoes
    Duck and Sweet Potato Hash with Quail Eggs, Sunny Side Up, 38
    Lemon Cheesecake, 158
    Panfried Mountain Rainbow Trout with Green Tomato and Lime Butter Salsa on Sweet Potato, Artichoke, and Crayfish Hash, 83
    Pork Tenderloin "au Poivre," 110
    Roasted Chicken with Collards, Red Onion, and Sweet Potato Chips, 92

T

Tamarind-Orange Honey Glaze, Sugar Cane-speared Shrimp with, 17
Tasso Gravy, Spicy Shrimp, Sausage, and, over White Grits, 59
Tempura-battered Frog Legs with Arugula Creamy Tartar Sauce, 36
Terrine, Grilled Vegetable, with Lobster and Red Pepper Coulis, 2
tomatoes
    basics, 221
    Panfried Mountain Rainbow Trout with Green Tomato and Lime Butter Salsa on Sweet Potato, Artichoke, and Crayfish Hash, 83
    Potato Crisp Pizza, 10
    Stuffed Strawberries with a Tomato-Cinnamon Confiture, Balsamic Vinegar, and Tomato Liqueur, 172
    Wild and Exotic Mushroom Salad on Marinated Tomatoes and Warm Sherry Bacon Vinaigrette, 46
tortes
    Chocolate Genoise Truffle Torte with Fresh Berries, 170
    Rich Dense Chocolate Pecan Torte, 166
    Shrimp and Plantain Torte, 13
Tropical Tiramisu, 135
trout
    Bacon-wrapped Trout Stuffed with Crawfish, 86
    Morel-crusted Trout Salad with Apple and Walnut Vinaigrette, 51
    Panfried Mountain Rainbow Trout with Green Tomato and Lime Butter Salsa on Sweet Potato, Artichoke, and Crayfish Hash, 83
truffles
    Gnocchi Stuffed with Fonduta in Parmesan Cheese-Cream Sauce, 11
    Guinea Hen "Souva Roff" Modern with Foie Gras, Truffles, and Morels, 99
tuna
    Grilled Barbecued Tuna, 74
    Grilled Yellowfin Tuna with Ratatouille, Risotto, Grilled Shallots, and Red Wine-Morel Sauce, 72
    Rice Paper-wrapped Tuna Loin with Ginger Sauce, 84
    Salad Niçoise, 49
Turbot and Fois Gras, Crepinet of, on Salsify Mousseline with White Asparagus and Morel Jus, 32

U

Uncooked Fruit Purée (Coulis), 217

V

vanilla
  Chocolate Crème Brûlée with a Sweet Basil
    Vanilla Sauce, 122
  Fresh Cracked Conch with Vanilla Rum Sauce
    and Spicy Black Bean Salad, 27
  Roast Bahamian Lobster with Chili, Saffron,
    Vanilla, and Rum, 63
  Salmon South by Southwest, 88
  Shrimp and Plantain Torte, 13
Veal or Beef Demi-Glace, 221
Veal or Beef Stock, 219
Vegetable Curls, 222
Vegetable Stock, 220
Vegetable Terrine, Grilled, with Lobster and Red
    Pepper Coulis, 2
Vidalia onions
  Barbecued Duck with Wilted Greens, 101
  Poached Vidalia Onions with Foie Gras and
    Marmalade, 44
  Pork Tenderloin "au Poivre," 110
  Roasted Game Hen with Goat Cheese and
    Spinach, 96
  Salmon South by Southwest, 88

W

walnuts
  Bananas Foster Chimichanga, 148
  Morel-crusted Trout Salad with Apple and Wal-
    nut Vinaigrette, 51
Warm Center Chocolate Pyramid Cake, 168
Warm Sherry Bacon Vinaigrette, Wild and Exotic
    Mushroom Salad on Marinated Tomatoes
    and, 46

White Chocolate Black Jack Ice Cream Sand-
    wiches, 160
Whole Sizzling Catfish with Chili-Black Bean
    Sauce, 82
Wild and Exotic Mushroom Salad on Marinated
    Tomatoes and Warm Sherry Bacon Vinai-
    grette, 46

Y

yellowfin tuna, *see* tuna
Yellowtail Snapper Encrusted in Yuca with Roasted
    Pepper-Orange Salsa and Sizzling Black
    Beans, 68
yuca
  Yellowtail Snapper Encrusted in Yuca with
    Roasted Pepper-Orange Salsa and Sizzling
    Black Beans, 68
  Yuca-stuffed Shrimp with a Sour Orange Mojo
    and Scotch Bonnet Tartar Salsa, 19

Z

zucchini
  Grilled Vegetable Terrine with Lobster and Red
    Pepper Coulis, 2
  Grilled Yellowfin Tuna with Ratatouille,
    Risotto, Grilled Shallots, and Red Wine
    Morel Sauce, 72
  Grouper Pibil, 75
  Pan-Seared Scallops with Zucchini and Sum-
    mer Squash, Cheddar Grits Soufflé, and
    Salmon Roe Butter Sauce, 56
  Rice Paper-Wrapped Tuna Loin with Ginger
    Sauce, 84
  Shrimp with Sugar Cane and Papaya Ketchup,
    22